Pro Azure Administration and Automation

A Comprehensive Guide to Successful Cloud Management

Vladimir Stefanovic
Milos Katinski

Apress®

Pro Azure Administration and Automation: A Comprehensive Guide to Successful Cloud Management

Vladimir Stefanovic
Belgrade, Serbia

Milos Katinski
Amsterdam, The Netherlands

ISBN-13 (pbk): 978-1-4842-7324-1
https://doi.org/10.1007/978-1-4842-7325-8

ISBN-13 (electronic): 978-1-4842-7325-8

Managing Director, Apress Media LLC: Welmoed Spahr
Acquisitions Editor: Joan Murray
Development Editor: Laura Berendson
Coordinating Editor: Jill Balzano

Cover photo courtesy of Gratisography

Distributed to the book trade worldwide by Springer Science+Business Media LLC, 1 New York Plaza, Suite 4600, New York, NY 10004. Phone 1-800-SPRINGER, fax (201) 348-4505, e-mail orders-ny@springer-sbm. com, or visit www.springeronline.com. Apress Media, LLC is a California LLC and the sole member (owner) is Springer Science + Business Media Finance Inc (SSBM Finance Inc). SSBM Finance Inc is a **Delaware** corporation.

For information on translations, please e-mail booktranslations@springernature.com; for reprint, paperback, or audio rights, please e-mail bookpermissions@springernature.com.

Apress titles may be purchased in bulk for academic, corporate, or promotional use. eBook versions and licenses are also available for most titles. For more information, reference our Print and eBook Bulk Sales web page at http://www.apress.com/bulk-sales.

Any source code or other supplementary material referenced by the author in this book is available to readers on GitHub via the book's product page, located at www.apress.com/9781484273241. For more detailed information, please visit http://www.apress.com/source-code.

Printed on acid-free paper

Table of Contents

About the Authors

Vladimir Stefanovic is a Microsoft Azure MVP and cloud solution architect with more than 15 years of experience in the IT industry. He has also been a Microsoft Certified Trainer for a long time and the MCT Regional Lead for the Serbian chapter. During his career as a solution architect, he has designed and delivered numerous projects in Microsoft Azure and on-premises environments, helping companies from diverse industries set their infrastructures in the best possible manner. As a technical trainer, he has delivered hundreds of courses and was a successful mentor to many students, from enthusiasts to IT professionals.

Vladimir is also an active conference speaker, having spoken at a number of conferences such as MCT Summits (in the United States and Europe), Microsoft Ignite Tours, and WinDays, KulenDayz, and Sinergija (regional conferences). He is a book author, leader of Azure UG Serbia, Azure Saturday – Belgrade edition conference organizer, and an active community member with a mission to share knowledge as much as possible.

Milos Katinski is an Azure solutions engineer with more than 12 years of rich experience in the IT industry, gained from numerous projects from on-premises to cloud-native solutions. Over the last few years, he is focused on cloud technologies and DevOps culture and helping companies to have a smoother transition to Microsoft Azure and transformation to DevOps culture.

Milos is an active blogger and conference/meetup speaker, Azure UG Serbia member, and one of the Azure Saturday – Belgrade edition conference organizers. These community activities were the main reason for getting the Azure Hero award in 2019, which gave him additional motivation to continue with a mission of sharing his knowledge of cloud as much as possible.

About the Technical Reviewer

Nishith Pathak is India's first and only Artificial Intelligence (AI) Most Valuable Professional (MVP), a Microsoft Regional Director (RD), lead architect, speaker, AI thinker, innovator, and strategist. Nishith's expertise lies in helping Fortune 100 companies design and architect next-generation solutions that incorporate AI, ML, cognitive services, Blockchain, and many more. It also lies in defining and strategizing technology road maps for customers and companies using emerging technologies. He sits on several technical advisory boards across the globe. He has also authored more than half a dozen international books for Springer Publication, USA. His last three books have been on Artificial Intelligence (AI). Previously, Nishith has also played the role of a PAN account enterprise architect where he was responsible for the overall architecture design of multiple projects. He is an internationally acclaimed speaker on technologies like AI, IOT, and Blockchain and regularly speaks at various technical conferences. He advises and mentors a lot of start-ups as a community initiative.

For his expertise in Artificial Intelligence, Microsoft awarded him the first Most Valuable Professional (MVP) from India in the Artificial Intelligence category. He is the only Artificial Intelligence MVP in India till date. Globally, he is among 19 MVPs on AI, recognized by Microsoft for their sheer expertise in AI. He has also received the "Microsoft Regional Director" award bestowed upon 150 of the world's top technology visionaries chosen specifically for their proven cross-platform expertise.

Nishith is also a gold member and sits on the advisory board of various national and international computer science societies and organizations. He is currently working as Global Chief Technologist of Emerging Technologies and Advanced Analytics for DXC Technology where he is focused on using emerging technologies to help companies architect solutions, laying out technology road maps, and curating the start-up ecosystem. He can be contacted at nispathak@gmail.com or through LinkedIn at www.linkedin.com/in/nishithpathak/.

Introduction

If you are a cloud engineer, a member of a DevOps team, or a system engineer for the on-premises systems who wants to improve skills in the cloud computing area, then this book is for you. Prior knowledge of the Microsoft Azure platform is not truly needed for reading this book, but experience and familiarity with IT concepts would be helpful and make understanding cloud computing easier.

Pro Azure Administration and Automation starts with the chapter "Foundations in Cloud Computing" as a general introduction to cloud computing, focusing primarily on Azure, which is a must-have for all people in the modern IT world. Chapter 2, "Azure Administration," covers tools that we can use for deploying and managing Azure resources, in which we will be able to see the differences between these tools. In Chapter 3, "Virtual Networks in Azure," real deployment and management start. We will discuss the Azure networking concept and why some network-related services are important. Starting from this chapter, almost all the following chapters will consist of a lot of scripts and templates, of which the main purpose is automation. Once networking in Azure becomes our "cup of tea," we will move forward to the "virtual machine and virtual machine scale sets (VMSSs)" in Chapter 4. In this chapter, we will learn why these services are important, how to deploy and manage them, and also the important configuration parameters.

In Chapter 5, "App Service and Containers in Azure Compute," we are slowly moving from IaaS to PaaS services in Azure. We will discuss services that are, most probably, the future of the application hosting infrastructure, but also we will see how we can build infrastructure that is based on these services. Chapter 6, "Azure Storage," is a logical step forward, and in this chapter, we will learn what Azure Storage is, why it is important, and what options there are to leverage this Azure resource. Chapter 7, "Advanced Azure Networking," will show Azure networking from different perspectives and will teach us what Azure resources are related to advanced networking, how we need to use them, and in what scenarios these resources could help us.

Chapter 8, "Monitoring and Data Protection," opens the door to monitoring and alerting for Azure resources, which is one of the most important parts of each infrastructure when it is deployed. In the same chapter, we will discuss data protection options in Azure and scenarios where they could be implemented. In Chapter 9, "Network Traffic Management," we will learn about Azure resources we can use if we need to have an additional traffic management layer. A couple of Azure services, which seem at first look the same, will be explained from a feature and use case perspective. Finally, we will discuss security in Chapter 10, "Azure Security and Compliance." This chapter covers the main security concepts and gives us a good starting point on how security in Azure works.

In this book, we will learn about basic concepts and what makes Azure the way it is today. We will explore different approaches to deploying Azure services, their differences, and the benefits they bring. As we progress, we will reveal different types of services, how they connect, and which type of service you should use based on your needs, but also we will learn how to deploy each one of them and how you could automate your future deployments.

By the end of this book, we will be more familiar with Azure resources and how they are related and will know what is important to each of the services and how we can deploy and maintain them. With this bigger picture of Azure, we would be able to select appropriate services for diverse workloads easily, which could lead to easier management and a more effective Azure environment.

CHAPTER 1

Foundations in Cloud Computing

Cloud computing was a mystery for a long time, but nowadays, it is our reality. Over the last few years, many companies, from start-ups to the enterprise-scale companies, moved their business to the cloud. However, the cloud is not magical by itself and will not perform the company's digital transformation without change in the mindset of its leaders. When compared to the traditional on-premises IT infrastructure, the cloud is a bit different. In the market all around the world, there is a high demand for cloud administrators, but the required skills and mindset are different in comparison with those of traditional IT administrators. This book will help those who want to become cloud administrators for Microsoft Azure or want to improve their cloud administration and automation skills.

This chapter covers the following topics:

- The history of cloud computing

- Cloud computing types

- Cloud service models

- Public cloud benefits

- Geographies, regions, and pairing

- Subscriptions and accounts

- Role-based access control (RBAC)

1

© Vladimir Stefanovic and Milos Katinski 2021
V. Stefanovic and M. Katinski, *Pro Azure Administration and Automation*,
https://doi.org/10.1007/978-1-4842-7325-8_1

The History of Cloud Computing

If we look at the late 1990s, the information technology world got one of the most significant innovations: *virtualization*. Although virtualization concepts are much older than the 1990s, we will not go back so far into history. In 1997, Connectix released the first virtual PC for Macintosh and later for Windows. In 1999, VMware started their journey into the virtualization world, and a few years later, Microsoft announced their virtualization platforms for Windows Server, Microsoft Virtual Server, and later Microsoft Hyper-V. Nevertheless, why is virtualization important for cloud computing? The core technology of each cloud computing platform is virtualization. Virtualization provides the possibility for creating a scalable system of multiple independent computing devices on the same physical infrastructure. Although virtualization is an essential part of cloud computing, we will not go deep into it. We will stay focused on public cloud computing concepts and how to leverage their benefits.

The popularization of public cloud computing started in 2006 when Amazon Web Services (AWS) was relaunched and its EC2 *(Elastic Cloud Compute)* service was released. In 2008, Google announced Google App Engine, and Microsoft announced the Windows Azure platform. Because this book focuses on Microsoft Azure, we will continue to talk about Microsoft Azure services and administration.

A Brief History of Microsoft Azure

As we mentioned, Microsoft announced Windows Azure in October 2008, with the code name "Project Red Dog." On February 1, 2010, Microsoft officially released the platform Windows Azure and made it commercially available. Later, in 2014, the platform changed its name to Microsoft Azure.

In its beginnings, Microsoft Azure did not have many services available. The initial management model, *Azure Service Management (ASM)*, started with a small set of services, including virtual machines, SQL databases, cloud services, and a few more. Over the years, the number of services has grown, and today, we have hundreds of different Azure services that can respond to all business requirements, and that number continues to grow daily. Some of these services will be explained in this book through theory and practical examples.

In April 2014, at the Microsoft Build conference, Microsoft announced two changes for the Windows Azure platform. One of them was rebranding into Microsoft Azure. There is an interesting theory about this platform rebranding that says that Microsoft had to change the platform name because they started to offer Linux workloads on the platform. Of course, from a marketing perspective, it would not be good to have an offer called "Windows Azure Linux Virtual Machine." The second change was significant from a platform perspective. Microsoft announced the new, completely redesigned portal with the new management model, called *Azure Resource Management (ARM)*. The new portal and management model brings new features, such as *role-based access control (RBAC)* and *resource groups*. With this ARM model, we can set user access permissions granularly on different levels, from the whole subscription to the single resource. With the previous ASM model, the only way to give access to other people to manage Azure resources was the co-administrator role. With this role, a specific user gets full access to an Azure subscription. Another significant improvement in the ARM model is a resource group. A resource group is a logical container for grouping Azure resources, depending on the chosen model. Resources can be grouped by location, purpose, environment, or any other appropriate model. Every single resource in Azure can be part of only one resource group, and one of the commonly used scenarios is grouping resources with the same lifecycle into one resource group. An additional benefit that the ARM model brings is the *ARM template*. The ARM template is a JSON-formatted file containing information about Azure resources that need to be deployed or edited. Later in this book, we will explain ARM templates in more detail. All chapter examples in this book will include the ARM template code. ARM templates allow us to have Infrastructure as Code (IaC) as a native Azure solution, which is very important in the modern IT world that relies on automation.

With all of these improvements in the ARM model and the growing number of services, Microsoft changed their cloud approach. Today, Microsoft is a public cloud provider with more than 60 regions worldwide, more than double their competitors. Also, Microsoft is the first public cloud provider that launched regions in Africa and the Middle East. Numerous countries, such as Italy, Spain, Mexico, Greece, Israel, and New Zealand, are announced as locations for new Azure regions.

Cloud Computing Types

Even though this book focuses on Microsoft Azure, we need to understand the cloud computing types that exist. For many of us, the phrase "cloud" means that resources are somewhere far away from us, but that is not a correct statement.

Private Cloud

In the private cloud, all infrastructure resources are located on-premises in our datacenter. In most scenarios, there is no need for Internet connectivity because all resources are located close to us. However, if we want to have a private cloud, we need to have our physical location and facilities. We need to take care of electricity, cooling, networking, physical servers, software and hardware licenses, and everything needed for one datacenter to function. Along with the location and physical resources, we need to have a staff dedicated to datacenter maintenance. Enabling a private cloud requires capital investment at the start so that we will have an upfront cost. After a few years, physical equipment needs to be renewed, as well as virtualization and other software. That will cause new capital investments and much work to migrate to new infrastructure.

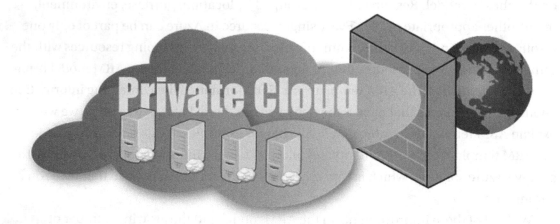

Figure 1-1. *Envisioning the private cloud. The image is used with permission from* https://go4hosting.in/blog/how-private-cloud-as-a-service-can-enhance-security/

Public Cloud

Over the years and as datacenters evolve, the public cloud has become one of the most crucial changes in the modern information technology world. Public cloud providers, such as Microsoft Azure, AWS, and Google, bring new IT concepts. In a nutshell, public cloud providers give us the ability to use their resources simply. Some of the benefits that come with the public cloud are a pay-per-use model, access to infrastructure over an Internet connection, resources available "on-click," and many others. These benefits forced us to think about the future of our local infrastructure. If we decide to use a public cloud, regardless of the company's size, we need to define a plan for how we will use it, activate subscriptions through one of the possible payment models, and start creating resources that we need. That is much easier than buying and installing complete local infrastructure, regardless of how extensive our infrastructure is. Also, the financial benefit is essential because resources in the public cloud are billed per usage, mostly per minute or per hour, resulting in a lower cost in many scenarios, especially for development and test environments. Since the infrastructure maintenance tasks are reduced significantly and the infrastructure scalability is almost endless, it is evident that the benefits of public cloud usage could be vast. For instance, we want to create a virtual machine in Microsoft Azure for application development. If we plan to work on that virtual machine only during work hours and then stop it until the next workday, we will pay only for the exact amount of time the virtual machine is powered up.

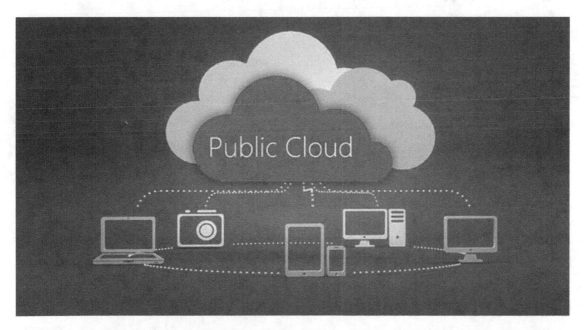

Figure 1-2. *Envisioning the public cloud. The image is used with permission from* `https://medium.com/@veritisgroup/7-ways-to-secure-your-public-cloud-experience-dc5388467b5a`

Hybrid Cloud

When we talk about hybrid cloud, we can just simply say that the hybrid cloud is a mix of the private and public clouds. Many large companies and enterprise-scale companies with their private cloud infrastructure that are interested in moving their workload to the public cloud are not able to do it quickly and easily. The most common blocking points are the infrastructure scale, legacy stuff, and legal compliance. However, many of them are eligible to use the hybrid cloud model and move the development environment, for example, to the public cloud. By establishing direct network connectivity between private and public cloud infrastructure, using a site-to-site VPN tunnel or ExpressRoute, resources can talk to each other without any restrictions. That approach gives them the possibility to leverage public cloud benefits, cut the costs for the resources that are not in use, and develop applications and processes in a cloud-native manner.

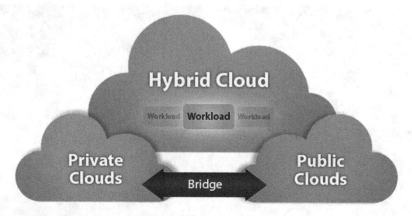

Figure 1-3. *Understanding the hybrid cloud model. The image is used with permission from* `www.rittal.us/contents/hybrid-cloud-explained/`

Cloud Service Models

When we talk about cloud computing, we need to know a few main cloud models. All of these models are applicable for cloud computing in general, as well as for Microsoft Azure:

- Infrastructure-as-a-Service (IaaS)

- Platform-as-a-Service (PaaS)

- Software-as-a-Service (SaaS)

Each of these cloud models has a different level of control given to the customer. As we can see in Figure 1-4, the control that customers have is significantly declining from the on-premises model to the SaaS model.

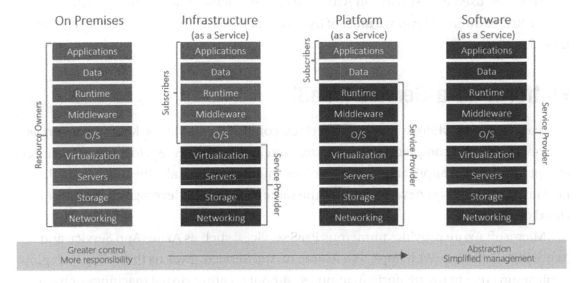

Figure 1-4. *Understanding the level of control in various cloud models. The image is used with permission from* www.itpromentor.com/what-is-azure/

Infrastructure-as-a-Service (IaaS)

In this cloud service model, Microsoft Azure is responsible for running and managing all physical resources, networking, and the complete virtualization layer of the infrastructure. The customer is responsible for deploying a virtual machine in one of the Azure datacenters. After that, the customer takes control of virtual machine configuration and management of the operating system. The underlying infrastructure is still the responsibility of Microsoft Azure.

Transformation to this cloud-native model is not an easy process. In most scenarios, business applications require a complete redesign, which is no quick task. Many customers that want to move infrastructure to the cloud quickly are forced to use the "lift and shift" migration model. In many cases, they will just deploy the same or similar virtual machine infrastructure and migrate the workload to the Azure virtual machine. That migration model is not the best possible option because we cannot use all cloud benefits. However, at the same time, the popularity and usage of Azure IaaS services are on a very high level. Also, there are many different scenarios where virtual machines are a "must-have" service for industries that are slow to change and adopt new technologies, such as enterprise-scale companies or the banking sector.

The most used IaaS services in Azure are virtual machines and virtual machine scale sets, which allow us to leverage most of the cloud benefits even though we use the IaaS model.

Platform-as-a-Service (PaaS)

The PaaS model is where we need to use cloud computing platforms. Microsoft Azure is responsible for the complete infrastructure, from bare-metal servers to the runtime layer, except for data and applications. With the PaaS model, we can take the business to the next level and focus on development. At the same time, we can leverage all benefits of cloud computing.

Microsoft Azure provides numerous PaaS services, such as Azure App Service and Azure SQL Database. Web Apps, as a feature of App Service, gives us the ability to deploy application code to the platform in minutes without creating virtual machines or more complex infrastructure. In just a few clicks, we will have a ready SQL database if we use Azure SQL Database, without the need to deploy and configure a virtual machine and install and configure SQL Server. Platform-as-a-Service services are a game-changer in the cloud computing world.

Software-as-a-Service (SaaS)

Finally, we have the Software-as-a-Service model. Each SaaS service is hosted and fully managed by Microsoft Azure. It is a multi-tenant architecture in most scenarios, and SaaS services are typically licensed through a monthly or yearly subscription. Microsoft Azure is fully responsible for the complete underlying infrastructure and the software upgrade and patching. The best example of a SaaS service is Microsoft 365. In the monthly- or yearly-based subscription, users get Microsoft Exchange, Microsoft OneDrive, Microsoft SharePoint, and many other Microsoft Office products.

Public Cloud Benefits

The public cloud, by itself, brings many benefits, and we need to organize our business to leverage all of those. Some of the benefits are readily enjoyed, like infrastructure high availability and global reach, but for some of them, we need to align our business to the public cloud.

Easier Management

On top of the list of benefits is infrastructure management, which is more comfortable than on-premises. If we talk about infrastructure, we do not need to think about hardware and software licenses, network equipment, storage space and drives, power and cooling, and many other things. However, for cloud administrators, there is no "magic stick" for all. If we use the IaaS model and have deployed virtual machines, we still need someone to manage Windows or Linux servers. As mentioned earlier, cloud administrators need to improve their skills and align with new technologies, but many of the "on-premises" skills will still be usable in the cloud.

Cost Efficiency

From a financial perspective, which is an inevitable part of digital transformation, the public cloud could be a big deal. When we decide to use the public cloud, we change Capital Expenditure **(CapEx)** to Operational Expenditure **(OpEx)**. In the CapEx model, we need to spend money to buy physical infrastructure, such as servers, network equipment, storage, and everything needed for the on-premises infrastructure. CapEx is an upfront cost that will decrease during a time of usage. Nevertheless, there is another problem. When we are buying infrastructure, we need to know what resources are needed at the moment and for the potential expansion. In most scenarios, that cannot be anticipated correctly, and on-premises infrastructure could be over-provisioned or under-provisioned, and in both scenarios, problems could arise. That means that we buy resources that we will not use (over-provisioning) or we do not have enough resources for our workload (under-provisioning). In the OpEx model, things are a bit different. We do not have capital investments in infrastructure. We will spend money just on services and products that we have used during a specific period.

For companies that are starting their new business or expanding a current business, the public cloud is the right choice. There are no capital investments so that companies can focus on business development. The consumption-based billing model means that users pay only for resources that they use. No upfront cost, no need to purchase hardware or licenses, and there is the ability to stop paying for the resources that are no longer in use.

Automation

Even though automation of infrastructure is possible and preferable in the on-premises environment and other cloud computing types, automation in the public cloud is a modus operandi. Like we said, in the Microsoft Azure ARM model, ARM templates are one of the options to automate provisioning and managing infrastructure. Along with ARM templates, the Microsoft Azure native tools for automation are PowerShell and Azure CLI. Also, there are a few third-party compatible tools, like Terraform, Ansible, or Pulumi.

Security

One of the biggest concerns for companies, regardless of their size, is security. Microsoft Azure, as a public cloud provider, invests over $1 billion yearly in security to protect customers' data and infrastructure. There are many aspects of security that are provided by Microsoft Azure, such as identity protection, network protection, and data protection. Most public cloud providers, including Microsoft Azure, rely on the shared responsibility model, which defines who is responsible for a specific security layer, which means responsibility is shared.

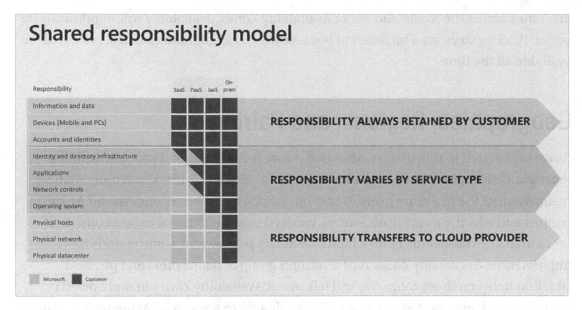

Figure 1-5. *The shared responsibility model. The image was taken from* `https://docs.microsoft.com/en-us/azure/security/fundamentals/shared-responsibility`

Scalability

Different industries have different requirements, and this is true for ecommerce, news portals, and law offices. If we have an ecommerce application, we will probably not have the same load throughout the day, and we will have spikes during a specific time. However, if we want to have a reliable platform and happy customers, we need to have a responsible application regardless of the number of customers. If we run our application on-premises, most probably, infrastructure will be over-provisioned. On the other hand, the public cloud gives us the possibility to use resources designed for auto-scaling. That will allow our application to scale up and down based on demands that helps us to cut costs and respond to spikes at the same time.

High Availability

High availability is one of the benefits of almost all services, mainly if we use PaaS services. Microsoft Azure, as a public cloud provider, must be resistant to various types of failures, so high availability and fault tolerance are concepts that are the core of the platform. IaaS services have slightly lower availability by design, but if we deploy virtual machines across the Availability set or Availability Zones, availability will significantly be better. PaaS services are a bit different because Microsoft guarantees that services will be available all the time.

Geographies, Regions, and Pairing

As we said earlier in this chapter, Microsoft Azure is a public cloud provider with the most available regions compared with other public cloud providers, and more than 50 regions across the world are ready to host our workload. To better understand Azure regions and why the term region is used, we need to know that one region consists of more than one datacenter. From a high availability perspective, some regions have implemented Availability Zones representing a group of datacenters and physical isolation between these zones. We will talk about Availability Zones in more detail in the following chapters. Also, we need to know that there are special Azure regions, along with publicly available regions. Customers can deploy and run their workloads in any publicly available region, while special regions are intended for specific workloads.

Azure US government regions are US DoD Central, US DoD East, US Sec East, US Sec West, US Gov Arizona, US Gov Texas, and US Gov Virginia. These regions are physically and logically isolated Azure regions for US government agencies and their partners. Only US screened persons are eligible to manage these regions. Azure regions for the US government must meet government security and compliance requirements to provide the best possible security, protection, and compliance for all services.

Germany Central and Germany Northeast are Azure regions in Germany, physically isolated to provide the best possible security and compliance service critical for German data privacy. These regions are under the control of Deutsche Telekom company T-Systems, acting as the German data trustee. These regions do not accept new customers since August 2018. Market evaluation statistics say that regions were a bit more expensive than global Azure regions, so Microsoft launched two new regions in Germany to provide customer data residency, connectivity to the global network, and competitive market price.

China East, China East 2, China North, and China North 2 are Azure regions available through the partnership between Microsoft and 21Vianet. Microsoft is not responsible for maintaining any of the datacenters in these regions. Regions are physically isolated to provide enterprise-compliant regulation based on China standards.

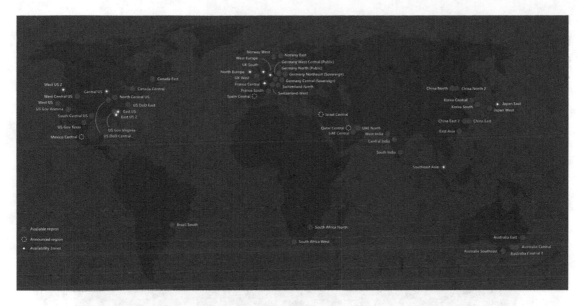

Figure 1-6. *A view of Microsoft Azure regions. The image was taken from* `https://azure.microsoft.com/en-us/global-infrastructure/regions/`

On top of the regions are *geographies.* A geography represents a market that contains two or more regions, which ensures that data residency, compliance, and resiliency stay within geographical boundaries. Customers that must meet a specific data residency and compliance requirement for their applications can leverage all benefits of the public cloud in a specific geography. A geography is fault tolerant in case of a complete region failure by virtue of underlying replication between paired regions within a geography and Azure's dedicated high-capacity network.

As we said, a geography contains two or more regions. Nevertheless, for one fully functional geography, two regions need to replicate each other to provide data resiliency. That concept is called *paired regions* and represents two regions within the same geography that replicate each other. When the Azure platform is under planned maintenance, that concept ensures that only one region in a pair updates at a time. In case of failure of multiple regions, at least one region in a pair is prioritized for recovery. By design, not all Azure services replicate data to the paired region. In some scenarios, replication and recovery need to be configured by the customer. When it is possible, Microsoft prefers to deploy regions with at least 300 miles of separation.

In most cases, regions are paired based on geography, but there are a few exceptions. Brazil South is the only region in South America, and there is no option to pair regions based on geography. That region is paired with South Central US, but at the same time,

Brazil South is not a replica region of South Central US. Other examples are regions in India. West India has one-direction pairing with South India, and the paired region for South India is Central India.

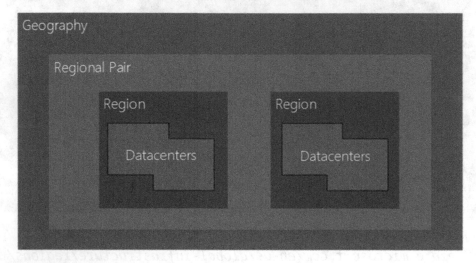

Figure 1-7. *Visualizing two regions within the same geography that replicate each other. The image was taken from* https://docs.microsoft.com/en-us/azure/ best-practices-availability-paired-regions

Subscriptions and Accounts

Now that we have a bigger picture of Azure's physical characteristics, we need to talk about essential logical things. Of course, a deep understanding of infrastructure is essential for architecting Azure solutions, but the understanding of logical components is also crucial from an organizational perspective. Two terms that are very often part of misunderstanding, especially for customers that are new in cloud technologies, are *subscription* and *account*. Let us talk about that.

Subscription

If we want to use Azure resources, we need to have a valid subscription. The subscription-based model is widely used in the public cloud world, which allows us to use Azure resources. Based on the subscription type, define how the usage of resources will be paid. Subscription is a high level of management of our Azure tenant, and without the subscription, we cannot start to use Azure resources. Subscriptions that are available for Microsoft Azure are separated into two main groups, free and paid.

When we talk about free subscriptions, at the top of the list is an *Azure free trial* subscription that includes $200 of credit for 30 days and is available for everyone. Free trial subscription will expire whatever comes first, and in most cases, there are no restrictions on what service is available for deploying. Of course, because that subscription is free, some publicly available regions are not available for deploying resources. Another important parameter that we need to consider when using a free subscription is resource pricing because $200 can go in a few days if we do not take care of it. For example, the smallest virtual machine with GPU costs approximately $25 per day. The second group of Azure free subscriptions is *sponsorship* subscriptions available in specific scenarios and for specific customers. There are a few different sponsorship subscriptions that include MSDN, Azure sponsorship, Visual Studio, and others, which are exclusively for customers that are eligible for sponsorship subscriptions, such as Microsoft MVPs, Microsoft Certified Trainers, cloud service providers, and others. These subscriptions have a monthly limit that varies depending on the plan that we have. MSDN subscriptions have a lower monthly limit than MPN sponsorship subscriptions.

Once we decide to go to the production workload in Azure, we need some paid subscriptions. Of course, there are a few options available, and we just need to choose one of them based on our needs. *Pay-as-you-go* is the first on the list of paid Azure subscriptions, which does not require anything more than a credit card. We just need to log in to our Azure tenant and select the option to buy a new subscription.

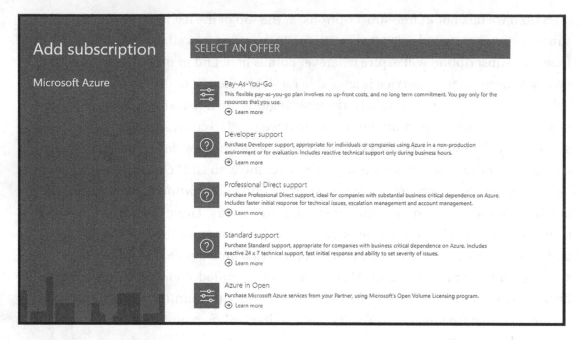

Figure 1-8. *Selecting "Pay-As-You-Go", the first option on the list of paid Azure subscriptions*

If that kind of subscription is not appropriate for our workload, other options are to buy a subscription through a reseller, such as a cloud service provider, or through the Enterprise Agreement directly with Microsoft. The difference between CSP and enterprise subscriptions is in yearly spending on resources in Azure. Enterprise customers need to define what amount will be spent on resources throughout the year. Based on that information, they will get a specific discount. Of course, enterprise customers are eligible for the hybrid benefit, which means that they can reuse their software licenses for Windows Server or SQL Server in Azure and cut the licenses' costs.

Tenant and Accounts

The core component of Azure, along with the subscription, is the *tenant*c. If we did not have a tenant when we decided to buy our first Azure subscription, we would need to create a new one. A tenant comes with Azure Active Directory (Azure AD), the enterprise identity service designed to provide authentication for the Microsoft cloud services. Many new Azure customers who use Office 365 in their organization are unaware that they already have Azure AD and the tenant. That gives them the possibility to start with Azure quickly because the tenant and accounts are already ready for use. As we said, Azure AD is an identity service, similar to the on-premises Active Directory, that contains user and group accounts. That concept has become more crucial when Azure transformed into the ARM model that we explained in this chapter earlier. Although, by default, the user account that created the subscription has the owner role, other user accounts can have the same or a different type of role on the same subscription.

Role-Based Access Control (RBAC)

In 2014, Microsoft started with the transformation of Azure from the ASM to the ARM model. One of the changes that ARM brings is *role-based access control (RBAC)*. RBAC gives us the possibility to manage access to Azure resources more granularly than we could with the ASM model and on different levels of the subscription. RBAC roles can be applied to a subscription, resource group, or single resource. Some of the built-in roles, such as Owner, Contributor, Reader, and User Access Administrator, could be found on all levels. Other roles, such as Virtual Machine Contributor or Storage Blob Data Owner, are resource-specific roles and define a specific task that the user can perform.

Along with users, RBAC can be assigned to groups, service principals, and managed identities. Also, if built-in roles are not fit for the organization, there is an option to create custom roles to meet the needs or compliance. RBAC roles work in an additive model, which means that an influential role is the sum of all applied roles to the identity. In some limited way, there is a possibility to apply for a role with "deny assignments," although RBAC native design is the allow-only model.

Chapter Recap

In this introduction chapter, we have learned what Microsoft Azure is and the main principles of public cloud in general. We were able to see the most essential physical and logical components in Microsoft Azure, which is crucial for better understanding. In the following chapter, we will take a look at tools that we can use for administering Azure workloads and understand why automation is vital in the IT world nowadays.

CHAPTER 2

Azure Administration

In Chapter 1 of this book, we were introduced to cloud concepts and what we can
expect from Microsoft's public cloud platform, Microsoft Azure. Now that we are more
familiar with the concepts, history, and underlying infrastructure principles, we can start
focusing on Azure administration.

This chapter focuses on administration tools that we can use for managing Microsoft
Azure. This chapter covers the following topics:

- Azure management using Azure Portal

- Azure PowerShell

- Azure CLI

- The ARM template – next generation of Azure management

Management Using Azure Portal

As we mentioned in the previous chapter, Microsoft Azure underwent a significant
change in late 2014 when the platform transformed from the ASM to the ARM model.
Like the complete underlying platform, Azure Portal was completely redesigned as well,
and the platform got a new access URL: `https://portal.azure.com`. Azure Portal is
the most used management tool because many customers are not familiar with other
management tools that require knowledge of command-line tools, scripting, and other
similar techniques. Using Azure Portal, we can build, manage, and monitor almost all
available resources in Microsoft Azure. Of course, there are Azure resources that cannot
be deployed or entirely managed through Azure Portal. One of the advantages of Azure
Portal is that we can easily find what new features are deployed and what regions are
available for our subscription and tenant and check usage metrics and many other
things.

© Vladimir Stefanovic and Milos Katinski 2021
V. Stefanovic and M. Katinski, *Pro Azure Administration and Automation*,
https://doi.org/10.1007/978-1-4842-7325-8_2

Azure Portal is improving daily, and over time, we are witnesses that the user interface is changing. For example, if we did not log into Azure for months, there is a big chance that we will struggle to find specific resource configurations or even resources. However, it is something we have to deal with. One of the first things that we need to configure once we are logged into Azure Portal is portal settings.

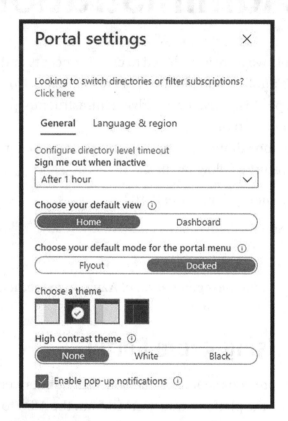

Figure 2-1. *View of the Azure portal settings*

As shown in Figure 2-1, we need to choose our default view, the mode for the portal menu, and a theme, language, and others. These configurations are saved and used as defaults whenever we log into Azure Portal. For example, if we configure that our default view is *Dashboard*, as shown in Figure 2-2, we can configure one or multiple dashboards with different important views. Maybe we want to have the necessary information in the graphical view whenever we log into Azure Portal, such as the number and list of virtual machines by size or operating system.

Figure 2-2. *Default view – Dashboard*

Otherwise, if we decide to use *Home* as the default view (Figure 2-3), we can see recently used resources.

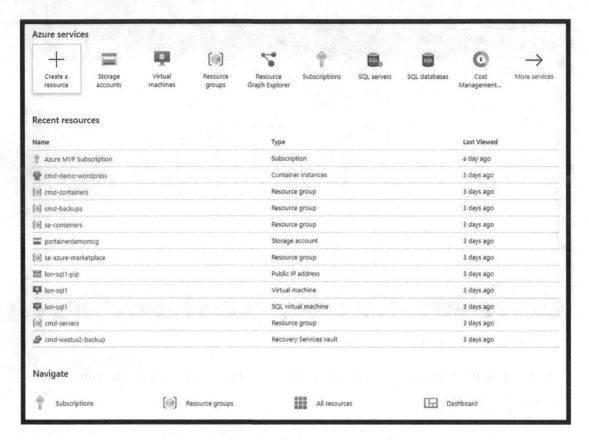

Figure 2-3. *Use "Home" as the default view to see recently used resources*

Although Azure Portal is frequently changing, the concepts of use remain the same. We can use the search bar at the top of the portal to find resources that we need or use the Favorites pane on the left side to pin frequently used resources. Azure Portal is a beneficial management tool for Microsoft Azure, especially for small environments and for customers with a limited set of technical skills. Of course, Azure Portal has limitations. We are not able to deploy and manage all Azure resources and their configurations, and we are not able to deploy multiple instances of resources without additional configuration. For instance, if we want to deploy five virtual machines simultaneously, we need to go through the same deployment procedure five times, which is a time-consuming process, or if we want to deploy Web Apps and Azure SQL Database and make a connection between these services manually using Azure Portal, we will spend more time for deployment and post-configuration, although we need to deploy one instance only of each of these services. However, deploying multiple instances of any of Azure services is much easier using any of the tools that we could use for automation in Azure, especially if deployment could be reused more than once. In addition, some of the services, such as virtual machine scale sets, do not have all configuration parameters available in Azure Portal for configuring. Some of the parameters will be used with a default value, whereas all of them could be configured with custom values if we use ARM templates or other automation and Infrastructure as Code tools.

Along with Azure Portal, accessible in a browser through URL `https://portal.azure.com`, there is also the Azure Portal Desktop App and the Azure mobile app. The Azure Portal Desktop App is available for download at `https://portal.azure.com/App/Download` and provides a similar experience to using Azure Portal in any of the browsers. The Azure mobile app, shown in Figure 2-4, is available for download for iOS and Android mobile devices. The application is limited, and we cannot deploy resources, but we can see metrics or status of resources or restart web apps or virtual machines.

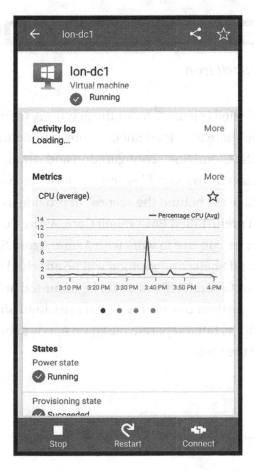

Figure 2-4. *The Azure mobile app*

Azure Cloud Shell

One of the essential Azure Portal features is Azure Cloud Shell. This feature, introduced in 2017, is a browser-based, interactive shell for managing Azure resources. Cloud Shell provides shell experience, either for Azure CLI or PowerShell, and allows us to work with command-line interfaces without having them installed locally. We said earlier that the Azure mobile app is not suitable for deploying Azure resources due to the limitations in functionalities. Nevertheless, Cloud Shell is available in the Azure mobile app, as well as the Azure Portal Desktop App. If we are comfortable with typing Azure CLI or Azure PowerShell commands on mobile device keyboards, there is no limitation in managing Azure resources.

Cloud Shell is accessible through the URL `https://shell.azure.com` or directly from Azure Portal by clicking the Cloud Shell icon at the top, as shown in Figure 2-5.

Figure 2-5. *The Cloud Shell icon*

When we open Cloud Shell (Figure 2-6) for the first time, we need to provide a storage account with a file share for Cloud Shell's proper configuration. A storage account will be used for the Cloud Shell configuration and simultaneously will provide us persistent data that allows us to reuse files and scripts whenever we use Cloud Shell. Instances that Cloud Shell uses "behind the scenes" to provide us browser-based shell are Linux containers with preinstalled PowerShell Core, Azure PowerShell, Azure CLI, and many other tools that we can use to work with Azure. Azure file share provided and configured during the Cloud Shell configuration will be attached to the Cloud Shell instance whenever we start Cloud Shell but could be mounted only from regions that are available for us. Also, if more than one user wants to use Cloud Shell, the same process of configuring needs to be done, but a separate file share needs to be created, whereas the storage account could be the same.

You have no storage mounted   ×

Azure Cloud Shell requires an Azure file share to persist files. Learn more
This will create a new storage account for you and this will incur a small monthly cost. View pricing

* Subscription

Azure Sponsorship 20-21   Show advanced settings

Create storage   Close

Figure 2-6. Opening Cloud Shell for the first time

Another good thing with Cloud Shell is that we are automatically authenticated to the Azure tenant and subscription. There is no need to run the command az login or Connect-AzAccount to log in to Azure. We just need to select whether we want to work in the PowerShell or Bash (Azure CLI) environment. Also, at any time of work, we can switch from Bash to PowerShell and vice versa. Another thing that we need to know is that the Cloud Shell sessions are limited to 20 minutes of inactivity and are not designed for long-running jobs.

Cloud Shell allows us to create or edit files and scripts that we need to use. By typing code in Cloud Shell, the built-in open source file editor, *Monaco Editor*, starts. Monaco Editor is a lightweight editor synced with the provided Azure file share, which allows us to create and edit files and scripts that need to be reused.

Azure PowerShell

As we saw, Azure Portal is a valuable management tool for building, managing, and monitoring Azure resources, especially if we combine the portal with Cloud Shell. Nevertheless, Azure Portal, by design, is not suitable for automation and mass-scale deployments. For those scenarios, we need to use other management tools, such as Azure PowerShell, Azure CLI, or ARM templates.

Fourteen years ago, Microsoft released the first version of the task automation and configuration management framework, PowerShell. PowerShell is designed to help Microsoft administrators in automation tasks and, over the years, has become an essential part of the administration of many different Microsoft products, as well as products from other vendors. In 2016, Microsoft introduced PowerShell Core, a cross-platform tool, to replace the initial Windows PowerShell designed for Windows systems. PowerShell Core is built on .NET Core, while Windows PowerShell is built on .NET Framework.

PowerShell is part of Azure management tools from the early days. However, we are not going back in history and going to check previous PowerShell modules for Azure administration. The Azure PowerShell module was available in the ASM model. When Azure transformed into the ARM model, the new *AzureRM* PowerShell module was released, which is deprecated today. The actual Azure PowerShell module nowadays is the *Azure PowerShell Az* module. At the time of writing this book, the last stable version of the *Az* module is 6.3.0. In December 2018, Microsoft released the first version of the *Azure PowerShell Az* module. The former *AzureRM* module is no longer in development, and because Az PowerShell modules have all the needed capabilities, Microsoft has decided to retire the AzureRM module completely on February 29, 2024. If we look at the years of releases of PowerShell Core and the new Az module, we can confirm that Microsoft decided to continue with a cross-platform concept.

Like all other PowerShell modules, the Azure PowerShell module is based on the *Verb-Noun* principle. Over the years, the library of cmdlets for Azure management has grown, and today a lot of Azure resources can be managed by Azure PowerShell. Unfortunately, there are still resources that are not included in modules and cannot be managed by PowerShell. Of course, the Azure PowerShell module must be installed before we decide to work with it. That can be done using the command `Install-Module Az`. So let us take a look at basic Azure PowerShell commands for logging in to Azure and selecting a subscription.

The cmdlet `Connect-AzAccount` is used if we want to log in to Azure using Azure PowerShell. This cmdlet supports several authentication methods, but the most crucial difference between Windows PowerShell and PowerShell Core, when we use this cmdlet, is the authentication process. If we use this cmdlet in Windows PowerShell 5.1, we can see that authentication is interactive, as shown in Figure 2-7, and we need to provide credentials.

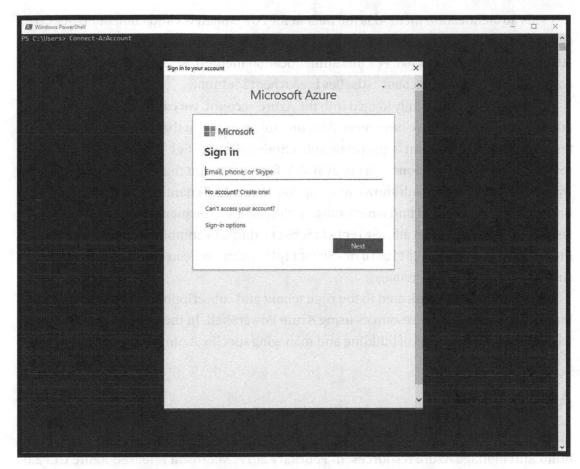

Figure 2-7. *The need for credentials*

If we use the same cmdlet in PowerShell Core, device code authentication is performed instead of interactive control (Figure 2-8), so we need to open the page `https://microsoft.com/devicelogin` and type the code for authentication.

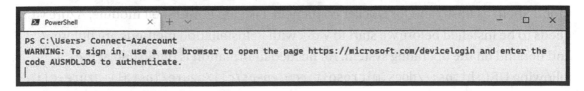

Figure 2-8. *Type the code for authentication*

This authentication method is the default for PowerShell 6.x and later, but is also available in Windows PowerShell by adding the switch parameter -UseDeviceAuthentication. For this authentication method, we need to use the command `Connect-AzAccount -UseDeviceAuthentication`.

Once we are successfully logged into the Azure account, we can start with administration tasks. If we have more than one subscription in the tenant, the first task should be selecting an appropriate subscription. Cmdlet `Get-AzSubscription` returns a list of subscriptions that are available for the account that is used for login. By default, the output result shows subscription Name, Id, TenantId, and State. This information is enough to find which subscription needs to be managed. Using cmdlet `Select-AzContext,` or its alias `Select-AzSubscription`, in combination with one of the parameters, `-SubscriptionId` or `-SubscriptionName`, we can select an appropriate subscription we want to manage.

When we are authenticated to the right tenant and subscription, we are ready to build and manage Azure resources using Azure PowerShell. In the following chapters, we will see various examples of building and managing specific Azure resources.

Azure CLI

Like PowerShell, Azure CLI (command-line interface) is a set of commands used to build and manage Azure resources. In February 2017, Microsoft released Azure CLI 2.0 as the successor of the previous version, 1.0. Azure CLI is designed as a cross-platform management tool, which can be installed on Windows, Linux, and macOS. At the time of writing this book, the latest stable version is 2.27.1. Azure CLI is no replacement for Azure PowerShell. Most of the resources have modules and commands for both management tools.

As we mentioned earlier, Azure CLI is available for all operating systems, as well as in Cloud Shell (as Bash) and for Docker containers. Like the PowerShell module, Azure CLI needs to be installed before we start to work with it. Installation methods are different and depend on the operating system. All needed information is published at the following URL: `https://docs.microsoft.com/en-us/cli/azure/install-azure-cli`. Once we have installed Azure CLI locally or in a Docker container, we can manage Azure resources with Azure CLI. Of course, if we do not want to install Azure CLI locally, we can start Cloud Shell with an appropriate subscription and start with work.

In the previous section, we used Azure PowerShell to log into Azure and an appropriate subscription. Let us see how the same process is accomplished by using Azure CLI. The command `az login` performs interactive authentication that uses a web browser and access token to sign into Azure. Once we are logged into Azure, the output returns JSON-formatted information about all subscriptions assigned to the account used for login. In some scenarios, we do not want to have any output on the screen with tenant and subscription information due to regulations or compliance. If we run command `az login --output none`, the same login process occurs, but there is no output information on the screen.

Once we are logged in, we have to check what the available subscriptions are and select an appropriate one to manage. By default, we are logged into the default subscription, which is maybe not appropriate for desired management tasks. Azure CLI command `az account show` gives us information about the current subscription. If we want to list all possible subscriptions, we need to run the command `az account list` or `az account list --output table`, if we prefer table output instead of default JSON-formatted output, as shown in Figure 2-9.

```
PS C:\Users> az account list --output table
Name                   CloudName    SubscriptionId                         State    IsDefault
---------------------  -----------  -------------------------------------  -------  ---------
Azure Pay-as-you-Go    AzureCloud   527bcc40-8db4-4d70-8e97-0e5156145327   Enabled  True
Azure Sponsorship 20-21 AzureCloud  4037a621-6966-40c1-b2f0-3e96cc57a667   Enabled  False
```

Figure 2-9. *To list all possible subscriptions, run the command* `az account list`

Once we decide on which subscription is appropriate for our management tasks, we need to run the command `az account set --subscription "mySubscription"` and put the subscription name or ID between quotes. When we are authenticated to the right tenant and subscription, we can build and manage Azure resources using Azure CLI.

ARM Template

In the previous chapter, we talked briefly about the history of Azure. We mentioned that in 2014, Microsoft began the transformation of Azure from the ASM to the ARM model. Also, we talked about the benefits that ARM brought and mentioned the ARM template as one of the significant benefits. Now is the time to talk about the ARM template a little bit more. In previous sections, Azure Portal, Azure PowerShell, and Azure CLI were covered as management tools provided by Microsoft.

If we compare the ARM template with Azure PowerShell and Azure CLI, the first thing that we can see is that they are very different. The ARM template is a JSON-formatted file thast defines the infrastructure to be deployed. Also, the ARM template is declarative and idempotent, unlike Azure PowerShell and Azure CLI, which are imperative. ARM allows us to create a template that can deploy complete infrastructure in a declarative fashion. Templates are reusable and every time give the same result. This is useful in scenarios where we need to have the same environment for test or development as we have in production. An additional benefit of the ARM template is extensibility of the deployment scripts, allowing us to run post-configuration scripts on the deployed environment and configure the end-to-end solution. The ARM template has built-in validation. The resource manager checks the template before the execution of deployment to confirm that the template is valid. In other words, the ARM template is a powerful Azure management tool that is a "must-have" in Azure management.

ARM Template Format

Before deploying resources with the ARM template, we need to know what each ARM template must include. The base ARM template has to look like the following example:

```
{
  "$schema": "https://schema.management.azure.com/schemas/2019-04-01/
  deploymentTemplate.json#",
  "contentVersion": "",
  "parameters": {},
  "variables": {},
  "functions": [],
  "resources": [],
  "outputs": {}
}
```

- Schema: Version of the template language that is used

- Content version: Version of the template (default is 1.0.0.0)

- Parameters: Values that need to be provided for deployment

- Variables: Values that are "hard-coded" in the template for reusage in the template language

- Functions: User-defined functions that are available in the template

- Resources: Resources that are to be deployed or updated

- Output: Values that return after deployment

Schema, content version, and resources are template elements that are required. Other elements are not required, but parameters, variables, and output are used in most of the templates.

ARM Template Example

Now that we know what is essential for a functional ARM template, let us create one ARM template and deploy resources. In this example, we are creating a basic ARM template that deploys a storage account:

```
{
    "$schema": "https://schema.management.azure.com/schemas/2019-04-01/
    deploymentTemplate.json#",
    "contentVersion": "1.0.0.0",
    "parameters": {
        "storageAccountName": {
            "type": "string"
        }
    },
    "functions": [],
    "variables": {
        "location": "[resourceGroup().location]"
    },
    "resources": [
        {
            "name": "[parameters('storageAccountName')]",
            "type": "Microsoft.Storage/storageAccounts",
            "apiVersion": "2019-06-01",
            "location": "[variables('location')]",
            "kind": "StorageV2",
            "sku": {
                "name": "Standard_LRS",
```

```
                    "tier": "Standard"
                }
            }
    ],
    "outputs": {
        "storageAccountName": {
            "type": "string",
            "value": "[parameters('storageAccountName')]"
        },
        "location": {
            "type": "string",
            "value": "[variables('location')]"
        }
    }
}
```

Before we deploy resources using this ARM template, let us see what is declared in this ARM template:

- One parameter (storageAccountName) that needs to be provided for deployment

- One variable (location) that collects the information about the location of the resource group and is reused in the template expression

- One resource (storage account) that is deployed with basic configuration by using the provided parameter and variable

- Two output values (storageAccountName and location) as the output result after deployment

ARM Template File

If the ARM template has configured parameters, some parameter values need to be provided for deployment. If we want to deploy the ARM template using Azure Portal by creating a custom deployment, the parameter file is unnecessary. Once we load the custom template file, we can provide the required values manually. Nevertheless, if we want to deploy the ARM template that requires parameter values using Azure PowerShell or Azure CLI, we need to have a template parameter file. This file defines values for the parameters that are required in the template file for deployment. Like an ARM template file, the template parameter file must have a schema and content version and the parameters element that provides the required values. The template parameter file for the ARM template that we are using in this example is as follows:

```
{
  "$schema": "https://schema.management.azure.com/schemas/2015-01-01/
  deploymentParameters.json#",
  "contentVersion": "1.0.0.0",
  "parameters": {
    "storageAccountName": {
      "value": "apressstorageaccount"
    }
  }
}
```

There is an option to define a *default value* for parameters in the ARM template that reduces the need for manually typing parameter values or using template parameter files. This is not a replacement for the template parameter file, but it could be helpful in specific scenarios. If the *default value* is configured, the resource manager can validate the ARM template even though we do not provide a template parameter file. For example, the default value for the parameters used in our example has to be configured as in the following example:

```
"storageAccountName": {
        "type": "string",
        "defaultValue": "apressazureadministration"
    }
```

ARM Template Deployment

There are a few different approaches to deploy the ARM template. We can deploy a custom ARM template using Azure Portal and Azure PowerShell or Azure CLI. If we decide to use Azure Portal for deploying the ARM template, we need to search for "deploy" in the search box and select *Deploy a custom template* and then click *Build your own template in the editor*. Then, we can copy the ARM template code or load the file and click *Save*, as shown in Figure 2-10.

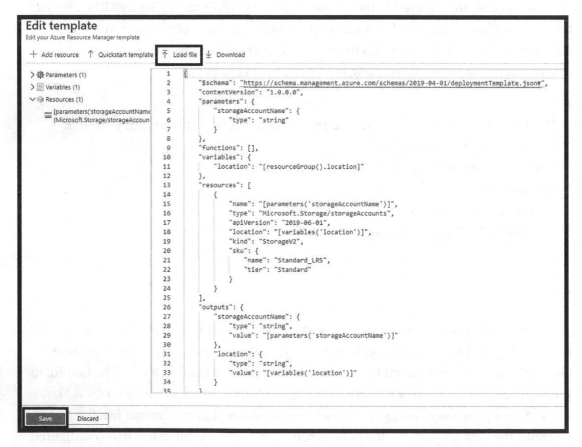

Figure 2-10. *Copy the ARM template code or load the file and click Save*

On the *Custom deployment* page, we need to select an appropriate resource group, existing or create new, and provide parameter values. If we do not want to provide parameter values manually, we can click *Edit parameters*, load the template parameter file, and click *Save* (Figure 2-11). Finally, we have to check the checkbox *I agree to the terms and conditions stated above* and click *Purchase*. Once the template validation is finished, the deployment starts.

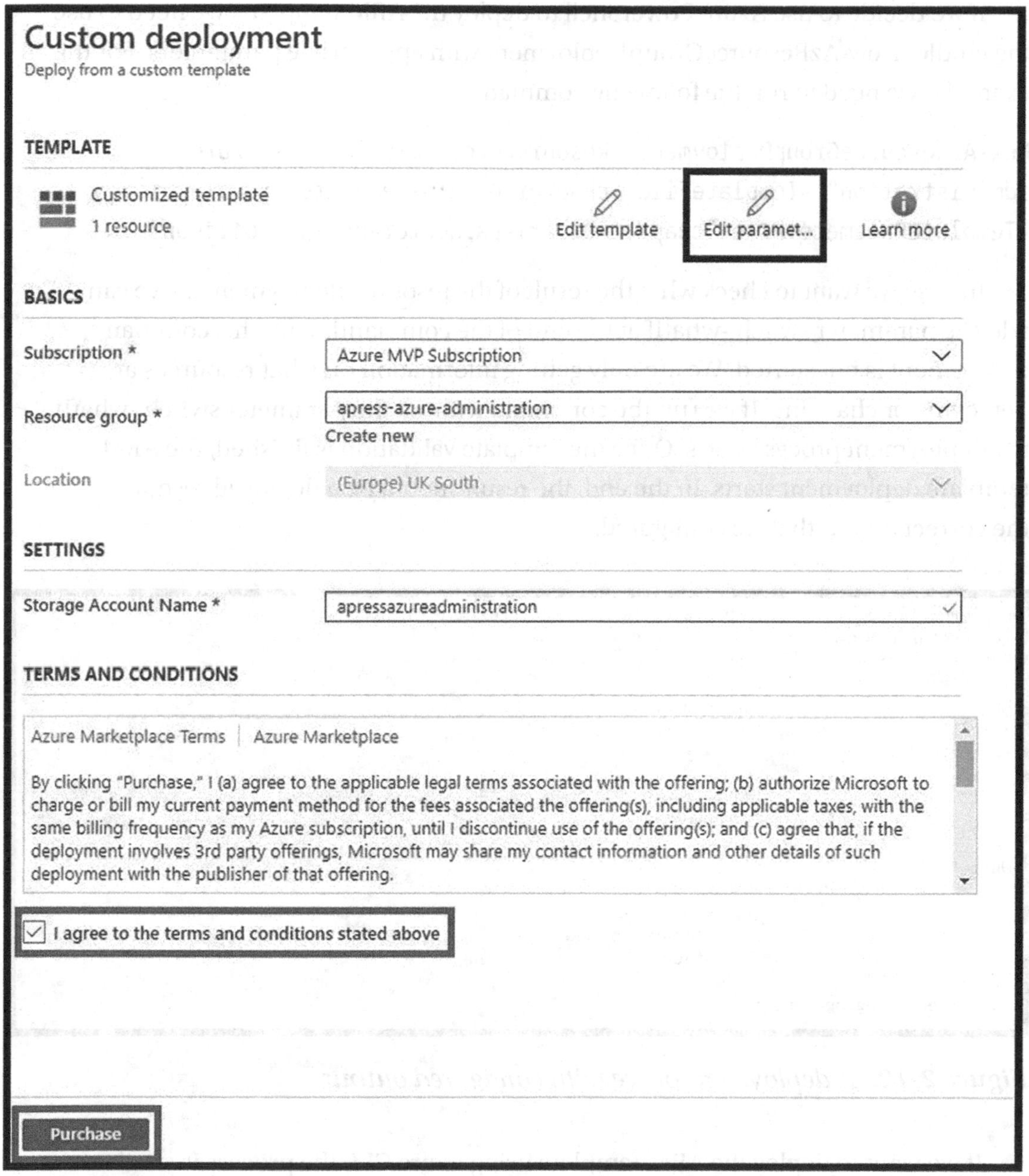

Custom deployment
Deploy from a custom template

TEMPLATE

■■■ Customized template
■■ 1 resource   Edit template   Edit paramet...   ⓘ Learn more

BASICS

Subscription *   Azure MVP Subscription   ⌄

Resource group *   apress-azure-administration   ⌄
                                  Create new

Location   (Europe) UK South   ⌄

SETTINGS

Storage Account Name *   apressazureadministration   ✓

TERMS AND CONDITIONS

Azure Marketplace Terms │ Azure Marketplace

By clicking "Purchase," I (a) agree to the applicable legal terms associated with the offering; (b) authorize Microsoft to charge or bill my current payment method for the fees associated the offering(s), including applicable taxes, with the same billing frequency as my Azure subscription, until I discontinue use of the offering(s); and (c) agree that, if the deployment involves 3rd party offerings, Microsoft may share my contact information and other details of such deployment with the publisher of that offering.

☑ I agree to the terms and conditions stated above

Purchase

Figure 2-11. *Click Edit parameters, load the template parameter file, and click Save. Check the checkbox agreeing to the terms and click Purchase*

If we decide to use Azure PowerShell to deploy the ARM template, we need to use the cmdlet New-AzResourceGroupDeployment with appropriate parameters. For this example, we need to run the following command:

```
New-AzResourceGroupDeployment -ResourceGroupName "apress-azure-
administration" -TemplateFile "chapter-02-arm-template-example-01.json"
-TemplateParameterFile "chapter-02-arm-parameter-example-01.json"
```

In case we want to check what the result of the resource deployment is, we can add the parameter switch -whatIf at the end of the command. With this command, deployment is not started. We are only getting information on what resources are deploying or changing. If we run the command without the parameter switch -whatIf, the deployment process starts. Once the template validation is finished, the ARM template deployment starts. In the end, the result should be a deployed resource with the correct output that we configured.

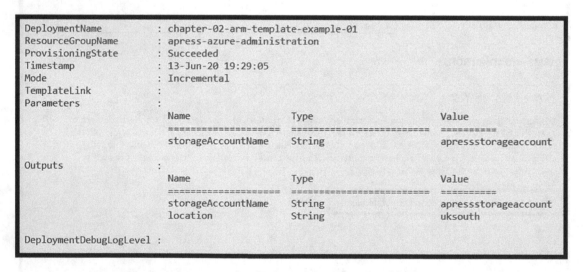

Figure 2-12. *A deployed resource with configured output*

If we want to deploy the ARM template using Azure CLI, the process is similar to that we used with Azure PowerShell, but the commands are different. If we want to test what resources are deploying or configuring, we can use the command

```
az deployment group what-if --resource-group apress-azure-administration
--template-file chapter-02-arm-template-example-01.json --parameters
chapter-02-arm-parameter-example-01.json
```

Once the command is completed, we get an output result on what happens when running this deployment. If we want to start deploying a custom ARM template using Azure CLI, we need to run the following command. Once the template is validated, the deployment starts:

```
az deployment group create --resource-group apress-azure-administration
--template-file chapter-02-arm-template-example-01.json --parameters
chapter-02-arm-parameter-example-01.json
```

To use what-if operations in Azure PowerShell or Azure CLI, we must install PowerShell Az module 4.2.0 or later and Azure CLI 2.5.0 or later. In these examples, we deployed a custom ARM template to a resource group. However, we need to know that the ARM templates can be deployed on the subscription and tenant level and management group level.

Chapter Recap

In this chapter, we were able to see the management options in Azure. As we will see in the following chapters, the majority of the Azure services could be deployed and managed using all of these management tools. What tool will be our first choice depends on many different factors, but we need to emphasize again that Azure Portal could not do automation.

In the next chapter, we will start with administration and automation topics. We will learn why the virtual network is essential, how to deploy and configure virtual networks using different management tools, what other networking resources in Azure are important, why we need them, and what is the process of their deployment and management.

CHAPTER 3

Virtual Networks in Azure

In Chapter 2 of this book, we covered four different tools to manage Azure resources. In the following chapters, we will see how we can deploy sAzure infrastructure using all these tools and decide on what is preferable for our needs.

This chapter will cover the basics of networking in Azure through the following topics:

- Virtual networks (VNets) and subnets
- Network interface card (NIC)
- IP addresses
- Network security groups (NSGs)
- Service endpoints
- Private endpoints

Virtual Networks and Subnets

Networking represents the core component of on-premises datacenters. The same goes for Azure. It is a vital component of each IaaS solution, hybrid implementations, and, with the latest service integrations, PaaS too. Azure networking components are giving us the possibility to design and build infrastructure based on our needs.

© Vladimir Stefanovic and Milos Katinski 2021
V. Stefanovic and M. Katinski, *Pro Azure Administration and Automation*,
https://doi.org/10.1007/978-1-4842-7325-8_3

Virtual Network (VNet)

An Azure virtual network enables us to connect our resources in Azure securely. It is very similar to the on-premises network that we are used to but gives us additional security layers, availability, and isolation. The main components of the virtual network are

- Address space: It is mandatory to create a private IP address space where we can use standard private ranges like 10.0.0.0/8 (class A), 172.16.0.0/12 (class B), and 192.168.0.0/16 or ones from the public scope (if your organization owns them).

- Subnet: Based on our needs, we are making segments of our address space that will later be used for deploying resources into them.

A virtual network is scoped to a specific region and a subscription where it is deployed (Figure 3-1). However, with some additional network services that we will cover in Chapter 7, virtual networks from different regions/subscriptions can be connected. This way, we can expand network reach to other parts of our cloud infrastructure.

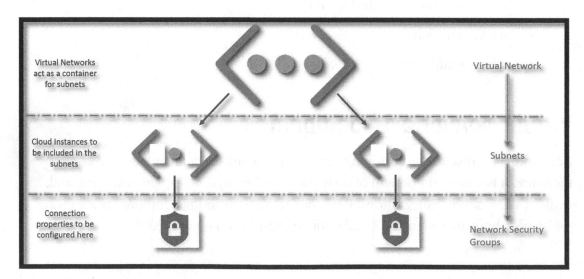

Figure 3-1. *A virtual network is scoped to a specific region and a subscription where it is deployed*

There are a couple of essential things and recommended practices that should be followed:

- We must pay attention that our virtual network address space is not overlapping with another one in our subscription or with our organization's on-premises ranges.

- One subnet should never cover the total address space. We need to plan up-front and have in mind additional services that might be deployed to the VNet. Having multiple subnets allows us to secure and filter traffic between different types of services.

- It is easier to manage few large virtual network address spaces than multiple small ones.

Subnet

Subnets represent the segments of our virtual network. Using them, we can improve the security, performance, and manageability of our network. Subnets are defined with a range of IP addresses under the scope of the virtual network address space. They must have a unique address range with no overlapping. An important thing to have in mind when designing the subnets is that when we create them, Azure "takes" five addresses for its purpose (the example is based on a /24 subnet range):

- x.x.x.0: Network address

- x.x.x.1: Reserved by Azure for the default gateway

- x.x.x.2, x.x.x.3: Reserved by Azure to map the Azure DNS IPs to the virtual network space

- x.x.x.255: Network broadcast address

Other things that need to be taken into consideration are

- Service requirements: Depending on the service that we plan to deploy to our subnet, we must think about routing and specific traffic that we need to allow. Certain services have exact prerequisites on subnet size and naming.

- Virtual appliances: By default, traffic between subnets in one virtual network is routed. By using virtual network appliances, we can either filter or entirely prevent a sort of traffic.

- Service endpoints: We will cover them later in this chapter. However, they will allow us to limit access to certain Azure resources to a specific subnet in a virtual network.

- Network security groups: Rule-based filtering service that we will also cover in this chapter.

Creating a Virtual Network and Subnets

In this part of the chapter, we will learn how to deploy a virtual network with subnets using the tools mentioned in the previous chapter.

Azure Portal

When we log into Azure Portal, from the menu, we can select **Create a resource**. From the Marketplace, we can then search for "virtual network" and select the proposed one from the results. On **Create virtual network** (Figure 3-2), we need to select the subscription for deployment, resource group where the virtual network will be deployed, name, and region.

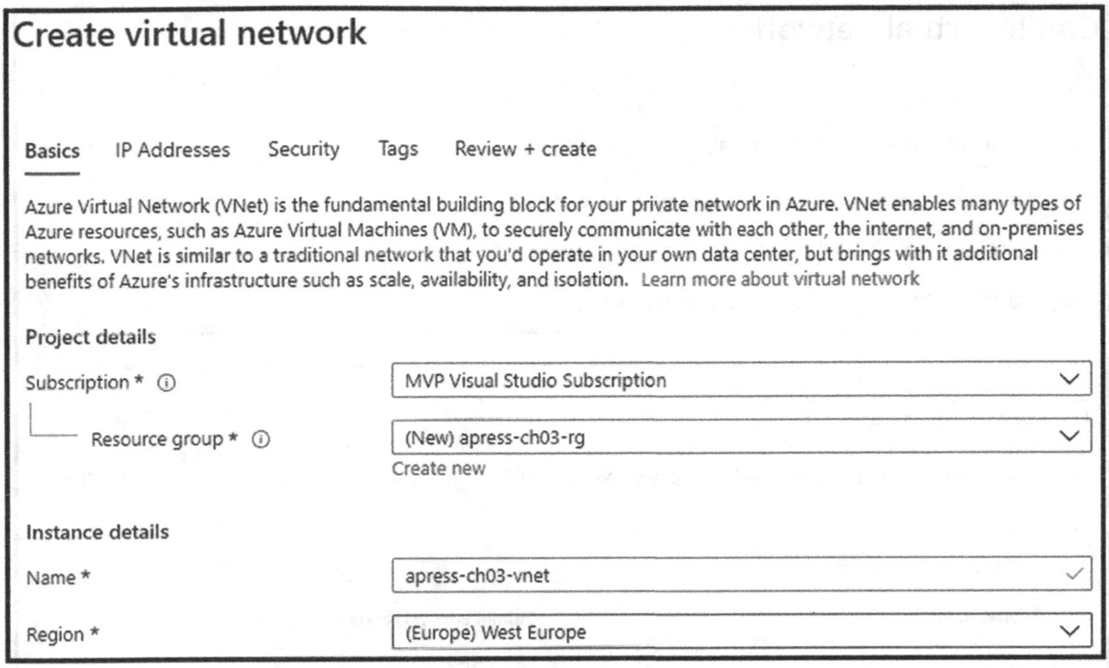

Create virtual network

Basics   IP Addresses   Security   Tags   Review + create

Azure Virtual Network (VNet) is the fundamental building block for your private network in Azure. VNet enables many types of Azure resources, such as Azure Virtual Machines (VM), to securely communicate with each other, the internet, and on-premises networks. VNet is similar to a traditional network that you'd operate in your own data center, but brings with it additional benefits of Azure's infrastructure such as scale, availability, and isolation. Learn more about virtual network

Project details

Subscription * ⓘ | MVP Visual Studio Subscription   ∨ |

　　└──── Resource group * ⓘ | (New) apress-ch03-rg   ∨ |
　　　　　　　　　　　　　　　　　　　　　　 Create new

Instance details

Name * | apress-ch03-vnet   ✓ |

Region * | (Europe) West Europe   ∨ |

Figure 3-2. *Select the subscription for deployment, resource group where the virtual network will be deployed, name, and region*

Tip   *Before we start deploying our resources, we should think about the naming convention. Microsoft has a best practice document for this, which we can adapt to our needs* – https://docs.microsoft.com/en-us/azure/cloud-adoption-framework/ready/azure-best-practices/naming-and-tagging.

In the next step, we need to decide about the address space used and create a subnet(s) if we have them designed (Figure 3-3).

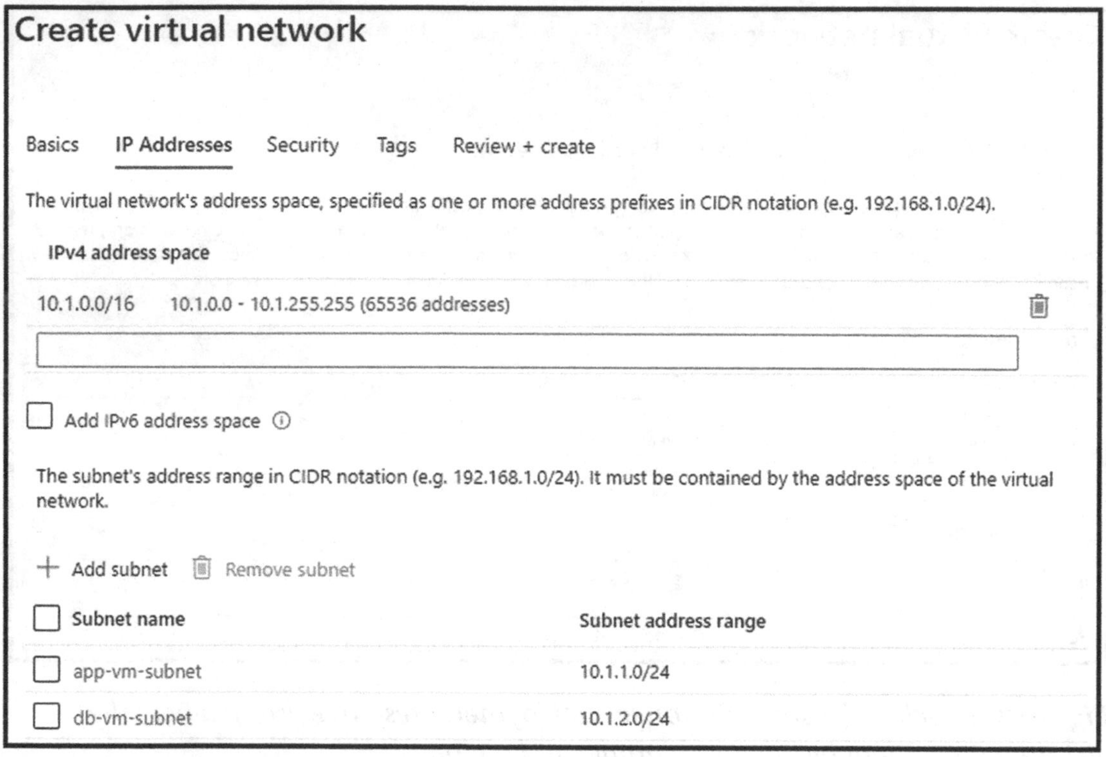

Figure 3-3. *Make a decision about the IP address*

On the **Security** tab, we will leave everything by default now. These services will be covered in later chapters. It is best practice to tag services (Figure 3-4), so we need also to design this.

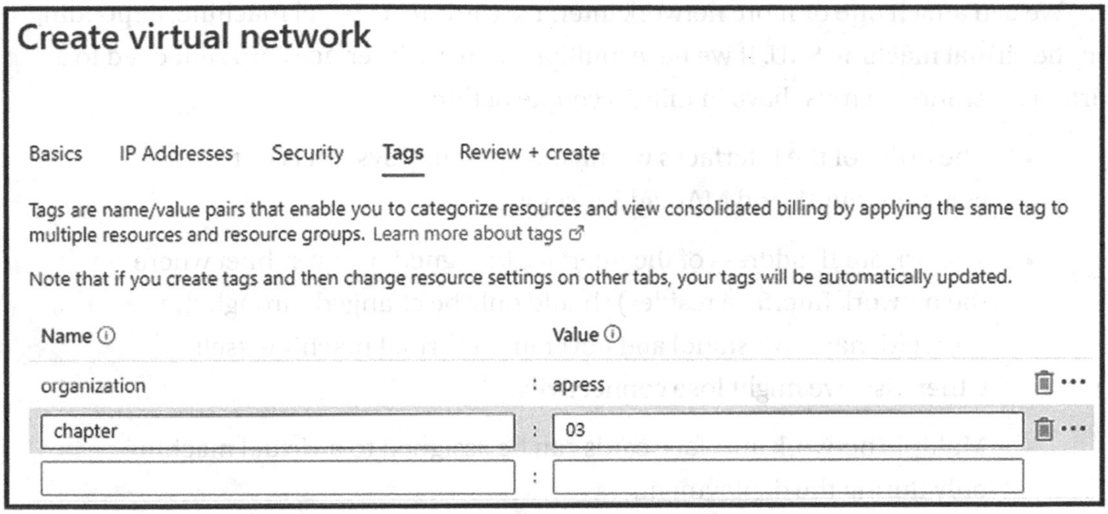

Create virtual network

Basics   IP Addresses   Security   **Tags**   Review + create

Tags are name/value pairs that enable you to categorize resources and view consolidated billing by applying the same tag to multiple resources and resource groups. Learn more about tags ☐

Note that if you create tags and then change resource settings on other tabs, your tags will be automatically updated.

Name ⓘ		Value ⓘ		
organization	:	apress	🗑	···
chapter	:	03	🗑	···
	:			

Figure 3-4. *It is a best practice to tag services*

When we select **Review + create**, Azure will validate entered data, and if everything is okay, we will be able to create our resource.

ARM Template, PowerShell, and Azure CLI

Since the deployment code could be pretty big, all ARM template, Azure PowerShell, and Azure CLI scripts are stored in the Apress GitHub account, available at the following URL:

`https://github.com/Apress/pro-azure-admin-and-automation`

Network Interface Card (NIC)

A network interface card is one of the resources being created while deploying a virtual machine in Azure, which will be covered in Chapter 4. It gives the virtual machine the possibility to communicate with other resources in Azure or on-premises and with the Internet. During the virtual machine deployment, Azure will create a NIC for us with some default parameters. If we want to use some custom settings, we can create a NIC on our own (Figure 3-5) or change an existing one.

We can attach one or more network interface cards to a virtual machine, depending on the virtual machine SKU. If we have multiple network interface cards attached to a virtual machine, we must have in mind a couple of things:

- The order of the interfaces within the operating system is not constant, but IP and MAC addresses are.

- The private IP address of the interface (assigned by the subnet where the network interface resides) should only be changed through the portal (dynamic or static) and never in the virtual machine itself. Otherwise, we might lose connectivity.

- Multiple network interface cards can be assigned to a virtual machine only during the deployment.

Creating a Network Interface Card

A network interface card will be deployed along with the virtual machine, and in most cases, that will be more than enough. If we need to add more network interface cards to virtual machines, we must create them before adding them. That could be done using all known management tools.

Azure Portal

If we want to deploy a network interface card using Azure Portal, the following steps will show us how to do that. When we log into Azure Portal, from the menu, we can select **Create a resource**. From the Marketplace, we can search for "network interface" and then select the proposed one from the results.

On **Create network interface**, we need to select the subscription for deployment, resource group where the network interface card will be deployed, name, and region. We also need to assign a network interface card to an existing virtual network and subnet. The next step would be to decide if we will use a dynamic or static IP address for our interface. In most cases, we will use static assignment, so we should choose this option. We can already insert an IP address that will be reserved for this network interface card. (Remember from the subnet explanation that we must skip the first three addresses used by Azure. Otherwise, our deployment will fail.)

We will cover the use of the **network security group** later in this chapter. For now, we will leave it by default – None.

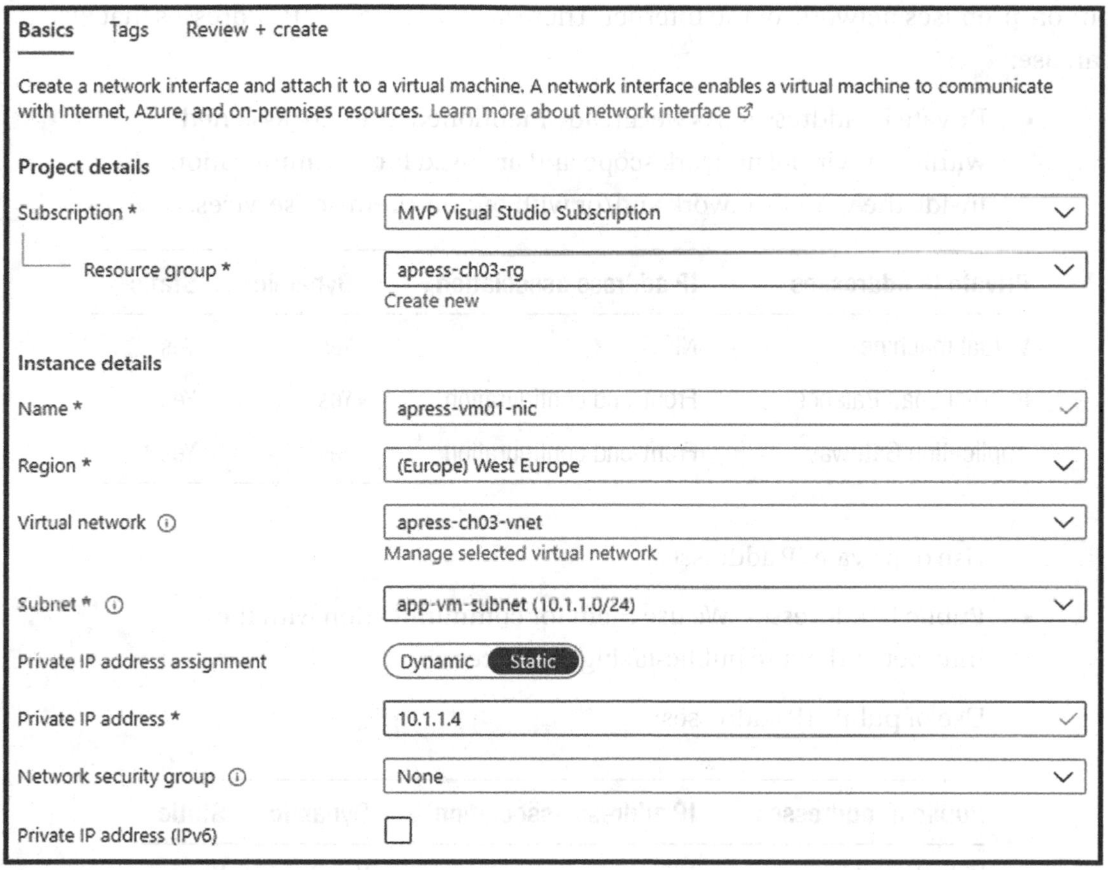

Basics   Tags   Review + create

Create a network interface and attach it to a virtual machine. A network interface enables a virtual machine to communicate with Internet, Azure, and on-premises resources. Learn more about network interface ⬚

Project details

Subscription *	MVP Visual Studio Subscription	⌄
Resource group *	apress-ch03-rg	⌄
	Create new	

Instance details

Name *	apress-vm01-nic	✓
Region *	(Europe) West Europe	⌄
Virtual network ⓘ	apress-ch03-vnet	⌄
	Manage selected virtual network	
Subnet * ⓘ	app-vm-subnet (10.1.1.0/24)	⌄
Private IP address assignment	Dynamic Static	
Private IP address *	10.1.1.4	✓
Network security group ⓘ	None	⌄
Private IP address (IPv6)	☐	

Figure 3-5. *If you want to use some custom settings, create a NIC or change an existing one*

After we populate tags as per design, we can review and create our resource.

ARM Template, PowerShell, and Azure CLI

Since the deployment code could be pretty big, all ARM template, Azure PowerShell, and Azure CLI scripts are stored in the Apress GitHub account, available at the following URL:

https://github.com/Apress/pro-azure-admin-and-automation

IP Addresses

We can assign IP addresses to Azure resources for them to communicate with each other, our on-premises network, or the Internet. There are two types of IP addresses that we can use:

- Private IP addresses: As we already mentioned, they are assigned within our virtual network scope and are used for communication inside the virtual network and/or with our on-premises services.

Private IP addresses	IP address association	Dynamic	Static
Virtual machine	NIC	Yes	Yes
Internal Load Balancer	Front-end configuration	Yes	Yes
Application Gateway	Front-end configuration	Yes	Yes

  Use of private IP addresses:

- Public IP addresses: We use them for communication with the Internet and Azure public-facing resources.

  Use of public IP addresses:

Public IP addresses	IP address association	Dynamic	Static
Virtual machine	NIC	Yes	Yes
Load Balancer	Front-end configuration	Yes	Yes
VPN Gateway	Gateway IP configuration	Yes	No
Application Gateway	Front-end configuration	Yes	No

Both private and public IPs can be set as **static** or **dynamic**. The Azure DHCP servers are the ones assigning the private IP address. When we say "static," we are making a reservation within our IP address space. When we assign a public IP address, it is by default a dynamic one. That means that when we deallocate a virtual machine, the address might change upon the next start. If we change the assignment to static, we will preserve the given IP until the public IP resource itself is deleted. Important notice regarding public IP addresses: Even if we create multiple consecutive resources with public IPs, that does not mean that we will get those IPs in the raw. If, for any reason, we need a logical address space, we need to obtain a public IP address prefix from Azure. The public IP prefix represents a reserved range of IP addresses.

Creating IPs

A public IP address is an Azure resource, unlike a private IP address, which is a logical representation and inevitable configuration parameter of a network interface card. In this part of the chapter, we will learn how to create a public IP address using all known Azure management tools.

Azure Portal

When we log into Azure Portal, from the menu, we can select **Create a resource**. From the Marketplace, we can search for "public IP address" and then select the proposed one from the results. On **Create public IP address** (Figure 3-6), we need to select the subscription for deployment, resource group where the IP will be deployed, name, and region. The next step would be to decide if we will use a dynamic or static IP address. We can also assign a DNS name for our public IP (it must be globally unique).

An important choice is the SKU of the IP: **Basic** or **Standard**. The choice between these two depends on the service to which we will assign our public IP. For this, we need to read the official documentation of the desired service and check for prerequisites. Notice that if we choose **Standard SKU**, the IP will be assigned as **Static**, and we will be able to set an additional option – **zone redundancy**.

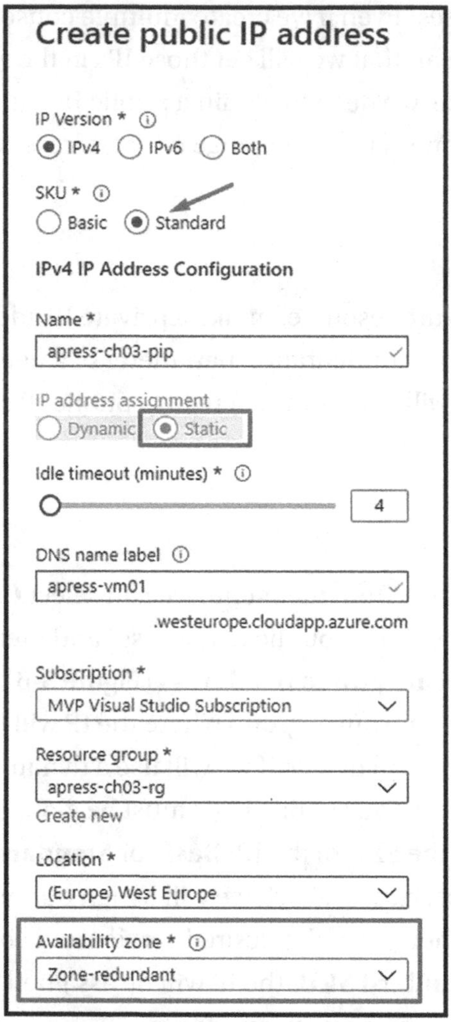

Figure 3-6. *Select the subscription for deployment, resource group where the IP will be deployed, name, and region*

We can now choose to create a public IP.

At this point, our new public IP is not associated with any service. In order to do that, we must do it manually.

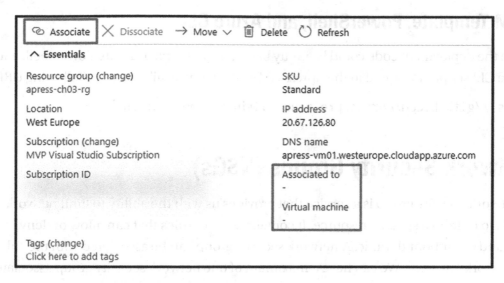

Figure 3-7. *Click the Associate button*

When we click the **Associate** button (Figure 3-7), we will choose the service for it (Figure 3-8).

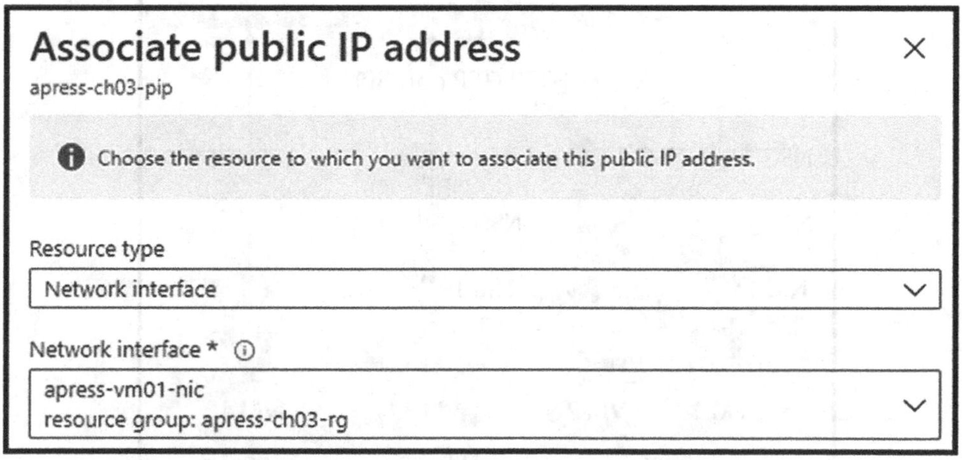

Figure 3-8. *Choose the service for the Associate button*

ARM Template, PowerShell, and Azure CLI

Since the deployment code could be pretty big, all ARM template, Azure PowerShell, and Azure CLI scripts are stored in the Apress GitHub account, available at the following URL:

`https://github.com/Apress/pro-azure-admin-and-automation`

Network Security Groups (NSGs)

A network security group is a service that provides us with the ability to limit network traffic to or from a specific resource. It contains a list of rules that can allow or deny inbound or outbound traffic. A network security group can be associated with the subnet or network interface. We can have a maximum of one network security group associated with a subnet or network interface card.

If we have a network security group associated with both the subnet and network interface card that our service uses (e.g., virtual machine), we need to make sure we have the same rules on both. Otherwise, our traffic will not flow as expected.

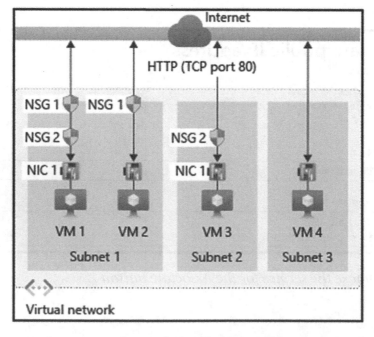

Figure 3-9. *Network security groups (NSGs). The image was taken from*
`https://docs.microsoft.com/en-us/azure/virtual-network/network-security-group-how-it-works`

For traffic coming to VM1, first, the rules from NSG1 would be processed, as it is bound to Subnet1. If we allow port 80 on NSG1, the traffic will then hit NSG2 (NIC1 associated). To allow port 80 to the virtual machine, both *NSG1* and *NSG2* must have a rule that allows port 80 from the Internet.

We need to be careful about with which subnet we are associating the network security group. For example, we should not put the network security group on the virtual network gateway because that could interfere with our VPN traffic. Also, the network security group associated with the subnet where our load balancers are has specific prerequisites to be used, and it is not the best idea to use the same network security group for other resources and services.

Creating a Network Security Group

A network security group is an essential defense line for all resources located in our virtual network subnets. In this part of the chapter, we will learn how to create them using all Azure management tools.

Azure Portal

When we log into Azure Portal, from the menu, we can select **Create a resource**. From the Marketplace, we can search for "network security group" and then select the proposed one from the results. On **Create network security group** (Figure 3-10), we need to select the subscription for deployment, resource group where the NSG will be deployed, name, and region.

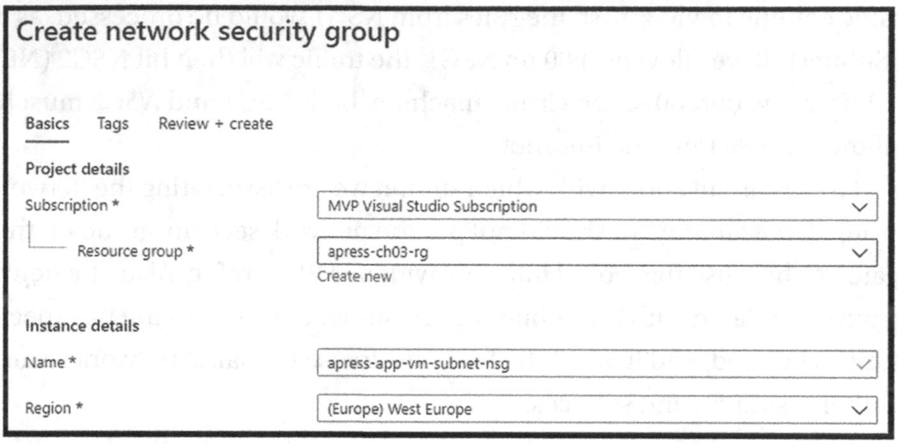

Create network security group

Basics   Tags   Review + create

Project details

Subscription * | MVP Visual Studio Subscription   ∨ |

└── Resource group * | apress-ch03-rg   ∨ |
                                   Create new

Instance details

Name * | apress-app-vm-subnet-nsg   ✓ |

Region * | (Europe) West Europe   ∨ |

Figure 3-10. *Select the subscription for deployment, resource group where the NSG will be deployed, name, and region*

After we populate tags as per design, we can review and create our resource.

Notice that there is no option to assign NSG to either subnet or NIC at this point. We can do it from the NSG settings after the deployment (Figure 3-11).

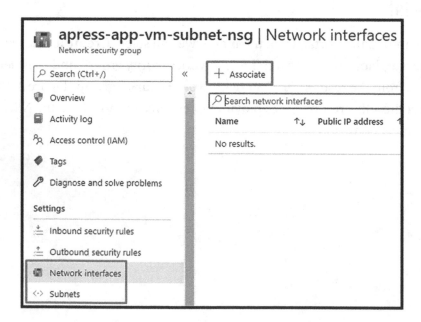

Figure 3-11. *Assign NSG to either subnet or NIC after the deployment*

ARM Template, PowerShell, and Azure CLI

Since the deployment code could be pretty big, all ARM template, Azure PowerShell, and Azure CLI scripts are stored in the Apress GitHub account, available at the following URL:

https://github.com/Apress/pro-azure-admin-and-automation

Service Endpoints

A virtual network service endpoint is an Azure resource that provides secure connectivity to Azure services over an Azure backbone network. Using them, we are securing critical service resources keeping the traffic within our virtual networks. A service endpoint uses private IP addresses in the virtual network to reach an Azure service endpoint without a public IP on the virtual network.

The main benefits are improved security, optimized routing from the virtual network to Azure services, and a simple setup. Several Azure services are capable of using service endpoints. Some of the most used ones are

- Azure Storage: Generally available in all Azure regions. Each storage account supports up to 100 virtual network rules.

- Azure SQL Database: Generally available in all Azure regions. The firewall security option controls whether the database server accepts communications sent from particular subnets in virtual networks.

- Azure Key Vault: Generally available in all Azure regions. The virtual network service endpoints for Azure Key Vault allow us to restrict access to a specified virtual network.

Creating a Service Endpoint

As we mentioned, a service endpoint is created under other resource settings. In this part of the chapter, we will learn how to create it using the storage account example, using all known Azure management tools.

Azure Portal

Since service endpoints are created on the virtual network level, we will go to our previously created VNet **apress-ch03-vnet**.

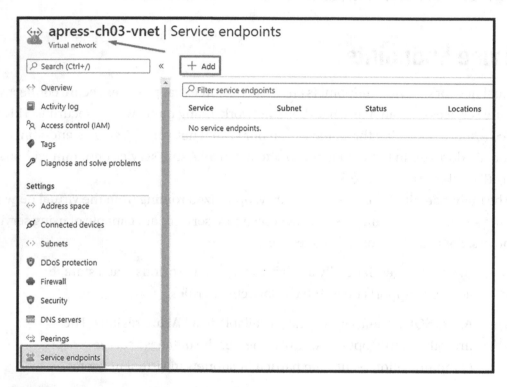

Figure 3-12.   *Choose to add a service endpoint*

When choosing to add one (Figure 3-12), we will be asked to choose a type of service and subnet bound to it (Figure 3-13).

Figure 3-13. *Choose a type of service and subnet bound to it*

That allows us to set a **firewall** in **storage account** settings and filter traffic from only a specific VNet and subnets (Figure 3-14).

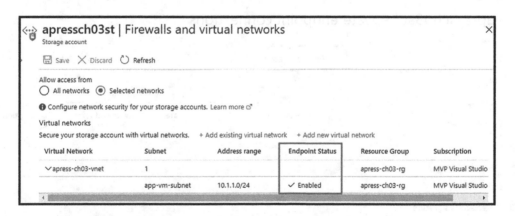

Figure 3-14. *Set a firewall in storage account settings*

ARM Template, PowerShell, and Azure CLI

Since the deployment code could be pretty big, all ARM template, Azure PowerShell, and Azure CLI scripts are stored in the Apress GitHub account, available at the following URL:

https://github.com/Apress/pro-azure-admin-and-automation

Private Endpoints

An Azure private endpoint is a network interface that allows us to create a private and secure connection toward a service that uses Azure Private Link. The private IP address from our virtual network will be assigned to an endpoint, which allows us to access services, such as Azure Storage, SQL, or Web Apps, through the virtual network.

Creating a Private Endpoint

As we mentioned in this chapter, a private endpoint has to be created on the service level. In the following examples, we will leverage Azure management tools to create a private endpoint for a storage account.

Azure Portal

From the **Settings** pane, we need to choose **Private endpoint connections** (Figure 3-15).

Figure 3-15. *From the Settings pane, choose Private endpoint connections*

When we choose to add one, we will be asked to choose a **Resource group**, **Name**, and **Region**. On the next tab (Figure 3-16), we need to choose the resource we are creating an endpoint for.

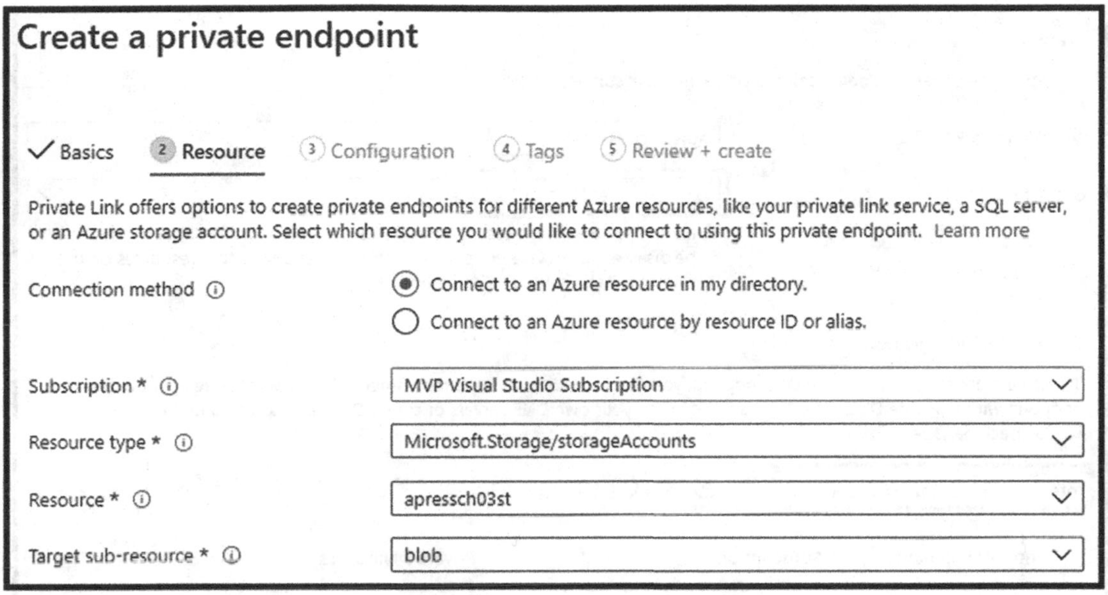

Create a private endpoint

✓ Basics   ② **Resource**   ③ Configuration   ④ Tags   ⑤ Review + create

Private Link offers options to create private endpoints for different Azure resources, like your private link service, a SQL server, or an Azure storage account. Select which resource you would like to connect to using this private endpoint. Learn more

Connection method ⓘ   ⦿ Connect to an Azure resource in my directory.
                                 ◯ Connect to an Azure resource by resource ID or alias.

Subscription * ⓘ | MVP Visual Studio Subscription   ⌄ |

Resource type * ⓘ | Microsoft.Storage/storageAccounts   ⌄ |

Resource * ⓘ | apressch03st   ⌄ |

Target sub-resource * ⓘ | blob   ⌄ |

Figure 3-16. *Choose the resource*

On the next tab (Figure 3-17), we need to choose a VNet and subnet that the endpoint will get an IP from. It is recommended to have a dedicated subnet for endpoints. Also, we are offered to make an integration with a private DNS zone (also recommended). If we do not have one, Azure will make it during the process.

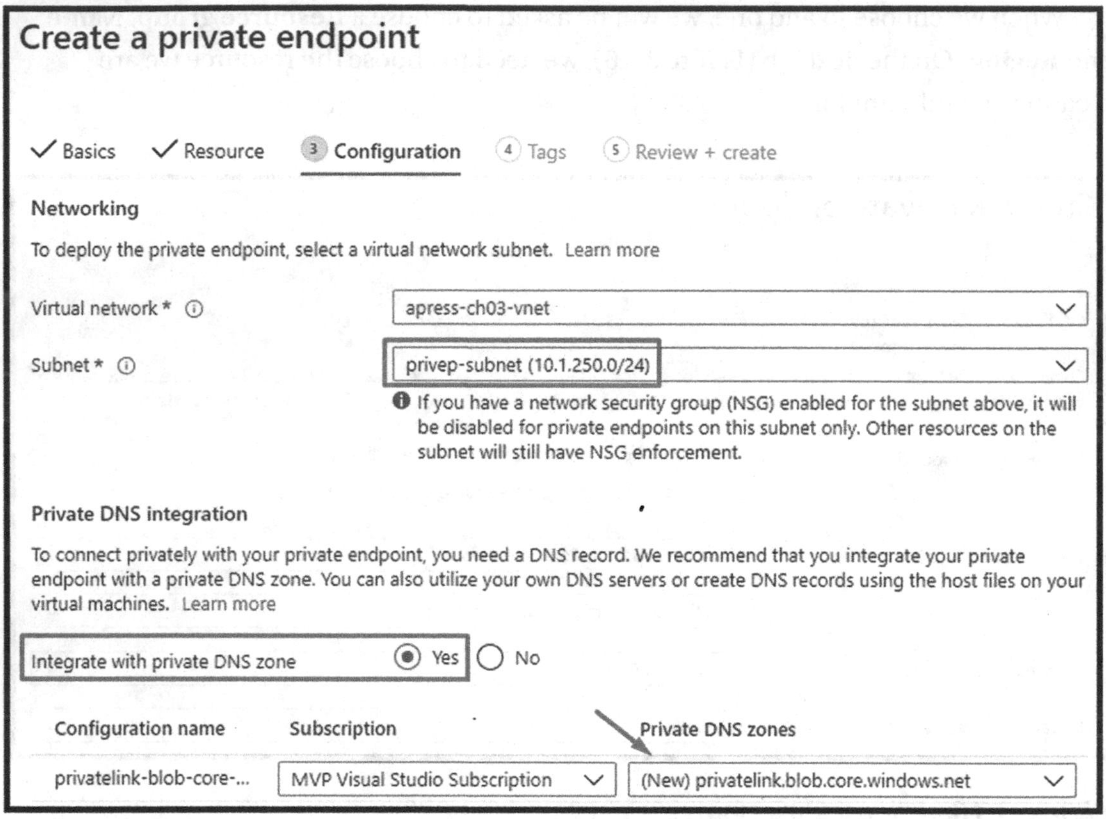

Create a private endpoint

✓ Basics   ✓ Resource   ③ **Configuration**   ④ Tags   ⑤ Review + create

Networking

To deploy the private endpoint, select a virtual network subnet. Learn more

| Virtual network * ⓘ | apress-ch03-vnet ⌄ |

| Subnet * ⓘ | privep-subnet (10.1.250.0/24) ⌄ |

ⓘ If you have a network security group (NSG) enabled for the subnet above, it will
be disabled for private endpoints on this subnet only. Other resources on the
subnet will still have NSG enforcement.

Private DNS integration

To connect privately with your private endpoint, you need a DNS record. We recommend that you integrate your private
endpoint with a private DNS zone. You can also utilize your own DNS servers or create DNS records using the host files on your
virtual machines. Learn more

Integrate with private DNS zone   ⦿ Yes   ○ No

| Configuration name | Subscription | Private DNS zones |
| privatelink-blob-core-... | MVP Visual Studio Subscription ⌄ | (New) privatelink.blob.core.windows.net ⌄ |

Figure 3-17. Choose a VNet and subnet that the endpoint will get an IP from

After we populate tags as per design, we can review and create our resource.

ARM Template, PowerShell, and Azure CLI

Since the deployment code could be pretty big, all ARM template, Azure PowerShell, and
Azure CLI scripts are stored in the Apress GitHub account, available at the following URL:

`https://github.com/Apress/pro-azure-admin-and-automation`

Chapter Recap

In this chapter, we have learned how to deploy a base for all our future resources – a
virtual network. Also, we got acquainted with the main principles of protecting our
resources. In all future chapters, we will rely on the resources created here.

In the next chapter, we will begin our journey through the IaaS part of the Azure cloud. We will learn how the most popular resource, the virtual machine, is created and handled. We will present the first solution for scaling our IaaS environment in Azure – a virtual machine scale set.

## CHAPTER 4

Virtual Machine: Virtual Machine Scale Sets in Azure Compute

In the previous chapter of this book, we have learned more about Azure networking, the core component of IaaS in Azure. Without the networking part, deploying virtual machines, which is a topic of this chapter, would not be possible.

This chapter covers the following topics regarding one of the most used cloud models (IaaS) and its services:

- Virtual machines – planning and usage

- Deploying virtual machines using various tools

- Virtual machine availability

- Virtual machine extensions

- Virtual machine scale sets

After this chapter, we will be able to design and implement a virtual machine workload in Azure. More importantly, we will understand the crucial steps for successful design, implementation, and management.

Virtual Machine: Planning and Usage

Based on researches conducted over the last year, virtual machines are one of the most used services in Azure, as well as IaaS in general. Although a virtual machine is not a cloud-native service like App Service or Azure Functions, more than 70% of overall

© Vladimir Stefanovic and Milos Katinski 2021
V. Stefanovic and M. Katinski, *Pro Azure Administration and Automation*,
https://doi.org/10.1007/978-1-4842-7325-8_4

cloud usage is IaaS. At the same time, there is a prediction that IaaS will continue to grow in the forthcoming years, although we are witnessing the growth of the usage of PaaS services as well. Two main reasons for these numbers are the complexity for refactoring applications and services from traditional to cloud-native models and the time needed for moving to the cloud in a cloud-native manner, especially for enterprise companies. For us, who are Azure architects, engineers, or administrators, this information is a pretty good sign for continuing to improve IaaS skills and understanding virtual machines in Azure and how they work.

Planning Checklist

When designing the IaaS workload in Azure, regardless of whether it is a migration project or a brand-new deployment, the principles we have to follow should be the same and have to start with detailed planning. Planning is one of the essential phases for every kind of infrastructure design, mainly because some configurations could not be changed later.

Virtual Machine Networking

Virtual networks in Azure, described and explained in the previous chapter, are used to provide connectivity between virtual machines in Azure and other resources through the isolated private network. By default, services that are outside of the virtual network are not able to reach nor connect to services inside of the virtual network, and additional actions are required if we want to provide access to external services. From a planning perspective, the virtual network must be on top of the rock because moving virtual machines from one virtual network to another is not allowed by design. We can move the virtual machine quickly from one subnet to another inside the same virtual network, but changing the virtual network requires additional effort and downtime of the virtual machines, even when leveraging automation skills. One of the potential solutions will require creating a copy of the virtual machine OS disk and then deploying a new virtual machine in the new virtual network, using the cloned OS disk.

Naming Convention

Like virtual networking, the naming convention for virtual machines, as well as for other resources, is an essential task. If we deploy a virtual machine with the name *vm-01* and want to change that later to *lon-svr-01* to align with company policy, that will not be possible. Although we can change the virtual machine's hostname inside the virtual machine, the resource name cannot be changed. From an operational perspective, misconfiguration will not harm infrastructure, but if we have hundreds or thousands of deployed machines in infrastructure, that could be problematic for managing.

Virtual Machine Location

When we talk about virtual machines' location, we must consider three important factors: *compliance*, *latency*, and *pricing*. Let's assume that our client is located in Germany. If the client's resources have to be deployed to datacenters inside Germany due to law regulations and compliance, we do not think so much about resource location. At the time of writing this book, there are two Azure regions in Germany for public use, *Germany North (Berlin)* and *Germany West Central (Frankfurt)*, and we can select one of them. Nevertheless, if the client does not have to meet law regulations and compliance and they can deploy a virtual machine outside of Germany, we have to check latency to Azure regions from the client's location. Deploying resources in an Azure region far from the client's location could lead to a slow response. The website https://azurespeedtest.azurewebsites.net/ will provide us with information regarding latency to Azure regions from the location of the machine that accesses the provided portal, ordered by the average latency, as shown in Figure 4-1.

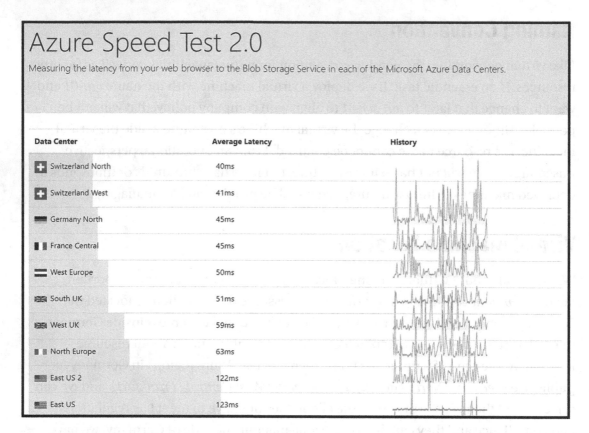

Figure 4-1. *Azure Speed Test*

And last but not least is pricing. The actual virtual machine pricing consists of two parameters: compute costs and storage costs. These prices are not the same in all Azure regions and could significantly differ, especially for compute costs. For instance, the virtual machine size Standard_D2s_v3 with a Linux operating system costs $109.50 in the Germany North region, whereas the same virtual machine size is $83.95 in the Germany West Central region. Even though we will pay for compute power per usage, we can see that the price difference between these regions is almost 30%.

To sum up, we must emphasize that a virtual machine must be deployed in a virtual network that is in the same Azure region as the virtual machine. We cannot deploy a virtual machine to Germany West Central if the virtual network has been deployed and configured in Germany North.

Virtual Machine Sizing

Sometimes, the virtual machine sizing could be part of a detailed analysis of the virtual machine workload, especially if we want to migrate the current on-premises workload to Azure. For instance, a client has their private datacenter and dozens of virtual machines with 8 vCPU and 8 GB of RAM, or even 16 vCPU and 4 GB of RAM. If we just want to replicate this sizing to Azure, that will not be possible since Azure has predefined types of instances and different sizes for each of the types. The general division is into

- General-purpose

- Compute-optimized

- Memory-optimized

- Storage-optimized

- GPU

- High-performance computing

Each of these types is different. Some have subdivision, like general-purpose, where we can find D-series as mainstream for the most common workloads and B-series as burstable sizes ideal for workloads that do not need the full-performance CPU continuously. General-purpose size has a CPU-to-memory ratio of 1:4, which means that for each CPU, we will get 4 GB of RAM. Unlike general-purpose sizes, compute-optimized sizes (F-series) have a CPU-to-memory ratio of 1:2, and processors are faster than general-purpose. If we need a high CPU-to-memory ratio, we need to think about memory-optimized sizes, such as E-series and some D-series, where we have 8 GB of RAM per CPU. These sizes are ideal for relational databases and cache services. If the workload needs high disk throughput and IO, storage-optimized sizes should be a perfect match. L-series are ideal for Big Data, SQL, NoSQL databases, data warehousing, and large transactional databases. NC-, ND-, and NV-series are GPU-optimized sizes, which are special virtual machines available with single, multiple, or fractional GPUs. If the workload is compute-intensive or graphics-intensive, these sizes will be our first pick. The H-series of Azure virtual machines are part of high-performance computing sizes, designed to deliver top-class performance.

Another important thing when we think about sizing, besides the compute power, is networking and storage limits. The number of network interface cards and network bandwidth are directly related to the instance size. For example, if we have a virtual machine with the size `Standard_D2s_v3`, we could add only two network interface cards, and bandwidth cannot exceed 1000 Mbps. The next virtual machine size, `Standard_D4s_v3`, can have the same number of network interface cards, but network bandwidth will be doubled.

If we compare these sizes from a storage perspective, the first one, `Standard_D2s_v3`, allows us to add four data disks, whereas the other instance, `Standard_D4s_v3`, gives us the ability to add eight data disks. Along with the number of data disks, another storage limitation is disk throughput. The `Standard_D2s_v3` size has a limit of 3200 IOPS and 48 Mbps, while the `Standard_D4s_v3` size has double these values. These storage limitations are essential if we want to run SQL Server on the Azure virtual machine. In that scenario, we have to analyze storage limitations in detail because a low level of these values can degrade data disk performances. For instance, the `Standard_D8s_v3` size has a limit of 12800 IOPS and 192 Mbps for disk throughput, and if we use a P30 premium SSD disk (1 TB) for databases, we will not be able to reach disk limits since these limits are higher than the virtual machine size limits.

Storage for Virtual Machines

Every virtual machine has to be equipped with storage. In the previous section, we have said that the number of data disks depends on virtual machine size, but that is not most important from a virtual machine storage perspective. Every virtual machine in Azure has an OS disk, which is mandatory because it holds an operating system. The most common size for an OS disk is 30 GB for the Linux distribution and 127 GB for the Windows operating system, but there are options to use small disk images for the Windows operating system that are 30 GB in size. The data disk is optional, and no rule will say that we have to use the data disk. These disks could be managed, which is the preferred option, or unmanaged. Because the Azure storage options will be explained in detail in Chapter 6, we will not talk about differences now.

Besides OS and data disks, almost every virtual machine in Azure has a temporary disk that is not a managed disk. This disk provides short-term storage for applications and processes. It is ideal for storing page or swap files because data may be lost during the maintenance or redeployment of the virtual machine. By default, on Windows virtual machines, the temporary disk is labeled as a `D:` drive, but that could be changed. On Linux virtual machines, the temporary disk is usually presented as a `/dev/sdb` and will be mounted to `/mnt` by the virtual machine agent. It is crucial to know that storing essential files on a temporary disk is not the best idea, as it leads to data loss.

Supported Operating Systems

Microsoft Azure, by default, provides a plethora of OS images that we can use for installing into the virtual machine. Along with the clean operating systems that include various Windows and Linux images, in the Azure Marketplace, we can find many images that include installed software besides operating systems, such as Microsoft SQL Server, WordPress, and Apache web server. If none of those provided images work for us, we can still create our image from any predefined images or upload a disk image to Azure and create a virtual machine from the uploaded disk. If we decide to upload a disk image to Azure, we have to know some limitations. Azure supports only 64-bit images, and the disk size has to be rounded, which means that the disk size cannot be 41.3 GB.

Another important thing regarding OS images in Azure is finding and selecting an appropriate one, especially if we want to deploy infrastructure using Infrastructure as Code (IaC) or command-line tools. Every official Azure Marketplace image is identified with *Publisher*, *Offer*, *SKU*, and *Version* information. If we want to deploy a virtual machine using Azure Portal, that will not be so important because we will search for the desired OS version in the Marketplace and just deploy it. If we want to deploy a virtual machine using any different method, we must specify all of these parameters. In the following JSON-formatted code, we can see the difference between OS image parameters for Windows Server 2019 and Ubuntu Server 19.04:

```
{
    "publisher": "MicrosoftWindowsServer",
    "offer": "WindowsServer",
    "sku": "2019-Datacenter",
    "urn": "MicrosoftWindowsServer:WindowsServer:2019-Datacenter:latest",
    "urnAlias": "Win2019Datacenter",
    "version": "latest"
}

{
    "publisher": "Canonical",
    "offer": "UbuntuServer",
    "sku": "19.04",
    "urn": "Canonical:UbuntuServer:19.04:latest",
    "version": "19.04.201908140"
}
```

As we can see, all the needed information is here, and we can use them if we want to deploy a virtual machine using the ARM template, Azure PowerShell, or Azure CLI. Input parameters for the ARM template and Azure PowerShell are the same, and we have to provide Publisher, Offer, SKU, and Version. In contrast, Azure CLI expects a little bit different input information. *Uniform Resource Name (URN),* presented in both outputs, combines all these values in a single line, separated by a colon (:) character: Publisher:Offer:SKU:Version. Additionally, some official virtual machine images have the urnAlias parameter, a shorter option to provide all needed parameters. If we want to deploy one of the most common images, such as Windows Server 2019 ("urnAlias": "Win2019Datacenter") or Ubuntu 18.04 ("urnAlias": "UbuntuLTS"), we can provide a urnAlias, instead of the full urn.

As we said, if we are using Azure Portal, we just need to search in the Azure Marketplace to find an appropriate image for deployment. Since we have to present these parameters if we want to deploy infrastructure using IaC or command-line tools, we must know how to find them. If we want to use Azure PowerShell, the following commands can provide us with the information:

```
Get-AzVMImagePublisher -Location 'North Europe'
Get-AzVMImageOffer -Location 'North Europe' -PublisherName
MicrosoftWindowsServer
Get-AzVMImageSku -Location 'North Europe' -PublisherName
MicrosoftWindowsServer -Offer WindowsServer
```

If we want to use Azure CLI to find this image information, we must use the following commands:

```
az vm image list-publishers --location northeurope
az vm image list-offers --publisher MicrosoftWindowsServer --location
northeurope
az vm image list-skus --publisher MicrosoftWindowsServer --offer
WindowsServer --location northeurope
```

Once we collect all needed information regarding a virtual machine image, we can write a fully functional template or script and deploy infrastructure in automated ways. Another benefit of deploying in these ways is finding a more specific version of an image that is not presented in the Azure Marketplace.

All installed Microsoft products in Azure have to be licensed. There is a scenario where we can use our license plans and avoid having license costs twice, but we need to have a Software Assurance agreement. In all other cases, we have to pay for licenses in the same manner as the compute power, pay-per-use. Also, Windows operating systems in Azure cannot be upgraded to a newer version. If we need that, we have to deploy a new virtual machine and migrate the workload. On the other hand, all Linux distributions supported by Azure can be upgraded to a newer version.

Virtual Machine Connectivity

Once we deployed the virtual machine in Azure, regardless of the operating system, we have to connect to that instance, and Azure provides us with several ways to do that. If we run a Windows operating system on a virtual machine in Azure, we can use the most common and native RDP access. Also, Windows operating systems support WinRM access, which could be used if we want to have access using PowerShell. To connect to a Linux-based virtual machine, we need to have any SSH client connect securely to the virtual machine.

One more option we have for connection to virtual machines is Azure Bastion. Azure Bastion is a fully platform-managed PaaS service that we can provision inside the virtual machine network. It will provide us with secure and seamless connectivity to virtual machines using RDP or SSH, directly over the SSL through Azure Portal. In this scenario, virtual machines do not need to have public IP addresses, nor we need to install any additional client or agent.

Creating Virtual Machines

Now that we have learned essential information about virtual machines in Azure, we can now see how to create a virtual machine using different management tools. In the following example, we will use the same input parameters to compare how different tools will achieve the same result.

Azure Portal

As mentioned many times, Azure Portal is the most popular management tool among the IT population, though it will not give us any kind of automation benefits. However, people that are not so familiar with other tools will be able to deploy infrastructure for demo or test purposes.

The first step in deploying a virtual machine in Azure is selecting an appropriate image from the Azure Marketplace. Once we find the desired image, a "*Create a virtual machine*" wizard will be opened. In configuring any virtual machines, we follow the wizard through the sections, although only the tab *Basics* is mandatory.

As shown in Figure 4-2, on the tab *Basics*, under *Project details*, we have to select a subscription that we want to use and use an existing resource group or create a new one. Under *Instance details,* we have to define a virtual machine name, select an appropriate region, define the availability option if applicable and needed, select the virtual machine image that we want, and select an appropriate size for the virtual machine. If our subscription is eligible, we can select deployment as an *Azure Spot instance*, which will give us the possibility to save a certain amount of money because virtual machines will be deployed for a lower price only if there are available resources. If we select a spot instance and there is a high demand for computing power in that region, the virtual machine will be powered off.

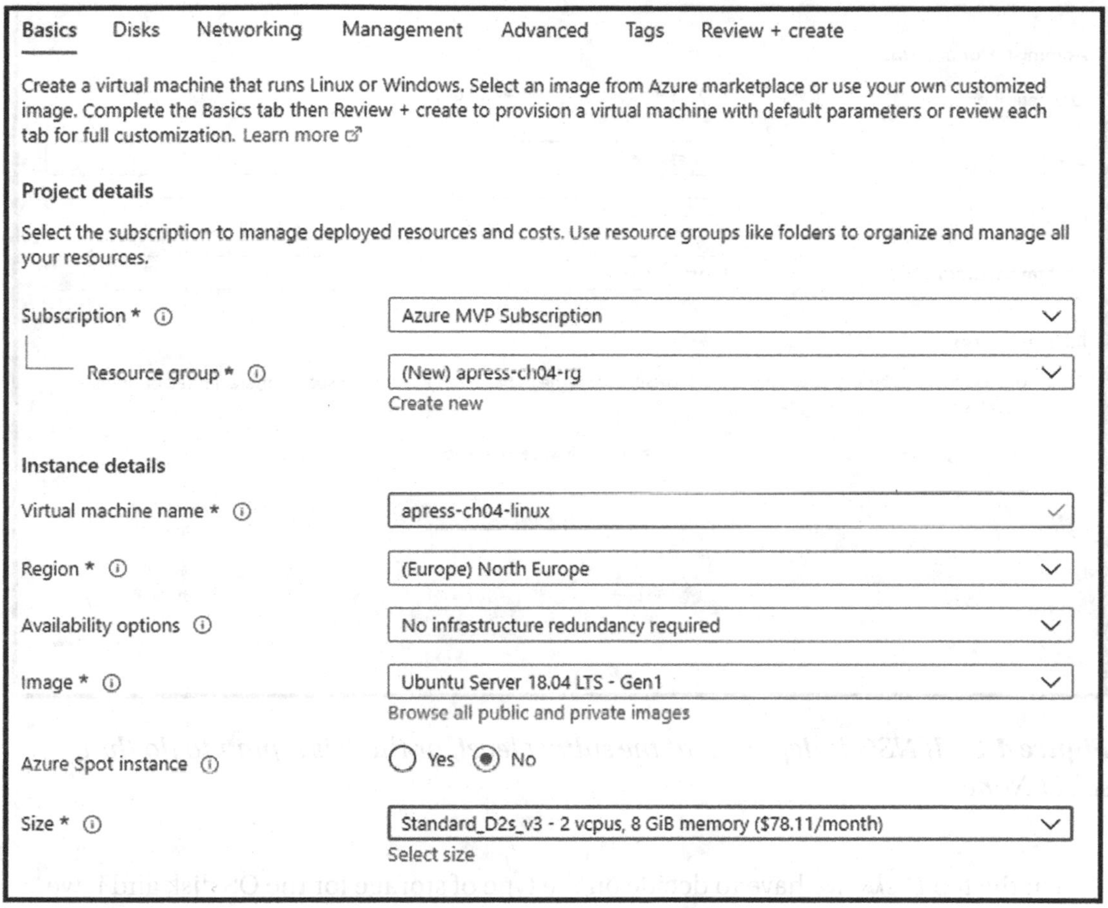

Basics   Disks   Networking   Management   Advanced   Tags   Review + create

Create a virtual machine that runs Linux or Windows. Select an image from Azure marketplace or use your own customized image. Complete the Basics tab then Review + create to provision a virtual machine with default parameters or review each tab for full customization. Learn more ⬀

Project details

Select the subscription to manage deployed resources and costs. Use resource groups like folders to organize and manage all your resources.

Subscription * ⓘ	Azure MVP Subscription ⌄
└─ Resource group * ⓘ	(New) apress-ch04-rg ⌄
	Create new

Instance details

Virtual machine name * ⓘ	apress-ch04-linux ✓
Region * ⓘ	(Europe) North Europe ⌄
Availability options ⓘ	No infrastructure redundancy required ⌄
Image * ⓘ	Ubuntu Server 18.04 LTS - Gen1 ⌄
	Browse all public and private images
Azure Spot instance ⓘ	◯ Yes ⬤ No
Size * ⓘ	Standard_D2s_v3 - 2 vcpus, 8 GiB memory ($78.11/month) ⌄
	Select size

Figure 4-2. *Select a subscription to use*

Under *Administrator account*, we have to define an admin username and password or add an SSH key if we are deploying a Linux virtual machine. The last configuration on the tab *Basics* is defining public inbound ports for the virtual machine, which will create a *network security group (NSG)* and assign it to the network interface card of the virtual machine. If we have deployed NSG at the subnet level, or we have a plan to do that, we can select *None* (Figure 4-3).

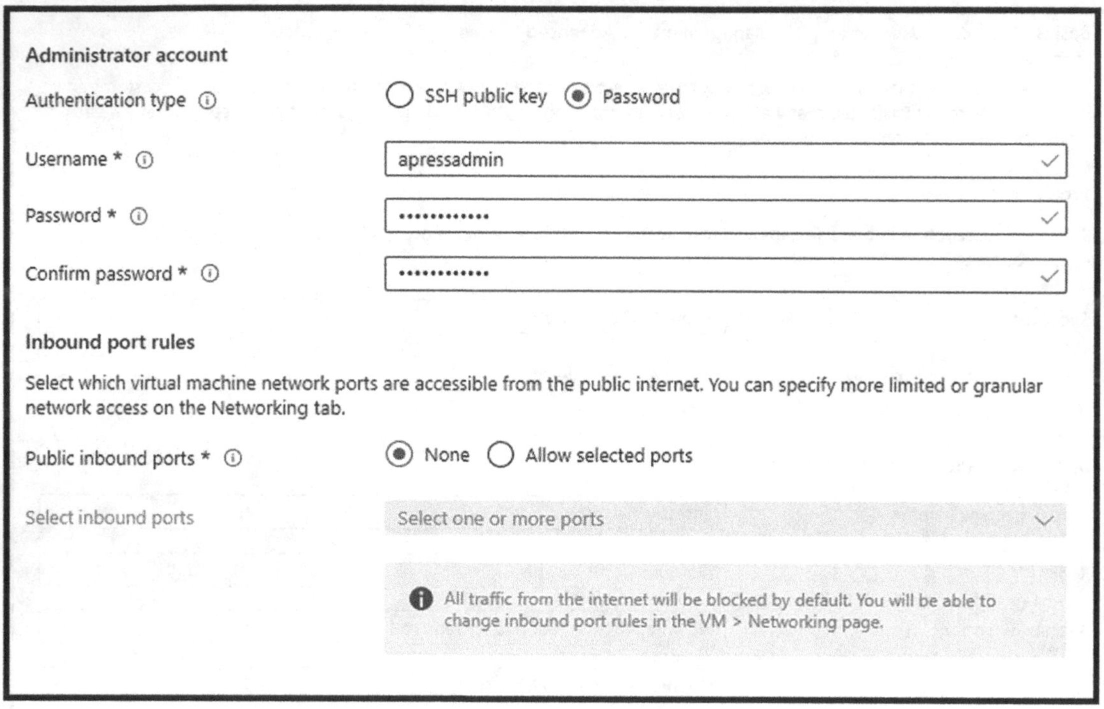

Administrator account

Authentication type ⓘ   ◯ SSH public key ⦿ Password

Username * ⓘ | apressadmin   ✓ |

Password * ⓘ | ••••••••••••   ✓ |

Confirm password * ⓘ | ••••••••••••   ✓ |

Inbound port rules

Select which virtual machine network ports are accessible from the public internet. You can specify more limited or granular network access on the Networking tab.

Public inbound ports * ⓘ   ⦿ None ◯ Allow selected ports

Select inbound ports | Select one or more ports   ⌄ |

> ⓘ All traffic from the internet will be blocked by default. You will be able to change inbound port rules in the VM > Networking page.

Figure 4-3. *If NSG is deployed at the subnet level, or there is a plan to do that, select None*

On the tab *Disks*, we have to decide on the type of storage for the OS disk and if we want to add any additional data disks at this stage. Additionally, we can define if we want to use a managed disk, which is the default, and if we need an ephemeral OS disk (Figure 4-4).

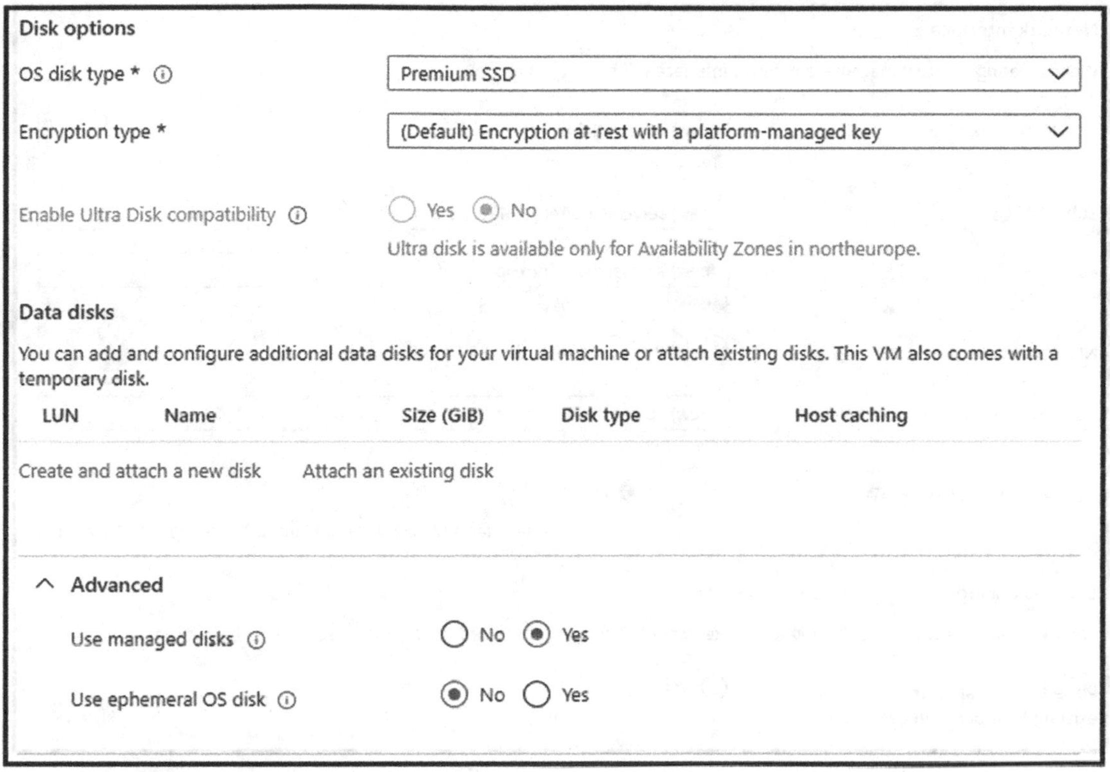

Disk options

OS disk type * ⓘ	Premium SSD	⌄

Encryption type *	(Default) Encryption at-rest with a platform-managed key	⌄

Enable Ultra Disk compatibility ⓘ   ◯ Yes ◉ No

Ultra disk is available only for Availability Zones in northeurope.

Data disks

You can add and configure additional data disks for your virtual machine or attach existing disks. This VM also comes with a temporary disk.

LUN	Name	Size (GiB)	Disk type	Host caching

Create and attach a new disk   Attach an existing disk

∧ **Advanced**

Use managed disks ⓘ   ◯ No ◉ Yes

Use ephemeral OS disk ⓘ   ◉ No ◯ Yes

Figure 4-4. *Managed disk is the default or an ephemeral OS disk*

As shown in Figure 4-5, on the tab *Networking*, we will select an existing virtual network for the virtual machine, or we will create a new one if there is no appropriate virtual network. Also, we will define if we need to deploy a new NSG or use an existing one. As a last configuration parameter, we can select or create a load balancer and place a virtual machine behind it.

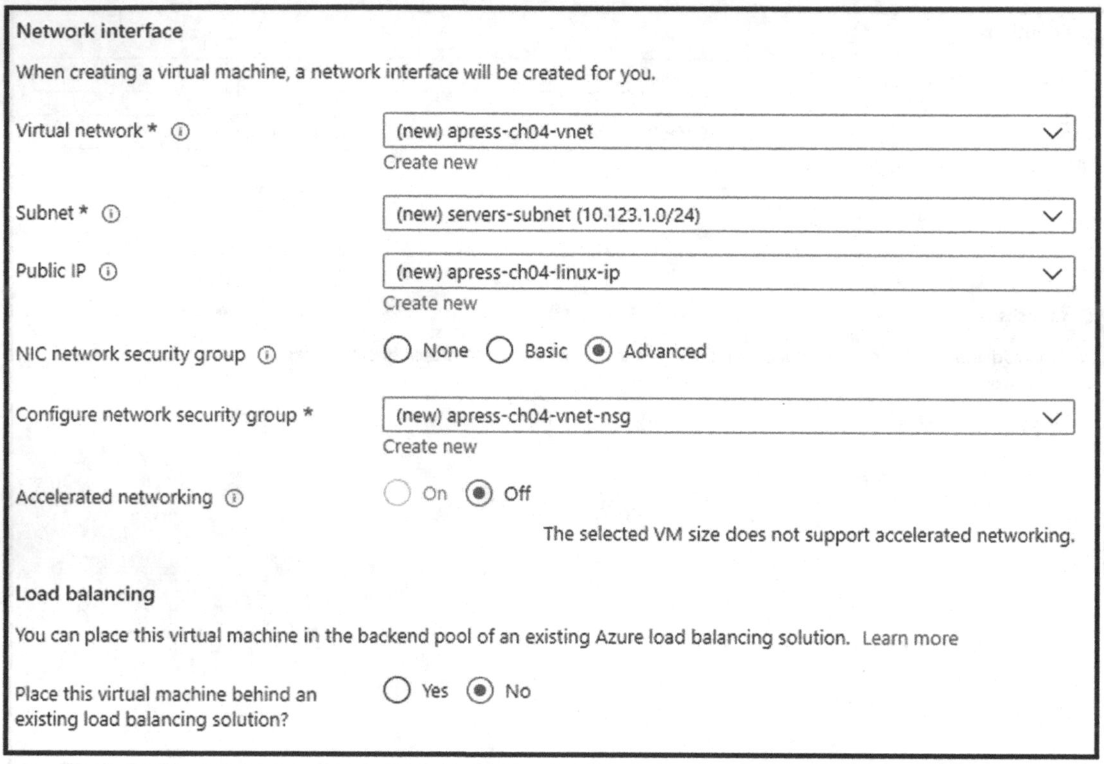

Network interface

When creating a virtual machine, a network interface will be created for you.

Virtual network * ⓘ

(new) apress-ch04-vnet ⌄

Create new

Subnet * ⓘ

(new) servers-subnet (10.123.1.0/24) ⌄

Public IP ⓘ

(new) apress-ch04-linux-ip ⌄

Create new

NIC network security group ⓘ   ◯ None   ◯ Basic   ⦿ Advanced

Configure network security group *

(new) apress-ch04-vnet-nsg ⌄

Create new

Accelerated networking ⓘ   ◯ On   ⦿ Off

The selected VM size does not support accelerated networking.

Load balancing

You can place this virtual machine in the backend pool of an existing Azure load balancing solution. Learn more

Place this virtual machine behind an   ◯ Yes   ⦿ No
existing load balancing solution?

Figure 4-5. Select an existing virtual network for the virtual machine or create a new one if there is no appropriate virtual network

The tab *Management* is reserved for management configuration parameters. We will define if we need boot diagnostics enabled, which is highly recommended. We have to define if we want to enable managed identity, auto-shutdown, or backup for a virtual machine (Figure 4-6).

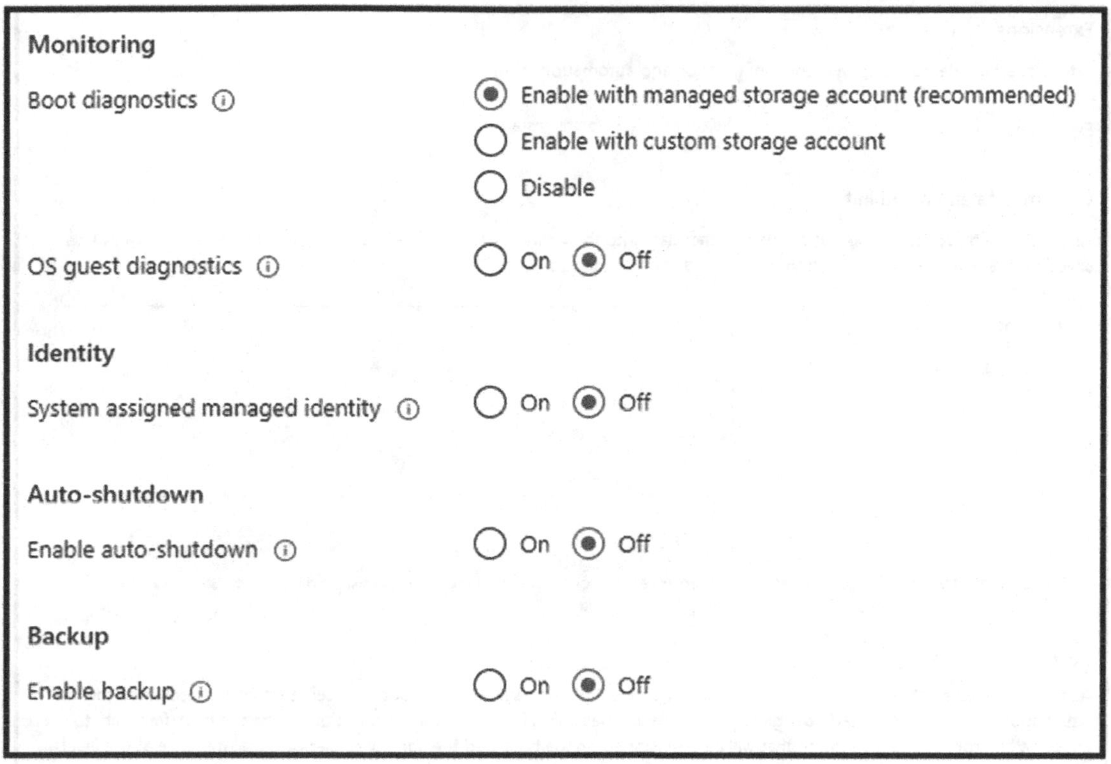

Monitoring

Boot diagnostics ⓘ

    ⦿ Enable with managed storage account (recommended)
    ◯ Enable with custom storage account
    ◯ Disable

OS guest diagnostics ⓘ   ◯ On ⦿ Off

Identity

System assigned managed identity ⓘ   ◯ On ⦿ Off

Auto-shutdown

Enable auto-shutdown ⓘ   ◯ On ⦿ Off

Backup

Enable backup ⓘ   ◯ On ⦿ Off

Figure 4-6. *Choose to enable managed identity, auto-shutdown, or backup for a virtual machine*

The *Advanced* tab gives us the ability to configure some additional features or parameters, such as extensions, or pass a cloud-init script. Additionally, we can select a proximity placement group or host group if we have a group of virtual machines and have better connectivity or availability, as shown in Figure 4-7.

Extensions

Extensions provide post-deployment configuration and automation.

Extensions ⓘ   Select an extension to install

Custom data and cloud init

Pass a cloud-init script, configuration file, or other data into the virtual machine while it is being provisioned. The data will be saved on the VM in a known location. Learn more about custom data for VMs ☑

Custom data

> ⓘ Custom data on the selected image will be processed by cloud-init. Learn more about custom data and cloud init ☑

Host

Azure Dedicated Hosts allow you to provision and manage a physical server within our data centers that are dedicated to your Azure subscription. A dedicated host gives you assurance that only VMs from your subscription are on the host, flexibility to choose VMs from your subscription that will be provisioned on the host, and the control of platform maintenance at the level of the host. Learn more

Host group ⓘ | No host group found   ⌄ |

Proximity placement group

Proximity placement groups allow you to group Azure resources physically closer together in the same region. Learn more

Proximity placement group ⓘ | No proximity placement groups found   ⌄ |

Generation 2 VMs support features such as UEFI-based boot architecture, increased memory and OS disk size limits, Intel® Software Guard Extensions (SGX), and virtual persistent memory (vPMEM).

VM generation ⓘ   ⦿ Gen 1   ◯ Gen 2

Figure 4-7. *Select a proximity placement group or host group if you have a group of virtual machines and have better connectivity or availability*

The tab *Tags* is the same for all Azure resources and provides us with a wizard for setting tags for the resources. The last tab, *Review + create*, gives us an overview of the configuration we prepared for the virtual machine deployment. Once we start with the creation process, as a first step, the system will run validation to check if everything is set correctly. Once the virtual machine is deployed, we will get a message that the deployment is completed.

ARM Template, PowerShell, and Azure CLI

Since the deployment code could be pretty big, all ARM template, Azure PowerShell, and Azure CLI scripts are stored in the Apress GitHub account, available at the following URL:

`https://github.com/Apress/pro-azure-admin-and-automation`

Virtual Machine Availability

By design, virtual machines in Azure are highly available from an infrastructure perspective. All virtual machines are deployed on the clustered infrastructure, resilient to datacenter hardware failures. Also, the virtual machine disks have multiple copies, regardless of whether we use managed or unmanaged disks. Nevertheless, although we do not need to think about infrastructure layers, we must know what we can expect from infrastructure and how we can improve virtual machine availability.

Maintenance and Downtime

Like every infrastructure, Azure also has planned and unplanned failures. From a downtime perspective, there are three potential scenarios:

- Unplanned hardware maintenance
- Planned maintenance
- Unexpected downtime

Unplanned hardware maintenance defines an event that occurs when datacenter engineers predict the potential failure of hardware or any platform component based on datacenter metrics and monitoring. In this case, Azure will migrate virtual machines to healthy hypervisors using *live migration* technology. This technology will pause a virtual machine for a short time, but reduced performance might happen before or after the event.

Planned maintenance is an event that happens periodically when Microsoft updates the underlying Azure platform to improve performance, reliability, and security. By design, most of these updates will not affect any virtual machine nor cloud services.

Unexpected downtime happens when a hardware or another platform component that can harm virtual machines or cloud services fails unexpectedly. This includes various types of failures, such as network failures, local disk failures, or rack-level failures. When any of these failures are detected, the platform will automatically migrate virtual machines to a healthy hypervisor. Since this event is unexpected, the virtual machine will be rebooted or redeployed, leading to losing data on temporary drives.

Availability Sets

An *Availability Set* is a feature that can help us improve the availability of a group of virtual machines that have the same workload, such as a web server. It is essential to know that an Availability Set will not help us improve the availability of services if we have only one virtual machine. If we have deployed and configured an Availability Set for virtual machines, Azure will ensure they will run across multiple hypervisors, rack, storage unit, and network switches. If any failure occurs, some virtual machines will be affected, but others will remain up and running to serve customers' applications. For instance, SLA for a single virtual machine is 99.9%, whereas SLA for multiple virtual machines in an Availability Set is 99.95%.

An Availability Set is a combination of *fault* and *update domains*. A fault domain is a group of hypervisor nodes that share a standard set of hardware, networking, and the same single point of failure. In the words of traditional administrators and engineers, the rack in the datacenter is represented as a fault domain. An upgrade domain is a group of hypervisor nodes that are upgraded together. Every update domain is composed of a set of nodes that can be upgraded and rebooted simultaneously. During planned maintenance, only one update domain is rebooted at a time. By default, during deployment, the number of the fault domains is 2, whereas the number of the update domains is 5. These numbers can be different, and the maximum number of fault domains is 3, while the maximum number of update domains is 20. For instance, if we select two fault domains and five update domains, that means that the first ten virtual machines in an Availability Set will be deployed on separate hypervisor nodes. Each subsequent virtual machine will be deployed along with any of the first ten virtual machines.

It is important to say that an Availability Set has to be selected only during virtual machine creation. At the moment, there is no possibility to add a virtual machine to an Availability Set at a later time. Creating an Availability Set and assigning a virtual machine is pretty straightforward and could be done using all management tools.

Azure Portal

Regardless of whether we want to create an Availability Set before creating a virtual machine or during that process, the steps are similar. If we want to add a virtual machine to an Availability Set, we just have to select an existing one or create a new one, as shown in Figure 4-8.

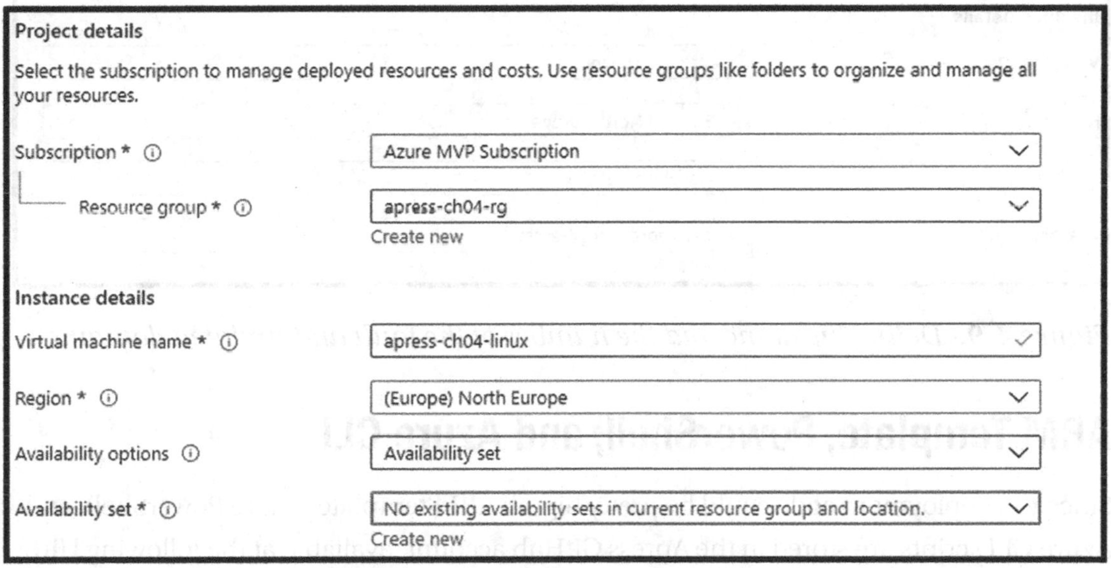

Project details

Select the subscription to manage deployed resources and costs. Use resource groups like folders to organize and manage all your resources.

Subscription * ⓘ | Azure MVP Subscription   ∨

　　　└─ Resource group * ⓘ | apress-ch04-rg   ∨
                                       Create new

Instance details

Virtual machine name * ⓘ | apress-ch04-linux   ✓

Region * ⓘ | (Europe) North Europe   ∨

Availability options ⓘ | Availability set   ∨

Availability set * ⓘ | No existing availability sets in current resource group and location. ∨
                                       Create new

Figure 4-8. *To add a virtual machine to an Availability Set, select an existing one or create a new one*

If there is no pre-deployed Availability Set, we have to click *Create new*, and a new wizard will be opened, where we have to define parameters for the Availability Set. Once we defined the name and the number of the fault and updated domains, a virtual machine will be added to the Availability Set (Figure 4-9).

Project details

Select the subscription to manage deployed resources and costs. Use resource groups like folders to organize and manage all your resources.

Subscription * ⓘ	Azure MVP Subscription ⌄
└── Resource group * ⓘ	apress-ch04-rg ⌄
	Create new

Instance details

Virtual machine name * ⓘ	apress-ch04-linux ✓
Region * ⓘ	(Europe) North Europe ⌄
Availability options ⓘ	Availability set ⌄
Availability set * ⓘ	(new) apress-ch04-avset ⌄
	Create new

Figure 4-9.   Define the name and the number of the fault and updated domains

ARM Template, PowerShell, and Azure CLI

Since the deployment code could be pretty big, all ARM template, Azure PowerShell, and Azure CLI scripts are stored in the Apress GitHub account, available at the following URL:

`https://github.com/Apress/pro-azure-admin-and-automation`

Availability Zones

While an Availability Set gives us the possibility to deploy virtual machines across an Azure region and theoretically deploy all virtual machines inside one datacenter only, *Availability Zones* provide us with the ability to select in which zone virtual machines will be deployed. An Availability Zone represents a unique physical location within an Azure region, composed of one or more datacenters equipped with independent power, cooling, and networking. Not all Azure regions are zoned, and that feature is not available in all Azure regions. SLA for virtual machines that are deployed across Availability Zones is 99.99%. Like an Availability Set, an Availability Zone has to be selected during virtual machine creation because there is no option to add a virtual machine to an Availability Zone later.

Unlike an Availability Set, which we have to create, assigning a virtual machine to an Availability Zone is an easier process and could be done using all management tools. We just need to define in what zone we want to deploy a virtual machine. Also, public IP addresses, if needed for the virtual machine, have to be deployed to the same Availability Zone.

Azure Portal

If we want to deploy a virtual machine and add it to a specific Availability Zone, we just have to define an Availability Zone during a virtual machine creation process, as shown in Figure 4-10.

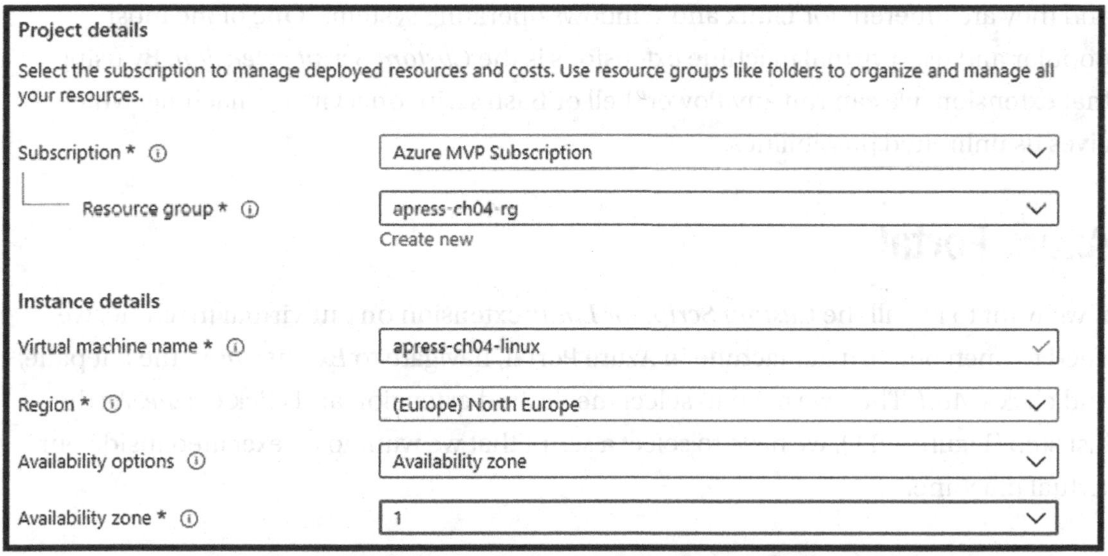

Figure 4-10. *Define an Availability Zone during a virtual machine creation process*

ARM Template, PowerShell, and Azure CLI

Since the deployment code could be pretty big, all ARM template, Azure PowerShell, and Azure CLI scripts are stored in the Apress GitHub account, available at the following URL:

`https://github.com/Apress/pro-azure-admin-and-automation`

Virtual Machine Extensions

In the modern, fast-paced IT world we live in today, creating and managing a virtual machine could be complicated and repetitive, especially in large-scale environments. The deployment process could be done in an automated way using ARM templates or any other IaC tools, even Azure PowerShell and Azure CLI, but what do we do if we talk about post-deployment configuration? One possible solution, which is native in Azure and supported by all management tools, is virtual machine extension.

Virtual machine extensions are small pieces of software that provide post-deployment configuration for Azure virtual machines. For instance, if a virtual machine must have installed specific third-party tools or just a specific Windows feature, that could be done by extensions. We can find many extensions for Azure virtual machines, and they are different for Linux and Windows operating systems. One of the most popular and used virtual machine extensions is the *Custom Script extension*. By using that extension, we can run any PowerShell or Bash script on a virtual machine, which gives us unlimited possibilities.

Azure Portal

If we want to install the *Custom Script for Linux* extension on our virtual machine, we need to open our virtual machine in Azure Portal, navigate to *Extensions* in the left pane, and click + *Add*. Then we need to select the desired extension and click *Create*. As the last step (Figure 4-11), we have to select a script that we want to be executed inside our virtual machine.

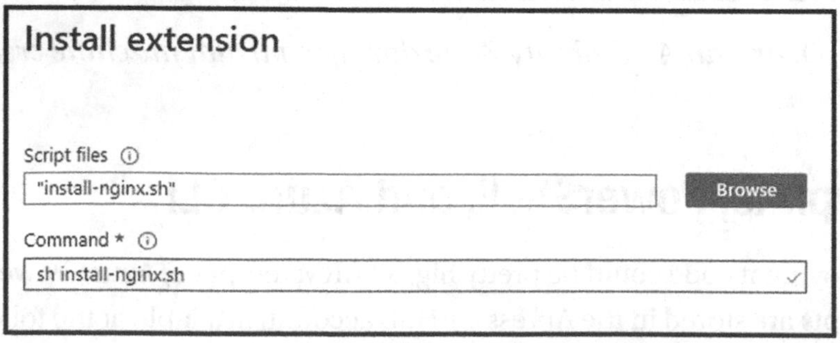

Figure 4-11. *Select a script to be executed inside our virtual machine*

ARM Template, PowerShell, and Azure CLI

Since the deployment code could be pretty big, all ARM template, Azure PowerShell, and Azure CLI scripts are stored in the Apress GitHub account, available at the following URL:

`https://github.com/Apress/pro-azure-admin-and-automation`

Virtual Machine Scale Sets

Earlier in this chapter, we have talked about the options for virtual machine availability in Azure. Even though Availability Sets and Zones can provide better virtual machine availability, in some specific scenarios, that may not be enough, especially if we host applications on virtual machines. A *virtual machine scale set (VMSS)* is an Azure resource representing a group of virtual machines with the same purpose, such as a web server. All virtual machines inside the scale set are called instances because the VMSS controls them to provide us with the cloud-native features, like auto-scaling or continuous deployment.

To have a fully functional and stable VMSS that can serve applications of customers, we have to plan in detail all layers in a VMSS architecture:

- Reference image
- Load balancing solution
- Auto-scaling plans
- Upgrading policy

Reference Image

Although a VMSS could be deployed from any Marketplace image and all instances can be configured later, that is not the best idea. In case that we have implemented auto-scaling and a new VMSS is deployed, an instance will be "clean" and without needed features, configuration parameters, or application code and will not be helpful. The recommended way to achieve this is by creating a custom reference image and deploying a VMSS from this image. This solution will ensure that every newly deployed VMSS instance will be the same as others. As a reference image source, we can use a managed disk or managed image or create a *shared image gallery* and then create an image definition. A shared image gallery allows us to implement versioning and save images into different Azure regions, which could be vital if we plan to distribute the application globally. Preparing the reference image is a straightforward process that includes deploying an appropriate virtual machine with a desired operating system, installing and configuring everything that is needed, generalizing the operating system, and then capturing the virtual machine into the managed image or shared gallery. All these steps are well documented and will not be a subject of this chapter.

Load Balancing Solution

Once we prepare the reference image for a VMSS that includes everything needed, we must decide what load balancing solution is the best for a specific deployment. In Azure, we can find many services that can balance network traffic between more than one virtual machine or service and numerous network virtual appliances (NVAs) for the same purpose. At the moment, only Azure Load Balancer and Application Gateway are supported for a VMSS as a native load balancing solution. Although we can use any other Azure service or third-party NVAs for this purpose, balancing management in a dynamic environment could be more complicated. In Chapter 9 of this book, load balancing services will be explained in more detail, and they will not be a subject of this chapter.

Auto-scaling Plans

If we want an application that runs on VMSS instances to remain responsive during the unpredictable peaks, regardless of whether they are during specific days in the week or times of the day, we have to leverage the auto-scaling feature. This is one of the most useful functionalities, and we have to implement this in VMSS deployment. Of course, as we said earlier, this is directly related to creating the custom reference image if we want to have fully functional and automated scaling. Many metric values could be used as a trigger for increasing or decreasing the number of instances in the VMSS, such as CPU percentage, disk read/write operations, or network bandwidth. Based on any of these metric values, we can define the behavior of the scaling plan. For instance, if the average CPU consumption across all VMSS instances is higher than 75% in a duration of 5 minutes, one new instance will be added to the VMSS, or if the average CPU consumption is lower than 30% in a duration of 5 minutes, one instance will be removed from the VMSS. We can define the minimum and the maximum number of instances in the VMSS, which is one of the vital configuration parameters for scaling since the default VMSS configuration allows us to have up to 100 instances in the VMSS. In specific cases, we can configure the VMSS to support up to 1000 instances.

Upgrading Policy

Once we have a custom reference image prepared and have decided on what load balancing solution is best for deployment and how we want to configure auto-scaling plans, we have to start to think about updating and upgrading the VMSS. There are two main factors why this is important: deploying a new image and changing VMSS parameters. Once we initially configure and deploy a VMSS, that VMSS will have its *configuration model,* and all deployed instances will pick up configuration parameters, such as virtual machine sizing, from the VMSS model. For instance, if we change a VMSS instance sizing and do not update instance(s), we can see a difference between VMSS configuration and instance configuration. Also, we can see that the instance(s) are flagged that the *latest model* is not yet deployed.

In Figure 4-12, we can see that the instance size is Standard_B1s, and that configuration applies to the two instances – on the VMSS level and the instance level.

Resource group (change)	: apress-ch04-rg		Public IP address	: 20.67.216.203
Status	: 2 out of 2 succeeded		Public IP address (IPv6)	: -
Location	: North Europe (Zones 1, 2, 3)		Virtual network/subnet	: apressvmss-vnet/apressvmss-subnet
Subscription (change)	: Azure MVP Subscription		Operating system	: Linux
Subscription ID	: 62cc79e0-66dd-4bb9-9aa0-77fdf43493da		Size	: Standard_B1s (2 instances)
Fault domains	: 5		Host group	: -
Colocation status	: N/A		Ephemeral OS disk	: Not applicable

Figure 4-12. *Configuration applies to two instances*

As shown in Figure 4-13, the size of the VMSS instances is still Standard_B2s. This discrepancy has occurred because the VMSS model is not applied yet to the VMSS instances. If we take a look at the VMSS instances, we will be able to see that information.

```
Instance ID              : 0

Status                   : Running, 1 more

Location                 : North Europe (Zone 1)

Provisioning state       : Succeeded

Latest model applied : No

Computer name            : apressvmss000000

Fault domains            : 5

SKU                      : Standard_B2s
```

Figure 4-13. *The size of the VMSS instances is still Standard_B2s*

At that moment, the upgrade policy will take care of that, using one of the three possible upgrade modes: *Manual*, *Automatic*, and *Rolling*. If we select to use the *Manual* upgrade mode, which is the default option, every change in the VMSS model will not affect instances automatically. If we want to upgrade instances, we have to do that manually, and we are in control of that process.

In case we want to avoid manual interactions and want that process automated, one of the options is to set the upgrade mode to *Automatic*. In this case, all instances will be upgraded automatically, simultaneously, in random order. Let us imagine that we have a production application on a VMSS with ten instances and we want to change just the size of the instances. All instances will be upgraded automatically, and the application will not be available until the first instance is up and running again. The main question is, do we want that scenario? Most probably, the correct answer is no.

The third upgrade mode, *Rolling*, is the best option to select, especially if we want to have automated upgrading of instances and ensure that the application will be responsive during that action. The prerequisite for enabling the Rolling upgrade mode is configuring *Enable application health monitoring* (Figure 4-14). That feature is part of the VMSS, and it will check the health of the application based on the provided probe parameters.

```
Enable application health monitoring  ⓘ
( Enabled   Disabled )
Application health monitor *  ⓘ
  Application health extension                                                    ⌄
Protocol *  ⓘ
  HTTP                                                                            ⌄
Port number  ⓘ
  80
Path *  ⓘ
  /

Automatic repair policy
Before enabling the automatic repairs policy, review the requirements for opting in  here

Enable automatic repairs  ⓘ
  ◉ On   ○ Off
Grace period (min) *  ⓘ
  30                                                                              ✓
```

Figure 4-14. *The prerequisite for enabling the Rolling upgrade mode is configuring Enable application health monitoring*

That configuration is essential because, in the *Rolling* upgrade mode, we have to configure how many instances can be upgraded simultaneously, how many unhealthy instances we can have in the VMSS, and how unhealthy instances will be upgraded. The health of instances can be checked only if we have configured application health monitoring. These numbers are represented in percentages, and a default value for all of these is 20%. For example, if we have a VMSS with ten instances and have configured the Rolling upgrade mode, only two instances at a time will be upgraded. If there are more than two instances with an unhealthy state, the upgrade mode will be aborted, and if there are more than two already upgraded instances that have an unhealthy state, the upgrade mode will be aborted as well. Also, we have to define how much time, in seconds, will be used as a pause between upgrade batches (Figure 4-15).

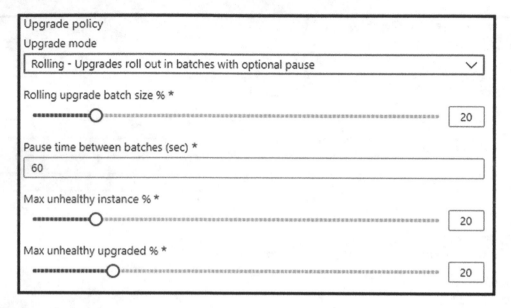

Figure 4-15. *Define how much time, in seconds, will be used as a pause between upgrade batches*

Creating a Virtual Machine Scale Set

Since deploying a VMSS can have so many variations that depend on specific needs, in the following examples, we will see how to deploy a VMSS from a custom reference image and with Azure Load Balancer as a load balancing solution. Also, the Rolling upgrade mode and application health monitoring will be configured.

Azure Portal

If we decide to use Azure Portal to deploy a VMSS, the very first we have to do is searching for "virtual machine scale set" in the Marketplace and clicking *Create*. The tab *Basics,* shown in Figure 4-16, is similar to the one we had when we created a virtual machine. We have to provide the subscription and resource group we want to use and then the name and location of the VMSS. If we want to deploy instances across the Availability Zones, we have to define that parameter. Under *Instance details*, we have to select a reference image and the VMSS instances' size. The last part of the *Basics* tab is information about an administrator account and credentials for the VMSS instances.

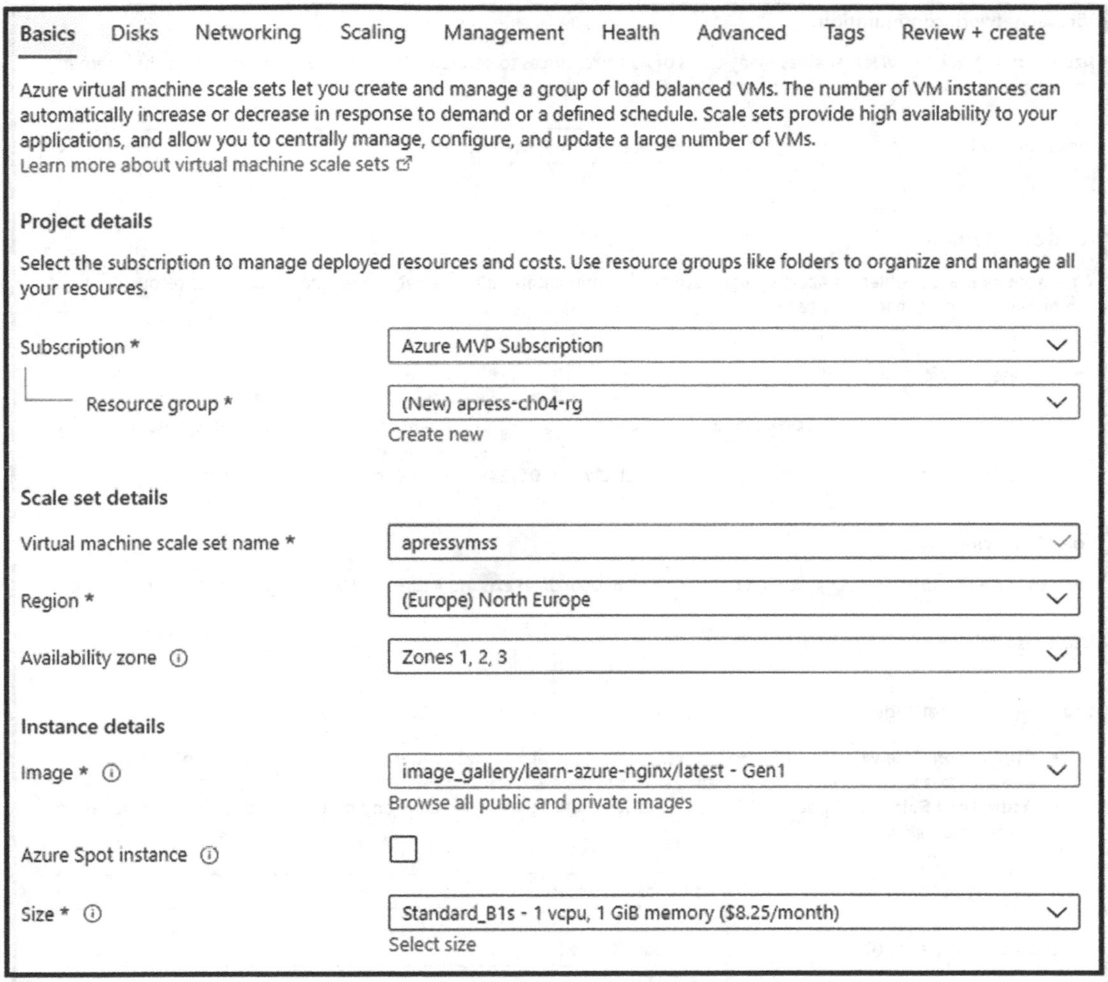

Basics	Disks	Networking	Scaling	Management	Health	Advanced	Tags	Review + create

Azure virtual machine scale sets let you create and manage a group of load balanced VMs. The number of VM instances can automatically increase or decrease in response to demand or a defined schedule. Scale sets provide high availability to your applications, and allow you to centrally manage, configure, and update a large number of VMs.
Learn more about virtual machine scale sets ⬚

Project details

Select the subscription to manage deployed resources and costs. Use resource groups like folders to organize and manage all your resources.

Subscription * | Azure MVP Subscription   ⌄ |

        └──── Resource group * | (New) apress-ch04-rg   ⌄ |
                                 Create new

Scale set details

Virtual machine scale set name * | apressvmss   ✓ |

Region * | (Europe) North Europe   ⌄ |

Availability zone ⓘ | Zones 1, 2, 3   ⌄ |

Instance details

Image * ⓘ | image_gallery/learn-azure-nginx/latest - Gen1   ⌄ |
                      Browse all public and private images

Azure Spot instance ⓘ   ☐

Size * ⓘ | Standard_B1s - 1 vcpu, 1 GiB memory ($8.25/month) ⌄ |
                      Select size

Figure 4-16. *The Basics tab is similar to the one used when creating a virtual machine*

On the tab *Disks*, we have to decide on the type of storage for the OS disk and if we want to add any additional data disks at this stage. If we use a custom reference image, a managed disk is mandatory, and we cannot change that. On the tab *Networking*, we will select an existing virtual network for the VMSS, or we will create a new one if there is no appropriate virtual network. A network interface card will be created that will be assigned to the VMSS instances. Under *Load balancing settings,* we can select what load balancing solution we want to implement, as shown in Figure 4-17. That configuration is not mandatory; that is recommended.

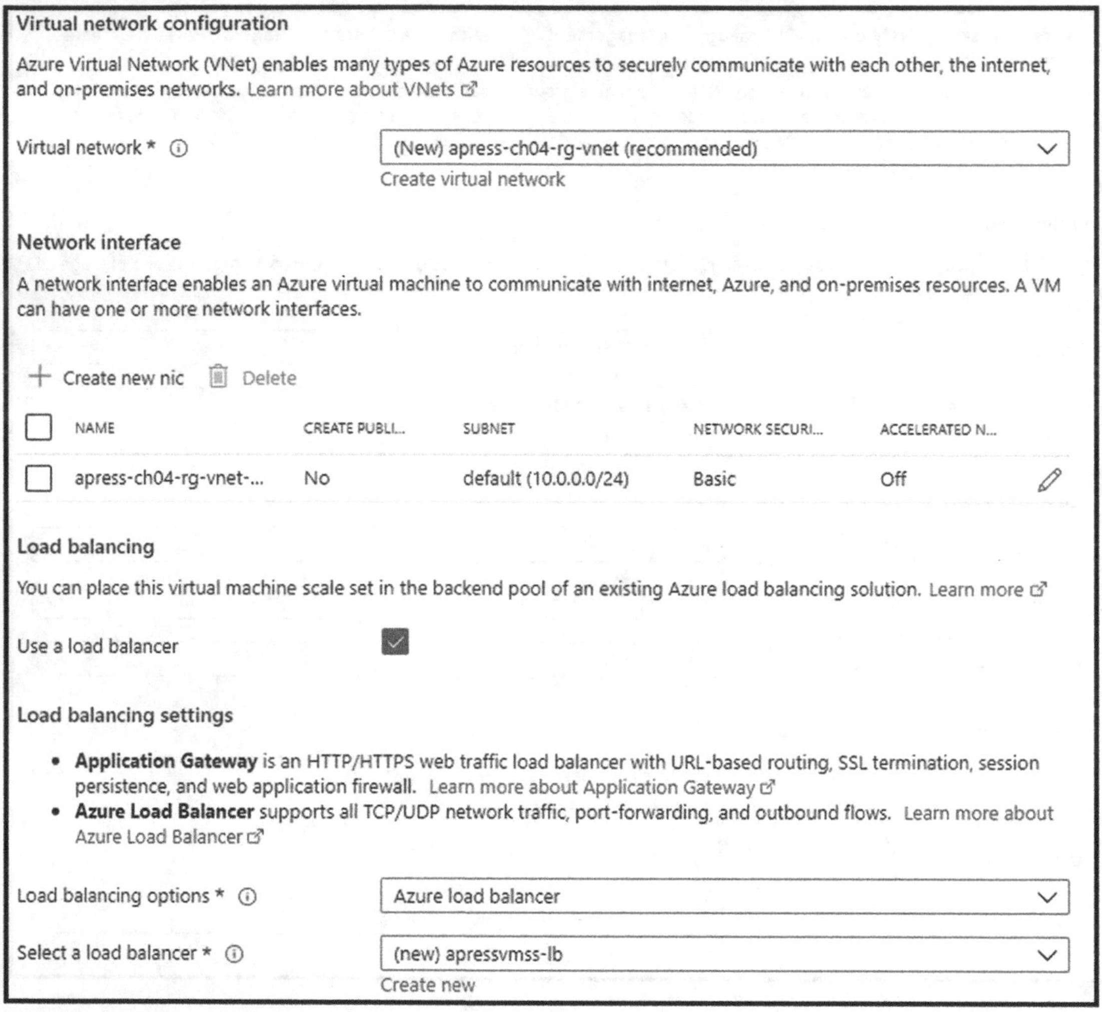

Virtual network configuration

Azure Virtual Network (VNet) enables many types of Azure resources to securely communicate with each other, the internet, and on-premises networks. Learn more about VNets ↗

Virtual network * ⓘ

| (New) apress-ch04-rg-vnet (recommended) | ⌄ |

Create virtual network

Network interface

A network interface enables an Azure virtual machine to communicate with internet, Azure, and on-premises resources. A VM can have one or more network interfaces.

＋ Create new nic   🗑 Delete

	NAME	CREATE PUBLI...	SUBNET	NETWORK SECURI...	ACCELERATED N...	
☐	apress-ch04-rg-vnet-...	No	default (10.0.0.0/24)	Basic	Off	✏

Load balancing

You can place this virtual machine scale set in the backend pool of an existing Azure load balancing solution. Learn more ↗

Use a load balancer   ☑

Load balancing settings

- **Application Gateway** is an HTTP/HTTPS web traffic load balancer with URL-based routing, SSL termination, session persistence, and web application firewall. Learn more about Application Gateway ↗
- **Azure Load Balancer** supports all TCP/UDP network traffic, port-forwarding, and outbound flows. Learn more about Azure Load Balancer ↗

Load balancing options * ⓘ

| Azure load balancer | ⌄ |

Select a load balancer * ⓘ

| (new) apressvmss-lb | ⌄ |

Create new

Figure 4-17. *Choose the load balancing solution to implement*

On the tab *Scaling* (Figure 4-18), we have to define the number of initial VMSS instances and the scaling method. If we want to implement auto-scaling, we have to select *Custom* and define initial configuration parameters for scale-in and scale-out. By default, the CPU metric is used for the scaling policy, but that can be changed later, or we can add more policies.

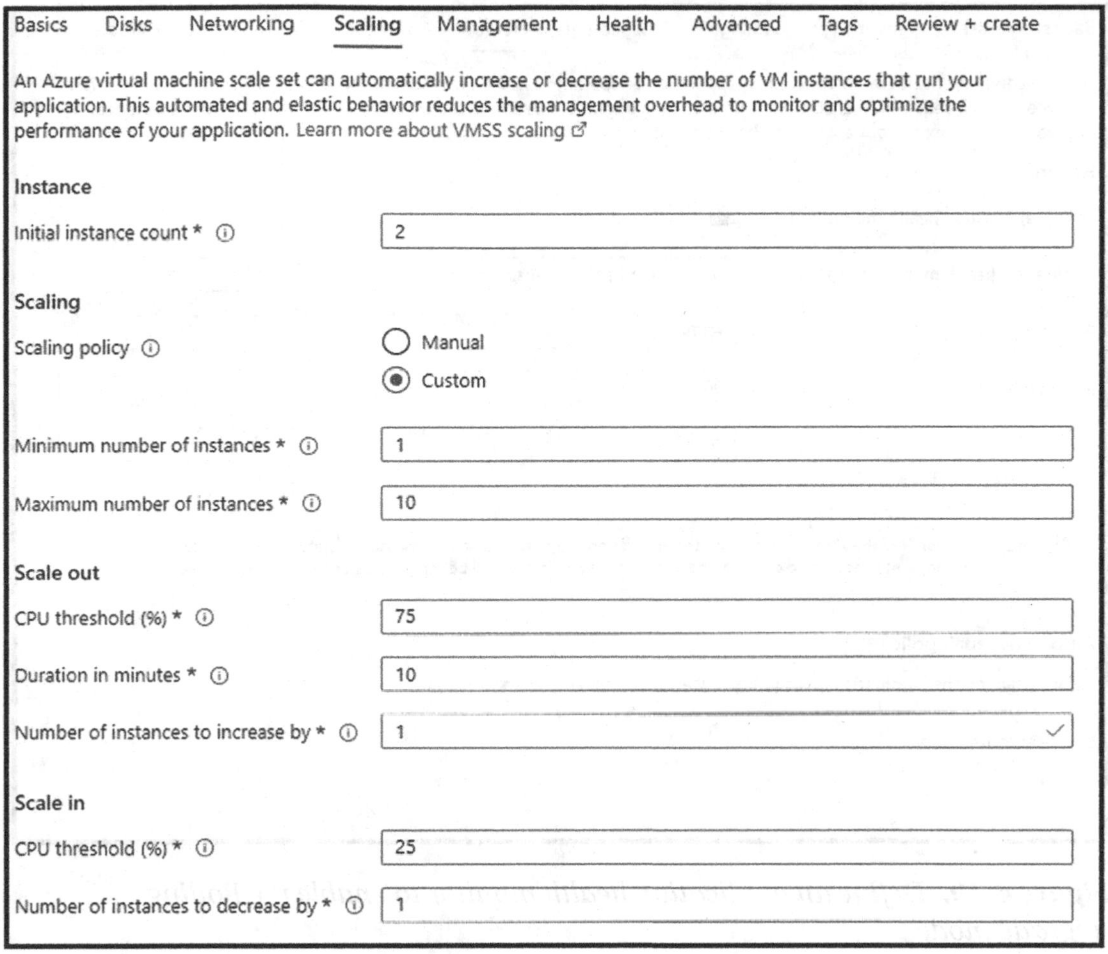

Basics   Disks   Networking   **Scaling**   Management   Health   Advanced   Tags   Review + create

An Azure virtual machine scale set can automatically increase or decrease the number of VM instances that run your application. This automated and elastic behavior reduces the management overhead to monitor and optimize the performance of your application. Learn more about VMSS scaling ☐

Instance

Initial instance count * ⓘ

> 2

Scaling

Scaling policy ⓘ

○ Manual
◉ Custom

Minimum number of instances * ⓘ

> 1

Maximum number of instances * ⓘ

> 10

Scale out

CPU threshold (%) * ⓘ

> 75

Duration in minutes * ⓘ

> 10

Number of instances to increase by * ⓘ

> 1   ✓

Scale in

CPU threshold (%) * ⓘ

> 25

Number of instances to decrease by * ⓘ

> 1

Figure 4-18. *Define the number of initial VMSS instances and the scaling method*

On the tab *Management*, we have to configure an upgrade policy and what upgrade mode will be used. We can configure system-managed identity, as well as disable over-provisioning, which is enabled by default. That functionality allows the VMSS to start with provisioning more instances than we precisely defined to provide us with the desired number of instances as soon as possible. That will not affect VMSS costs because once the desired number of instances is reached, other instances will be destroyed. Also, we can set automatic OS upgrades and the notification when an instance is terminated. On the tab *Health*, as shown in Figure 4-19, we have to define an application health monitor, which we explained in this chapter earlier, if we want to enable the Rolling upgrade mode.

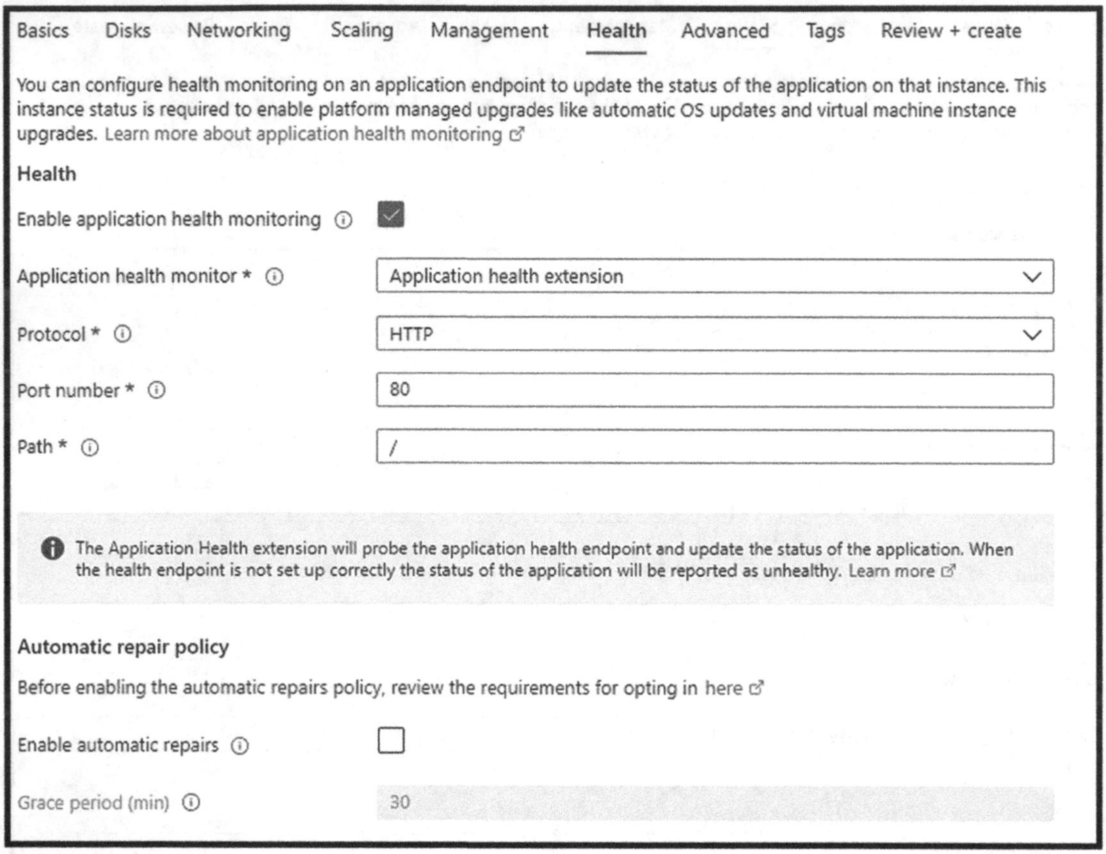

Figure 4-19. *Define an application health monitor to enable the Rolling upgrade mode*

The tab *Advanced* is reserved for the advanced configuration parameters, such as if we need more than 100 instances in the VMSS, what the spreading algorithm is, and how many fault domains we need for the VMSS. Also, we can define any extension for installing or a Custom Script that will be executed on the instances as a part of the post-deployment configuration. The tab *Tags* is the same for all Azure resources and provides us with a wizard for setting tags for the resources.

The last tab, *Review + create*, gives us an overview of the configuration we prepared for the VMSS deployment. Once we start with the creation process, as a first step, the system will run validation to check if everything is set correctly. Once the VMSS is deployed, we will get a message that the deployment is completed.

ARM Template, PowerShell, and Azure CLI

Since the deployment code could be pretty big, all ARM template, Azure PowerShell, and Azure CLI scripts are stored in the Apress GitHub account, available at the following URL:

`https://github.com/Apress/pro-azure-admin-and-automation`

Chapter Recap

In this chapter, we have learned what is essential for virtual machines and virtual machine scale sets, the most used IaaS Azure resources. Although we live in a fast-paced IT world and everything is moving so fast, virtual machines are one of the most used resources regardless of whether we use a cloud provider or on-premises infrastructure.

In the next chapter, we will partially stay in the IaaS world because containers in Azure could be run on a virtual machine with Docker installed. However, we will start to talk about Platform-as-a-Service services, why they are important, what benefits they give us, and how we can leverage them to improve infrastructure and business processes.

CHAPTER 5

App Service and Containers in Azure Compute

In the previous chapter of this book, we have learned more about, still the most popular, the IaaS cloud model. This chapter covers services within the second cloud model – PaaS:

- App Service overview

- App Service plans

- Web Apps deployment and configuration

- Publishing a web application

- CI/CD with Web Apps

- Auto-scaling with Web Apps

- Web Apps monitoring

- Docker on Azure

- Azure Container Registry (ACR)

- Azure Container Instances (ACI)

- Azure Kubernetes Service (AKS)

© Vladimir Stefanovic and Milos Katinski 2021
V. Stefanovic and M. Katinski, *Pro Azure Administration and Automation*,
https://doi.org/10.1007/978-1-4842-7325-8_5

After this chapter, we will be able to design an environment for our application and deploy it in a DevOps way of working. We will learn how to deploy a highly available application, use Blue-Green deployments, and much more. In order to choose the right environment/service for our application, Microsoft offered a flowchart that can help us make the decision (Figure 5-1).

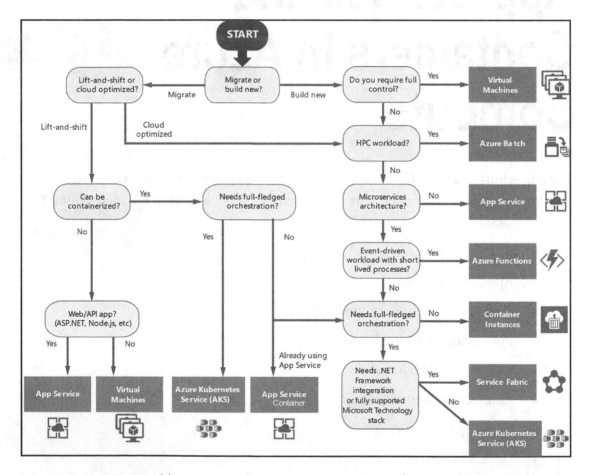

Figure 5-1. *Microsoft's compute decision tree flowchart (Source: https://docs. microsoft.com/en-us/azure/architecture/guide/technology-choices/ compute-decision-tree)*

App Service Overview

App Service is a cloud-native service in Azure. It is usually the first choice within DevOps teams during the transition from the previously mentioned IaaS model. It enables us to host Web Apps, mobile back ends, and APIs using one of the many supported languages:

- ASP.NET (Windows)

- ASP.NET Core (Windows or Linux)

- PHP (Windows or Linux)

- Java (Windows or Linux)

- Python (Linux)

- Ruby (Linux)

- Node.js (Windows or Linux)

One of the main advantages of using App Service is built-in high availability and auto-scaling functions. From an operating system perspective, both Windows and Linux are supported (in most cases – we will cover options later in the chapter). An additional benefit of moving to PaaS solutions is using various DevOps capabilities, like continuous deployment from Azure DevOps or GitHub and other similar CI/CD tools.

The App Service feature that developers should have in mind is that it automatically patches OS and language frameworks. If the application depends on a specific version of a framework, we need to include it in the build pipelines.

App Service Plans

An App Service plan covers the definition of computing resources for a web app(s) hosted under App Service. Those compute resources are reserved in the region where we create App Service and are used by any app we put under the same plan. An App Service plan is defined by

- Region (e.g., West Europe)

- Number of VM instances

- Size of VM instances

- Pricing tier (currently available are Free, Shared, Basic, Standard, Premium, PremiumV2, PremiumV3, Isolated – they are offering different options)

Pricing tier categories:

- Free and Shared: They are considered Shared compute tiers. That means that our App Service could be on the same VM as, for example, the App Service of another customer. Scaling out is not available.

- Basic, Standard, and Premium (V1, V2, V3) have dedicated compute resources:

  - The Basic tier offers to scale for up to three instances and a custom domain option.

  - The Standard tier offers scaling for up to ten instances, a custom domain, a maximum of five staging slots, a maximum of ten daily backups, and possible use of Traffic Manager (will be covered in Chapter 9).

  - The Premium tier adds up to 20 staging slots and offers a maximum of 50 daily backups and scaling for up to 20 instances.

- The Isolated tier also runs on a dedicated VM, but it offers network isolation by being connected to a dedicated virtual network. It has a maximum of scale-out options.

Each tier has a couple of different versions offering a wide range of compute options. We have mentioned scaling a few times. There are two types:

- Scale-up: Changing the tier of the App Service plan

- Scale-out: Changing the number of instances within the plan

Auto-scaling offers us an option to support the high demand for our application. We can manually scale resources or set custom policies that automatically scale our App Service based on metric thresholds.

Creating App Service

For this resource, too, we will first show how to create it via Azure Portal and then automate the same process differently.

Azure Portal

As mentioned many times, Azure Portal is the most popular management tool among the IT population, but we have to choose each option manually. When we choose to create a new resource and search for an App Service plan, we will need to populate few basic parameters – Resource Group where App Service will be deployed, Name, Operating System, Region, and Tier (Figure 5-2).

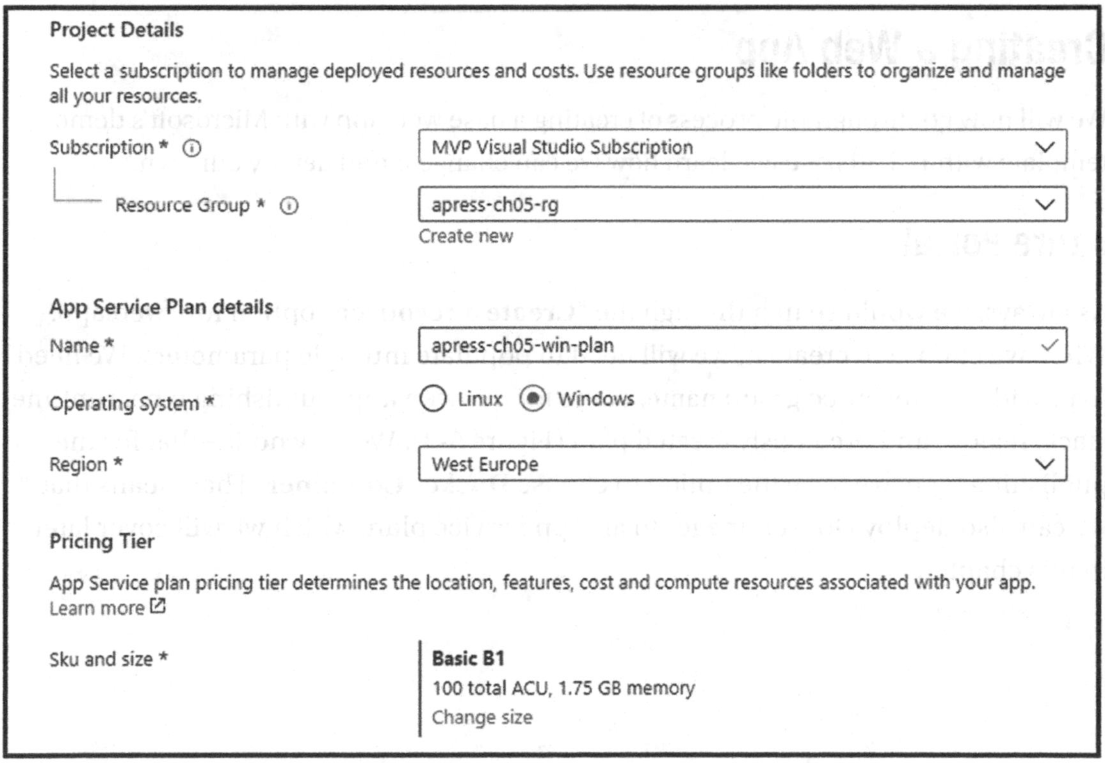

Project Details

Select a subscription to manage deployed resources and costs. Use resource groups like folders to organize and manage all your resources.

Subscription * ⓘ   MVP Visual Studio Subscription ⌄

    └── Resource Group * ⓘ   apress-ch05-rg ⌄
                                Create new

App Service Plan details

Name *   apress-ch05-win-plan ✓

Operating System *   ◯ Linux ◉ Windows

Region *   West Europe ⌄

Pricing Tier

App Service plan pricing tier determines the location, features, cost and compute resources associated with your app.
Learn more ☑

Sku and size *   **Basic B1**
                           100 total ACU, 1.75 GB memory
                           Change size

Figure 5-2. *Resource Group where App Service will be deployed, Name, Operating System, Region, and Tier*

We can then review and create our resource.

ARM Template, PowerShell, and Azure CLI

Since the deployment code could be pretty big, all ARM template, Azure PowerShell, and Azure CLI scripts are stored in the Apress GitHub account, available at the following URL:

```
https://github.com/Apress/pro-azure-admin-and-automation
```

Web Apps Deployment and Configuration

Web apps are actual applications written in one of the mentioned languages, deployed to an App Service plan. When we deploy the initial one out of the box, we will get base template code, which we can then modify.

Creating a Web App

We will now go through the process of creating a base web app with Microsoft's demo template within. Later, we will learn how we can change it and deploy our own.

Azure Portal

As always, we would search through the **"Create a resource"** option for "web app." When we choose to create it, we will need to populate multiple parameters. We need to provide the resource group name, name for our web app, publishing type, runtime stack, region, and previously created plan (Figure 5-3). We may notice that for the publishing type, we have the option to choose **Docker Container**. That means that we can also deploy Docker images to an App Service plan, which we will cover later in this chapter.

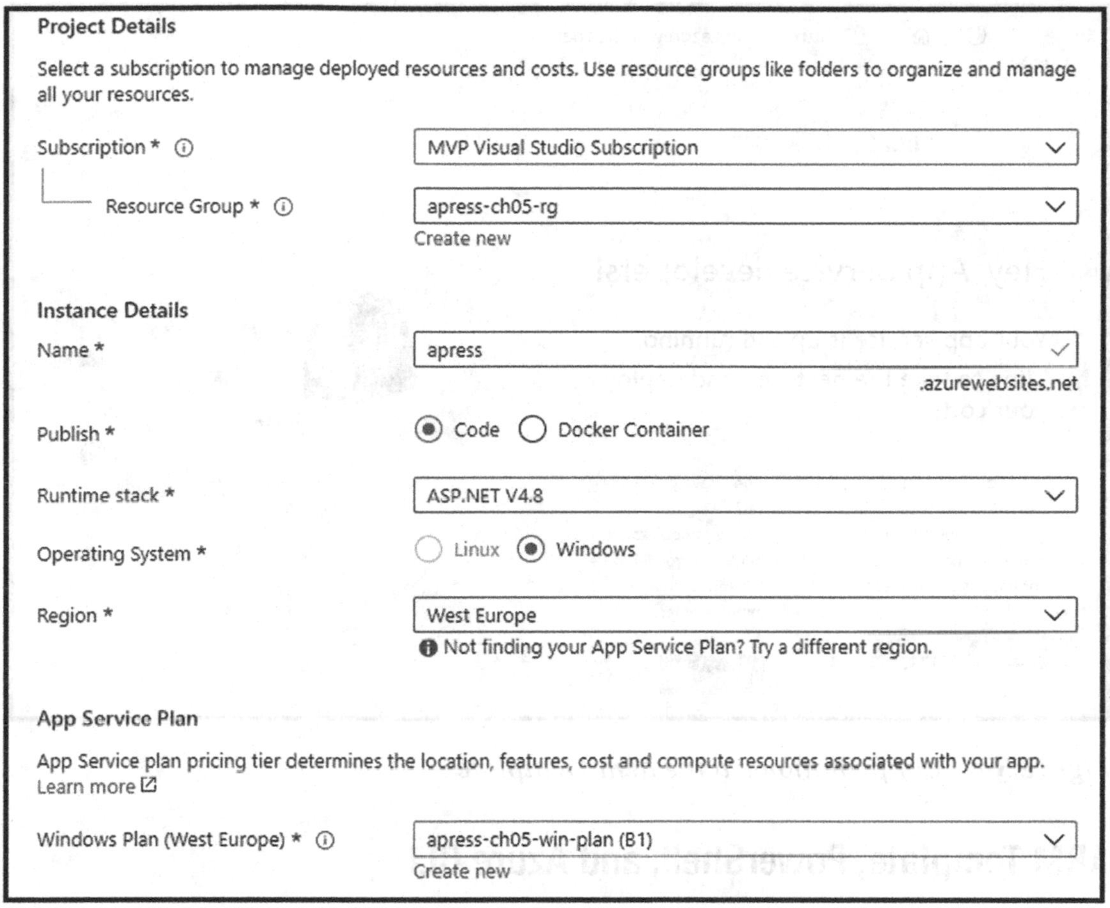

Project Details

Select a subscription to manage deployed resources and costs. Use resource groups like folders to organize and manage all your resources.

Subscription * ⓘ

MVP Visual Studio Subscription ⌄

└─── Resource Group * ⓘ

apress-ch05-rg ⌄

Create new

Instance Details

Name *

apress ✓

.azurewebsites.net

Publish *

◉ Code ○ Docker Container

Runtime stack *

ASP.NET V4.8 ⌄

Operating System *

○ Linux ◉ Windows

Region *

West Europe ⌄

ⓘ Not finding your App Service Plan? Try a different region.

App Service Plan

App Service plan pricing tier determines the location, features, cost and compute resources associated with your app.
Learn more ↗

Windows Plan (West Europe) * ⓘ

apress-ch05-win-plan (B1) ⌄

Create new

Figure 5-3. *Provide the resource group name*

In the next step, we can enable Application Insights (an Azure service that provides us with the ability to monitor other services and applications – we will cover this in this chapter too), but we will skip this. Finally, we just need to review our choices and create a web app. After the app is created, we will be able to visit the page (name of the web app) to confirm that all went well for now. We should get the demo template as in Figure 5-4.

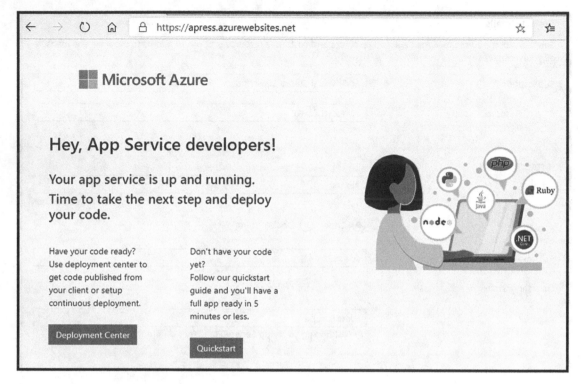

Figure 5-4. *Confirmation via the demo template*

ARM Template, PowerShell, and Azure CLI

Since the deployment code could be pretty big, all ARM template, Azure PowerShell, and Azure CLI scripts are stored in the Apress GitHub account, available at the following URL:

`https://github.com/Apress/pro-azure-admin-and-automation`

Publishing a Web Application

Now that we have successfully deployed our web app, it is time to work on deploying our code into it. As always, we have multiple choices to do that.

Running from the Package

Azure App Service gives us an option to run our app directly from a deployment ZIP package file. To use this option, we need to create a ZIP archive of everything in our project (should contain files like index.html, index.php, and app.js). The uploaded ZIP will be mounted as the read-only wwwroot directory.

The prerequisite is to enable a specific option in the web app – **WEBSITE_RUN_ FROM_PACKAGE.** We can do that with the Azure CLI command

```
az webapp config appsettings set --resource-group apress-ch05-rg --name
apress --settings WEBSITE_RUN_FROM_PACKAGE="1"
```

Running the package is achieved with this command:

```
az webapp deployment source config-zip --resource-group apress-ch05-rg
--name apress --src <filename>.zip
```

Deploying a ZIP

The same ZIP that was created in the previous step can be deployed to a web app. In this case, our project files will be deployed to a default folder (/home/site/wwwroot) in the app. To deploy the package, we need to visit the https://apress.scm.azurewebsites. net/ZipDeployUI page and drag the ZIP file to the file explorer area on the web page.

We can also use the Azure CLI command to do this, which will deploy the files and directories from ZIP to the default App Service application folder and restart the web app:

```
az webapp deployment source config-zip --resource-group apress-ch05-rg
--name apress --src <filename>.zip
```

Deploying via FTP

Within our web app, there is a Deployment menu. There, we can choose **Deployment Center** and **FTP** as one of many (Figure 5-5).

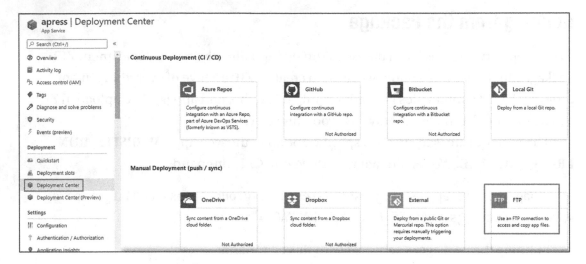

Figure 5-5. *Choose Deployment Center and FTP*

This will give us the necessary parameter information for the deployment – FTPS Endpoint, Username, and Password.

Cloud Sync

With this option, we can use services like Dropbox and OneDrive to sync our content. We can find these options under the same **Deployment Center** menu.

Continuous Deployment

This option can be used with GitHub, Bitbucket, and Azure Repos. Within **Deployment Center**, we can authorize access from the web app to our repository:

- Continuous deployment for custom containers – we will cover this later in the chapter.

Deploying from Local Git

If we want to leverage this, we need to have the repository cloned locally. Initiate the following command to test:

```
# Cloning template repository
git clone https://github.com/Azure-Samples/app-service-web-html-get-started
# Configuring a deployment user
```

```
az webapp deployment user set --user-name 'apress' --password
'V3ryStrOngPa55!'
# Get the deployment URL
$url = az webapp deployment source config-local-git --name apress
--resource-group apress-ch05-rg
$url
# Deploy the Web App
git remote add azure "https://apress@apress.scm.azurewebsites.net/apress.git"
git push azure
# You will be asked to enter the password you created for the deployment user
```

The result should look similar to the one in Figure 5-6.

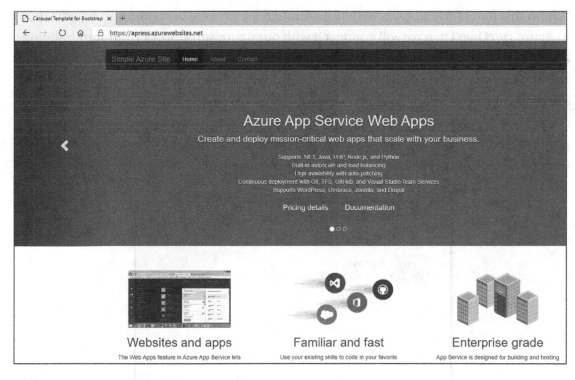

Figure 5-6. *Confirming results*

Deploying via GitHub Actions

GitHub actions can easily automate software workflows, using CI/CD directly from GitHub (not part of this book).

Deploy Using the ARM Template

A great example provided by Microsoft can be found on this link – `https://github.com/azure-appservice-samples/ToDoApp`.

Click the **Deploy to Azure** button and populate parameters.

CI/CD with Web Apps

Within this part of the chapter, we will go through the process of creating an organization in Azure DevOps. Then we will connect it with our Azure subscription and start building the first CI/CD pipelines for our application. When we visit the page dev.azure.com, we will be taken to the home page of Azure DevOps. There, we need to log in with a Microsoft account.

We will then be asked to create an organization under which we will create our projects later on. When we create an organization, we can then create multiple projects under it. Inside the projects, we will have our repositories, CI/CD pipelines, and others.

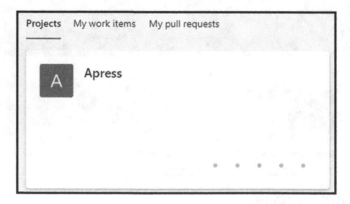

Figure 5-7. *Create a project*

To use Azure DevOps, we need to connect it to our Azure subscription. Under **Organization Settings**, we need to choose **Azure Active Directory** and **Connect directory** (Figure 5-8).

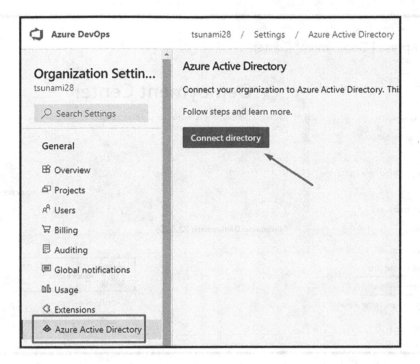

Figure 5-8. *Choose Azure Active Directory and Connect directory*

The easiest way to proceed after connecting Azure DevOps and the subscription is to go back to our previously deployed App Service and choose **Deployment Center ➤ Azure Repos**.

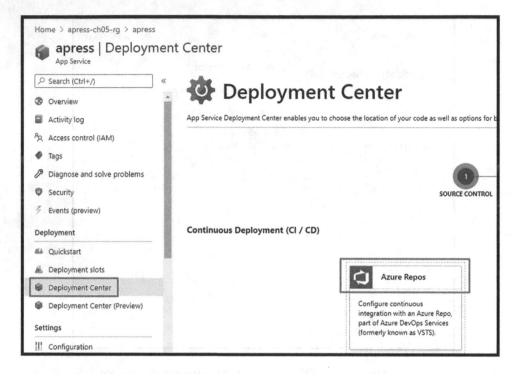

Figure 5-9.   Choose Deployment Center ➤ Azure Repos

In the next step, choose **Azure Pipelines** and continue. Then we will need to choose from the dropdown menus the organization we created, project, repository, branch, and framework used for the application (Figure 5-10).

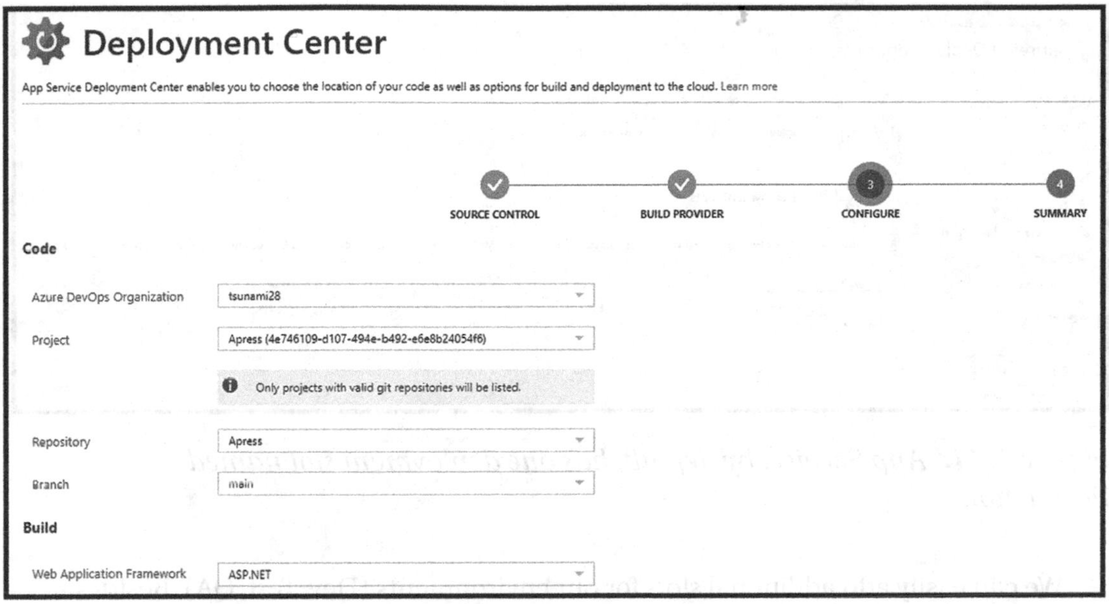

*Figure 5-10. Choose **Azure Pipelines** and continue*

Ending this process will create all needed CI/CD pipelines within the Azure DevOps project. We can now switch to our Azure DevOps project and continue working on our code. Each new push to the repository will trigger a new build. A successful build will then trigger release. That easy. Furthermore, we now have an automated CI/CD process for our application.

Blue-Green Deployment

With the Standard S1 App Service plan comes one more great functionality – staging slots. When we create App Service, by default, it has one deployment slot named Production (Figure 5-11).

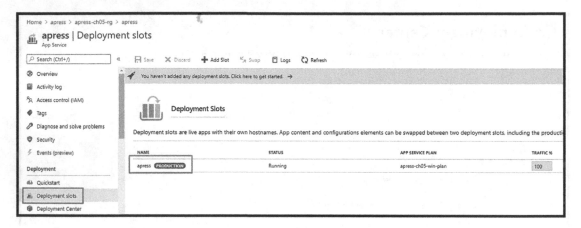

Figure 5-11. *App Service, by default, has one deployment slot named Production*

We can easily add additional slots for our environments (Dev, Test, QA). Besides giving it a name, we can choose to clone the current state from the Production slot.

Now we can set up multiple stages within our release pipeline that would target different slots of App Service. When we are done testing new features or any kind of change, we can easily, with just one click, swap the slots (Figure 5-12). That way, the one that was Production would become a Development one.

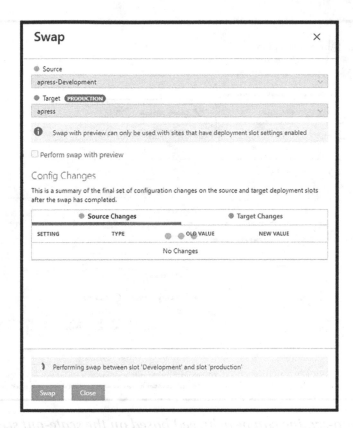

Figure 5-12. *When testing new features or changes is complete, click to swap the slots*

If, by any chance, we notice that there is a problem with the new code, we can always make an additional swap reverting to the previous state. All this is done with minimal downtime. One more thing we can use before swapping is traffic percentage – this gives us the option to send a specific % of traffic to the Development slot and track further how the new code is working with the load of the Production one.

Auto-scaling with Web Apps

When it comes to scaling, we already mentioned that there are two types of it:

- Scale-up

- Scale-out

Auto-scaling can be achieved based on the scale-out scenario (Figure 5-13). The first App Service plan that allows us to use auto-scaling as a feature is Standard S1.

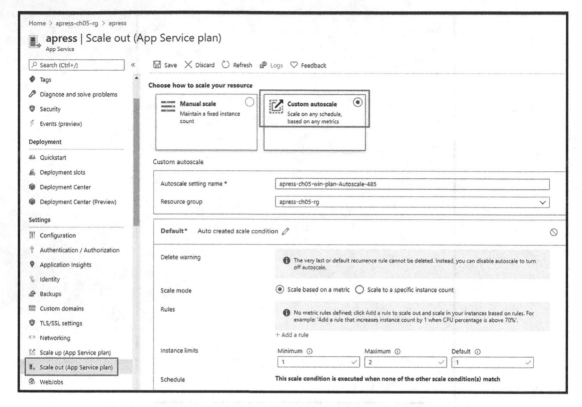

Figure 5-13. *Auto-scaling can be achieved based on the scale-out scenario*

To use this feature in an automated way, we need to create rules that will trigger both the increase and decrease in the number of instances (scale-out or scale-in), as shown in Figure 5-14.

Rules are created based on the specific metrics that are available for App Service like

- CPU percentage

- Memory percentage

- Data in or out

- Disk or HTTP queue length

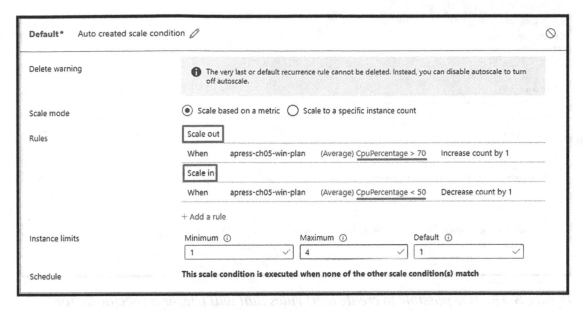

Figure 5-14. *Create rules that trigger both the increase and the decrease in the number of instances (scale-out or scale-in)*

It is also essential to set the minimum and the maximum number of instances. That could save us from potential money loss in case of an unpredictable scale-out.

Web Apps Monitoring

There are multiple options for monitoring App Service:

- Alerts: It is possible to create alert rules that will trigger a specific action (Figure 5-15). For example, we can monitor the number of connections, and if it goes beyond a specific value, the Send email action will be triggered.

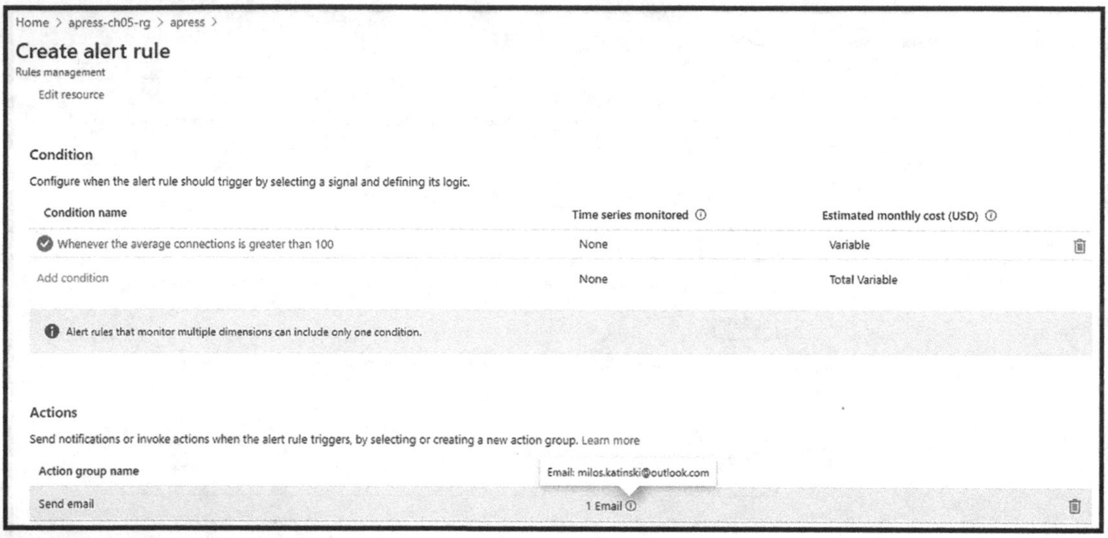

Figure 5-15. *It is possible to create alert rules that will trigger a specific action*

- Metrics: This is live monitoring of the different App Service metrics. They can also be added to the dashboard for teams monitoring apps in real time.

- Logs: They are powered by Azure Log Analytics. To use them, we need to set a few more things so that our App Service sends data to the Log Analytics workspace (LAW).

- Diagnostic settings: This is where we set all the available logs to be sent to LAW (Figure 5-16).

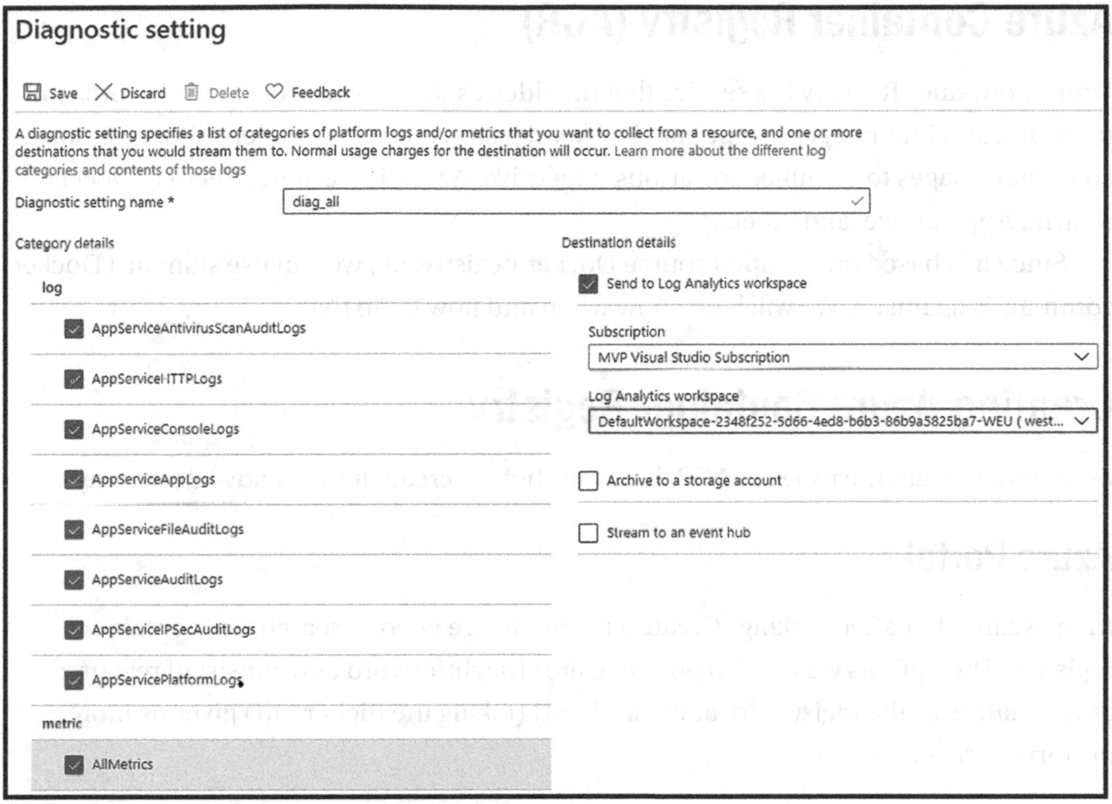

Diagnostic setting

🖫 Save   ✕ Discard   🗑 Delete   ♡ Feedback

A diagnostic setting specifies a list of categories of platform logs and/or metrics that you want to collect from a resource, and one or more destinations that you would stream them to. Normal usage charges for the destination will occur. Learn more about the different log categories and contents of those logs

Diagnostic setting name *   [diag_all   ✓]

Category details   **Destination details**

log   ☑ Send to Log Analytics workspace

  ☑ AppServiceAntivirusScanAuditLogs   Subscription
                                                             [MVP Visual Studio Subscription   ⌄]
  ☑ AppServiceHTTPLogs
                                                             Log Analytics workspace
  ☑ AppServiceConsoleLogs   [DefaultWorkspace-2348f252-5d66-4ed8-b6b3-86b9a5825ba7-WEU (west... ⌄]

  ☑ AppServiceAppLogs   ☐ Archive to a storage account

  ☑ AppServiceFileAuditLogs   ☐ Stream to an event hub

  ☑ AppServiceAuditLogs

  ☑ AppServiceIPSecAuditLogs

  ☑ AppServicePlatformLogs

metric

  ☑ AllMetrics

Figure 5-16.   Set all the available logs to be sent to LAW

- App Service logs: Here, we can enable additional/detailed logging if we need to troubleshoot the behavior of our application.

- Log stream: Live representation of the application logs.

After we have set diagnostic settings and our App Service started sending data to the Log Analytics workspace, we can start using logs and the Microsoft Kusto query language to read needed data. Many predefined queries can help us in the beginning.

Docker on Azure

Docker is the most popular container management and imaging platform. It enables us to efficiently work with containers on any operating system that supports the Docker platform. Along with the many operating systems, including Windows and various Linux distributions, today we can find Docker on Azure in many different variations.

Azure Container Registry (ACR)

Azure Container Registry is a service that provides us with the ability to build, store, and manage container images in a private Docker registry. It is used as a repository for our container images to be pulled to various targets like Azure Kubernetes Service, Docker Swarm, App Service, and others.

Since it is based on the open source Docker Registry 2.0, we can use standard Docker commands against it. We will later show when and how to do that.

Creating Azure Container Registry

Before we explain the usage of ACR, let us see how to create it in already known ways.

Azure Portal

In the search bar after clicking "Create a resource," we need to search for "container registry." The options we need to populate are straightforward and consist of resource group, name for the registry, location, and SKU (taking the higher SKU gives us more performance and scale).

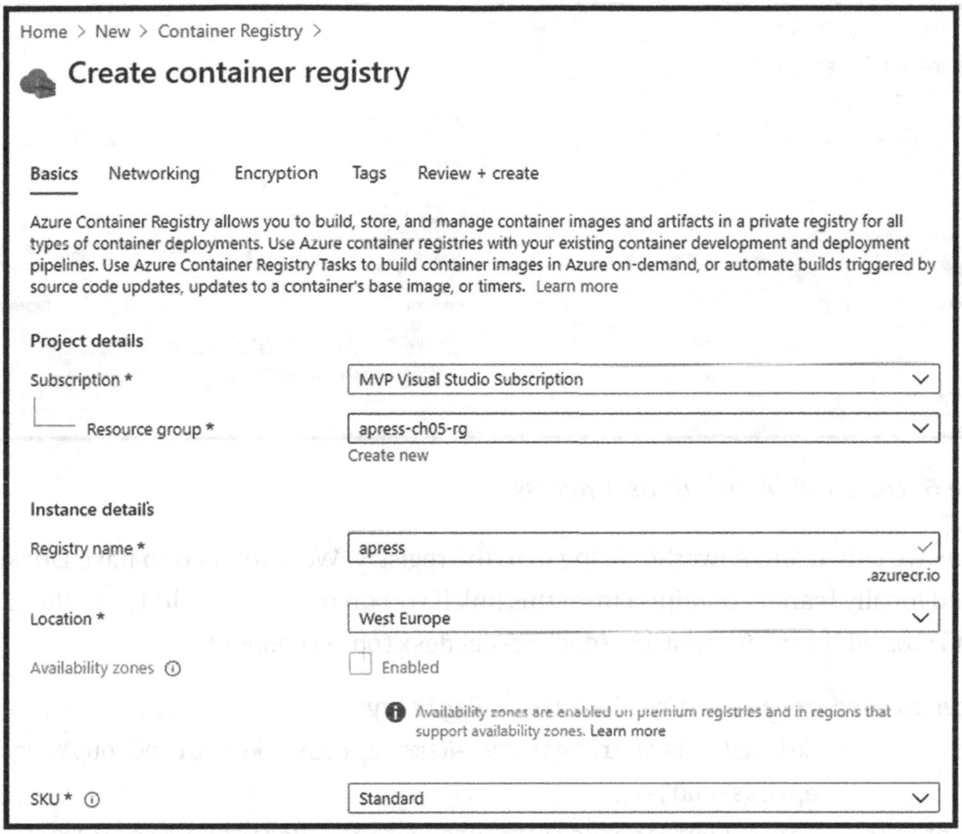

Figure 5-17. *Population the fields*

Since we have chosen to go with Standard SKU, Private Endpoint and Encryption are not available (need Premium for both). We can now review and create our resource.

ARM Template, PowerShell, and Azure CLI

Since the deployment code could be pretty big, all ARM template, Azure PowerShell, and Azure CLI scripts are stored in the Apress GitHub account, available at the following URL:

https://github.com/Apress/pro-azure-admin-and-automation

Now when we have our Container Registry prepared, we can, with few more prerequisites, upload our first image. First, we need to enable admin user access (Figure 5-18), which is vital for interaction with ACR if we cannot leverage RBAC.

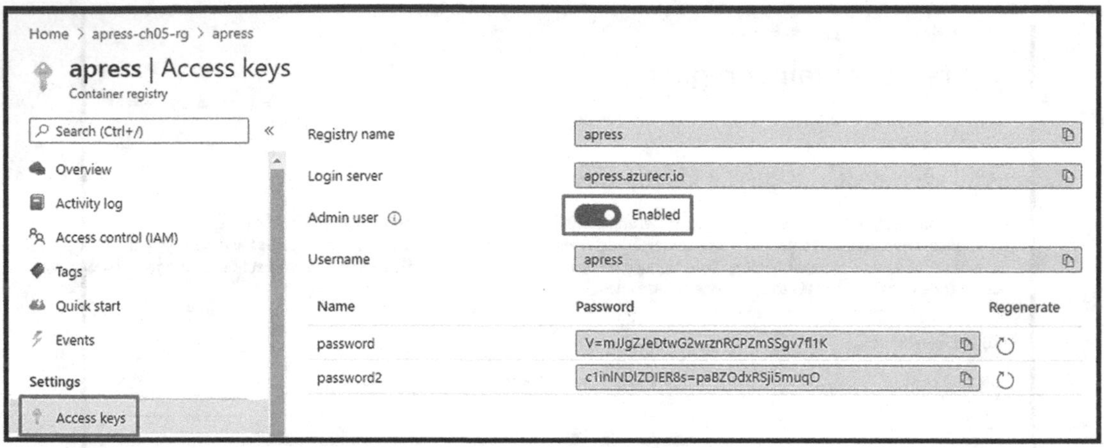

Figure 5-18. *Enable admin user access*

Now we can, using PowerShell, log in to the registry. We also need to have Docker installed locally (can be obtained from this link if you do not have it – https://hub. docker.com/editions/community/docker-ce-desktop-windows/):

```
# Login procedure for Azure Container Registry
$registry     = Get-AzContainerRegistry -Name apress -ResourceGroupName
               apress-ch05-rg
$credentials = Get-AzContainerRegistryCredential -Registry $registry

$credentials.Password | docker login $registry.LoginServer -u $credentials.
Username --password-stdin
```

The next step would be to push the image to the registry and run it from there:

```
# Pull the image from the official Docker registry
docker pull hello-world
# Tag the image
docker tag hello-world apress.azurecr.io/hello-world:v1
# Push image to the registry
docker push apress.azurecr.io/hello-world:v1
# Local cleanup
docker rmi apress.azurecr.io/hello-world:v1
# Run from registry
docker run apress.azurecr.io/hello-world:v1
```

The output of previous commands should look like this:

```
PS C:\drscoding> docker pull hello-world
Using default tag: latest
latest: Pulling from library/hello-world
0e03bdcc26d7: Pull complete
Digest: sha256:31b9c7d48790f0d8c50ab433d9c3b7e17666d6993084c002c2ff1ca09b9
        6391d
Status: Downloaded newer image for hello-world:latest
docker.io/library/hello-world:latest
PS C:\drscoding> docker tag hello-world apress.azurecr.io/hello-world:v1
PS C:\drscoding> docker push apress.azurecr.io/hello-world:v1
The push refers to repository [apress.azurecr.io/hello-world]
9c27e219663c: Pushed
v1: digest: sha256:90659bf80b44ce6be8234e6ff90a1ac34acbeb826903b02cfa0da11c
            82cbc042 size: 525
PS C:\drscoding> docker rmi apress.azurecr.io/hello-world:v1
Untagged: apress.azurecr.io/hello-world:v1
Untagged: apress.azurecr.io/hello-world@sha256:90659bf80b44ce6be8234e6ff90a
          1ac34acbeb826903b02cfa0da11c82cbc042
PS C:\drscoding> docker run apress.azurecr.io/hello-world:v1
Unable to find image 'apress.azurecr.io/hello-world:v1' locally
v1: Pulling from hello-world
Digest: sha256:90659bf80b44ce6be8234e6ff90a1ac34acbeb826903b02cfa0da11c82c
        bc042
Status: Downloaded newer image for apress.azurecr.io/hello-world:v1

Hello from Docker!
This message shows that your installation appears to be working correctly.
```

Azure Container Instances

Azure Container Instances is a service that provides us with the fastest way to run a container in Azure. It is the best solution for isolated containers. With Azure Container Instances, we avoid provisioning and managing VMs or App Service as host for our containers. During the creation of the Container Instance, we can specify a DNS name for our application and make it reachable over the Internet.

ACI offers exact specifications of CPU and memory, and we are billed by the second of our application uptime. It offers connectivity via an Azure virtual network. That means that it can communicate securely with other resources within the VNet or through peering.

Creating Azure Container Instances

With the already known options, we will see how easy and quickly it is to create an Azure Container Instance and be live with the containerized application.

Azure Portal

After choosing **Create a resource**, we should search for "container instances." We need to provide a resource group for deployment, name, region, and – the most crucial parameter – image source (Figure 5-19).

An image source could be chosen from

- QuickStart images: Provided by Microsoft

- Azure Container Registry: If we have built one of our own

- Docker Hub or other registries

For this deployment, we will choose a QuickStart image:

- "mcr.microsoft.com/azuredocs/aci-helloworld:latest"

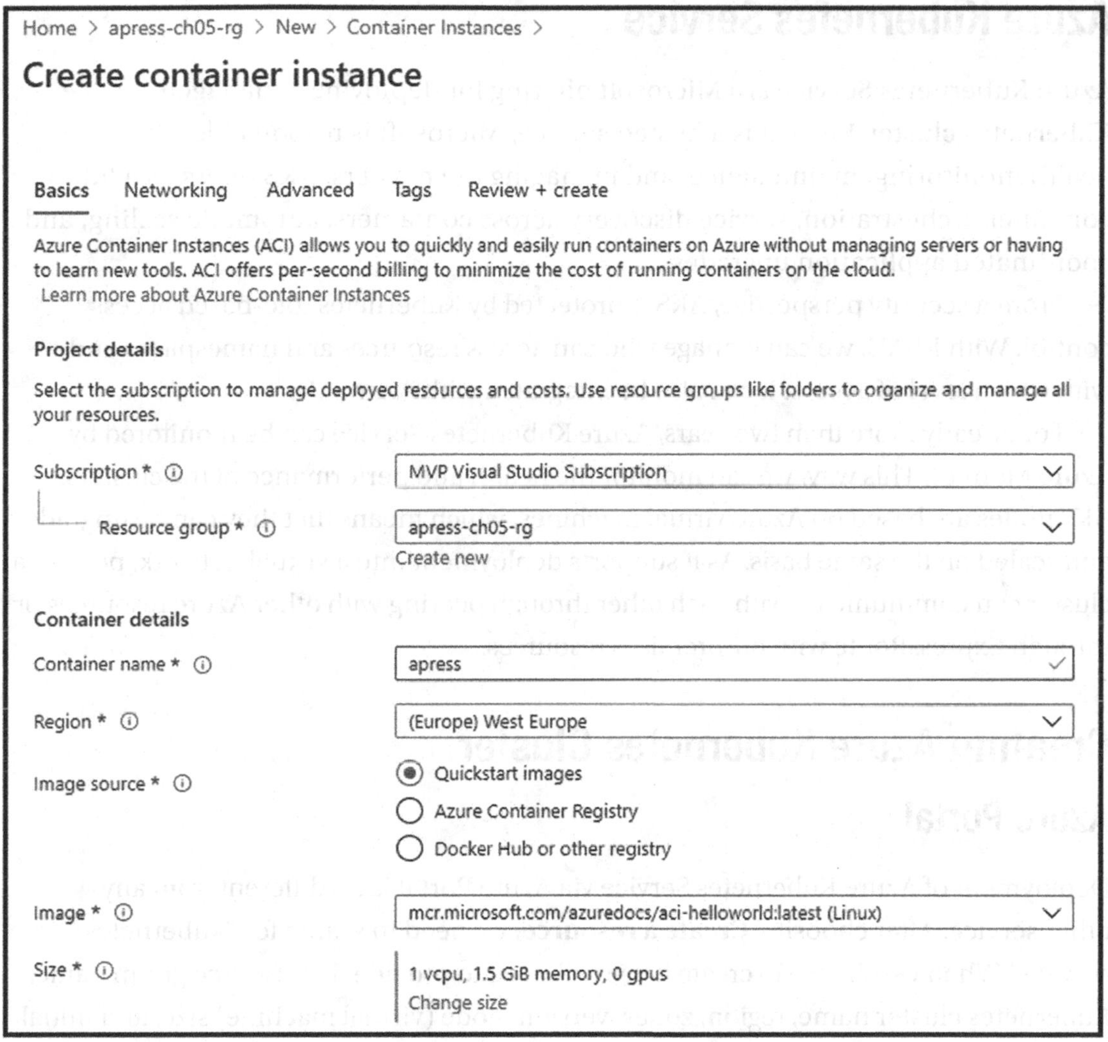

Home > apress-ch05-rg > New > Container Instances >

Create container instance

Basics   Networking   Advanced   Tags   Review + create

Azure Container Instances (ACI) allows you to quickly and easily run containers on Azure without managing servers or having to learn new tools. ACI offers per-second billing to minimize the cost of running containers on the cloud.
Learn more about Azure Container Instances

Project details

Select the subscription to manage deployed resources and costs. Use resource groups like folders to organize and manage all your resources.

Subscription * ⓘ | MVP Visual Studio Subscription |

  Resource group * ⓘ | apress-ch05-rg |
     Create new

Container details

Container name * ⓘ | apress |

Region * ⓘ | (Europe) West Europe |

Image source * ⓘ   ◉ Quickstart images
                     ◯ Azure Container Registry
                     ◯ Docker Hub or other registry

Image * ⓘ | mcr.microsoft.com/azuredocs/aci-helloworld:latest (Linux) |

Size * ⓘ | 1 vcpu, 1.5 GiB memory, 0 gpus |
                       Change size

Figure 5-19. *Provide a resource group for deployment, name, region, and – the most crucial parameter – image source*

After successful deployment, we should be able to open the FQDN assigned to the instance.

ARM Template, PowerShell, and Azure CLI

Since the deployment code could be pretty big, all ARM template, Azure PowerShell, and Azure CLI scripts are stored in the Apress GitHub account, available at the following URL:

```
https://github.com/Apress/pro-azure-admin-and-automation
```

Azure Kubernetes Service

Azure Kubernetes Service is a Microsoft offering for deploying a managed Kubernetes cluster. Since it is a hosted service, Microsoft is responsible for health monitoring, maintenance, and managing the masters. AKS offers us a full container orchestration, service discovery across containers, automatic scaling, and coordinated application upgrades.

From a security perspective, AKS is protected by Kubernetes role-based access control. With RBAC, we can manage who can access resources and namespaces and with which level of access. It can also be integrated with Azure AD.

For already more than two years, Azure Kubernetes Service can be monitored by Azure Monitor. This way, we can monitor the health and performance of the clusters. AKS nodes are based on Azure virtual machines, which means that they can be upgraded and scaled on the same basis. As it supports deployment into a virtual network, pods in a cluster can communicate with each other through peering with other Azure resources or through ExpressRoute with on-premises resources.

Creating Azure Kubernetes Cluster

Azure Portal

Deployment of Azure Kubernetes Service via Azure Portal is no different from any other service. After choosing **Create a resource**, we need to search for "kubernetes service." When we choose to create it, we will need to provide the resource group name, Kubernetes cluster name, region, zones, version, node (virtual machine) size, and initial number of nodes. The next step is to define node pools – we will have one predefined. We now need to choose the authentication method, networking options, monitoring, and possible integration with Azure Policy. Finally, review and create the resource.

ARM Template, PowerShell, and Azure CLI

Since the deployment code could be pretty big, all ARM template, Azure PowerShell, and Azure CLI scripts are stored in the Apress GitHub account, available at the following URL:

https://github.com/Apress/pro-azure-admin-and-automation

Chapter Recap

In this chapter, we have learned more about the most used Platform-as-a-Service product – App Service. We have seen how easily we can use it to deploy our applications and even Docker containers. We have also covered the basic deployment of Azure Kubernetes Service.

In the next chapter, we will talk about one of the most used Azure services. We will cover the types and use cases for it.

CHAPTER 6

Azure Storage

In the previous chapters, we discussed and explained the most used cloud services in Azure, such as virtual machines, scale sets, and App Service, and learned how to use them. One Azure service that we mentioned but still did not go into details about is Storage Account, which will be the subject of this chapter.

This chapter covers the following topics regarding one of the most used Azure services:

- Storage Account and its features
- Storage Account management
- Security of storage accounts
- Azure disks
- Data transfer

After this chapter, we will be able to design, implement, and deploy a storage workload in Azure in various scenarios and using various tools.

Storage Accounts

When we talk about storage, in general, we are aware that without it, we will not be able to do almost anything. Storage is everywhere around us, in computers, mobile phones, tablets, even smartwatches and TVs, and logically any kind of cloud. If we focus our talk on Microsoft Azure, there are many storage options, but Storage Account is the most used. Easy and quick deployment and scaling are some of the most significant benefits of using storage accounts in Azure. Also, we are witnesses that pricing for storing data in Azure decreases over the years, with a tendency to be lower. For instance, 1 TB of stored data in a blob container in the archive tier is only 1$ per month.

127

© Vladimir Stefanovic and Milos Katinski 2021
V. Stefanovic and M. Katinski, *Pro Azure Administration and Automation*,
https://doi.org/10.1007/978-1-4842-7325-8_6

At first look, we could say that Azure storage accounts will be perfect for our needs, but let's go more in depth to see what we can expect from Storage Account and what it offers.

Account Types and Performance Tiers

The very first things that we need to choose when designing or implementing storage accounts are the account type and performance tier. A few options are on the table, and a few combinations as well, so we need to know what we exactly want to achieve.

In the first place, we have to decide what kind of performance we need: Standard or Premium. Storage accounts in the Standard tier will be created on magnetic drives, whereas storage accounts in the Premium tier will be created on SSDs, which is the first significant difference on the physical layer. Since the price is very different between these tiers and there is no possibility of upgrading or downgrading between storage tiers, we have to plan carefully what performance tier will be used. The Standard tier is sufficient for most workloads. However, there are also scenarios where the Premium tier is needed due to better performance and lower latency in the first place. In addition, constant improvement of Azure Storage service features and the possibility to store block and page blobs in the Premium tier could be crucial for choosing this performance tier.

Once we define our needs, we have to select an appropriate storage account performance tier and account type from the following:

- Standard: General-purpose V2

- Premium: Page blobs

- Premium: Block blobs

- Premium: File shares

The general-purpose account type is most used and can fit most Azure workloads because it could be used for storing all types of data, blobs, file shares, tables, and queues, inside of one storage account. Of course, since the Standard performance tier is cheaper than Premium, and if we do not need low latency, it will be our first choice in most cases. On the other hand, a premium storage account can be used for storing page and block blobs, as well as file shares, but not in one single storage account. If we need to use all these account types in the Premium performance tier, we need to separate them into different storage accounts. Also, append blobs, tables, and queues are still not supported in the Premium performance tier.

In conclusion, if we do not need high performance and do not need to deploy anything, the general-purpose storage account will be more than enough for our needs. Otherwise, if we need better performance for our data, we have to plan a bit more because one account type does not cover all storage services in the Premium performance tier. Last but not least, the pricing schemes for these performance tiers are very different. For instance, blob storage in the Standard performance tier costs approximately $22 per TB, whereas the Premium performance tier will cost us approximately $185 per TB. If we have to think about financial matters, it will be an additional task before deciding on the performance tier that we will use.

Storage Account Replication

In real-world scenarios, if our data are not backed up or replicated, we cannot say that we are protected. For the storage accounts in Azure, there are a few different replication plans that we can use to protect our data, and fortunately, we can benefit from them. We can divide replication plans into two main categories: replication in the primary region and replication in the secondary region.

Replication or redundancy in the primary region includes *locally redundant storage (LRS)* and *zone-redundant storage (ZRS)*. LRS is the lowest-cost redundancy option, and all our data will be replicated three times within a datacenter where a storage account is created. Even though LRS is the lowest-cost option for redundancy, Microsoft guarantees 99.999999999% (11 nines) SLA in a year. Another option for replication in the primary region is ZRS, which can be implemented only in regions with zones. This replication plan gives us three copies of our data in three separate zones in the region, with 99.9999999999% (12 nines) SLA in a year.

If we want to protect our data better, we can select one of the replication plans that replicate our data to the secondary region: *geo-redundant storage (GRS)* and *geo-zone-redundant storage (GZRS)*. Both options will give us three copies in the primary region and three copies more in the secondary region. Also, for both options, Microsoft guarantees 99.99999999999999% (16 nines) SLA in a year and an RPO of 15 minutes. Additionally, GRS and GZRS can be implemented as *read-access geo-redundant storage (RA-GRS)* and *read-access geo-zone-redundant storage (RA-GZRS)*, where replicas in the secondary region will be readable. One of the essential things when considering storage account replication is that not all redundancy options are available in all regions. However, since the improvements on the Azure infrastructure are continually processed, we can expect that "missing" features will come to specific regions in the future.

In the replication plans that include the secondary region, we must be aware of potential data loss since replication between regions is asynchronous. Microsoft does not guarantee any SLA for this replication since the data replication time depends on the amount of data.

Creating a Storage Account

Like almost all Azure resources, a storage account can be created using all management tools used in the previous chapters.

Azure Portal

Before we go to the next discussion about storage services, let us create one general-purpose V2 storage account in the Standard performance tier. If we decide to use Azure Portal to perform this operation, the first step is to click **+ Create a resource**, search for "storage account" in the *Marketplace*, and click **Create**. In our cases, we will configure parameters just on the *Basics* tab, and all other things we will configure later in this chapter. As with all other Azure resources, we need to define Subscription and Resource group under *Project details*. Under *Instance details,* we will define Storage account name, which must be unique across Azure, Location, Performance tier, Account type, and Replication type. Once these parameters are filled, click **Review + create** and then **Create** to create a storage account. All these parameters are shown in Figure 6-1.

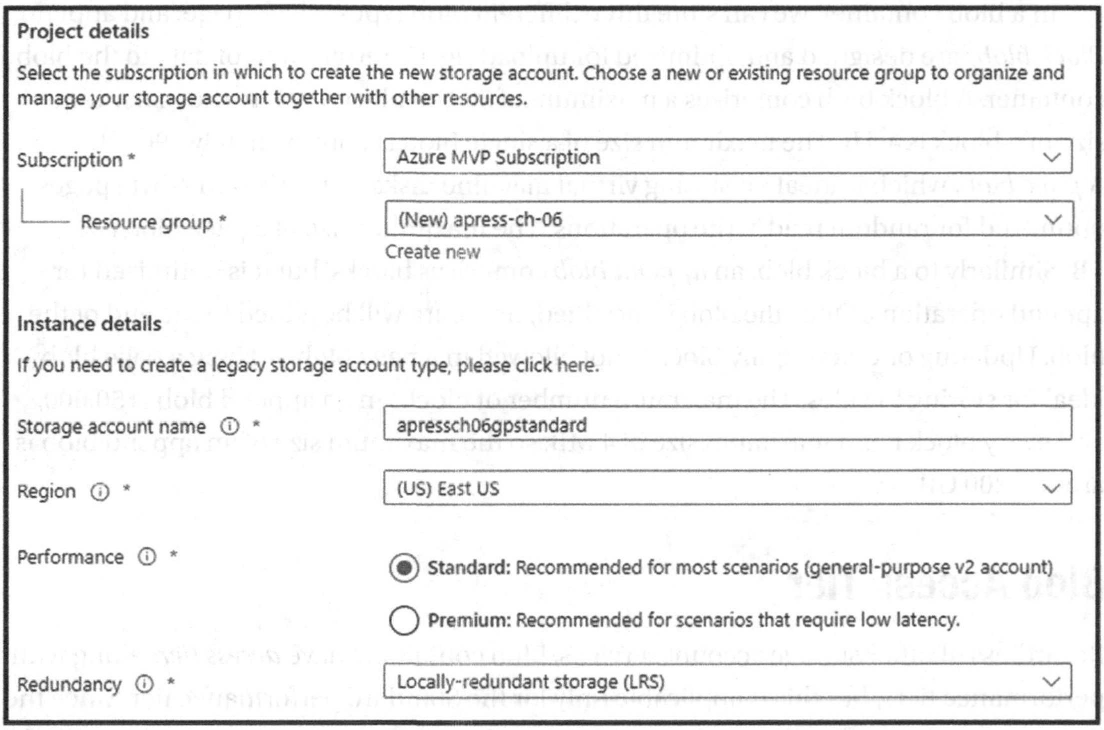

Project details

Select the subscription in which to create the new storage account. Choose a new or existing resource group to organize and manage your storage account together with other resources.

Subscription *   Azure MVP Subscription

└─ Resource group *   (New) apress-ch-06
                          Create new

Instance details

If you need to create a legacy storage account type, please click here.

Storage account name ⓘ *   apressch06gpstandard

Region ⓘ *   (US) East US

Performance ⓘ *   ⦿ Standard: Recommended for most scenarios (general-purpose v2 account)

                         ○ Premium: Recommended for scenarios that require low latency.

Redundancy ⓘ *   Locally-redundant storage (LRS)

Figure 6-1. *Define Subscription and Resource group under Project details*

ARM Template, PowerShell, and Azure CLI

Since the deployment code could be pretty big, all ARM template, Azure PowerShell, and Azure CLI scripts are stored in the Apress GitHub account, available at the following URL:

```
https://github.com/Apress/pro-azure-admin-and-automation
```

Blob Containers

One of the most used storage services is the blob container that could be used for various workloads, such as storing logs, pictures, SQL backup files, and many others. Also, the blob container is the storage service that is used by many other Azure services for storing their data. For instance, if we want to configure a disaster recovery location in Azure or prepare an on-premises environment for migrations, Azure Site Recovery will use a storage account and blob containers to store migrated data. As we mentioned earlier, blob containers are available in both performance tiers, with some limitations based on the account type.

In a blob container, we can store three different blob types: block, page, and append. *Block blobs* are designed and optimized for uploading a large amount of data to the blob container. A block blob comprises a maximum of 50.000 blocks, where the maximum size of a block is 4 TB. The maximum size of a single blob is approximately 190 TB. A *page blob*, which is ideal for storing virtual machine disks, comprises 512-byte pages optimized for random read/write operations. The maximum size of a page blob is 8 TB. Similarly to a block blob, an *append blob* comprises blocks, but it is optimized for append operations. Once the blob is modified, new data will be added to the end of the blob. Updating or deleting any block is not allowed in a page blob, making a page blob ideal for storing log files. The maximum number of blocks in an append blob is 50.000, and every block has a maximum size of 4 MB, so the maximum size of an append blob is around 200 GB.

Blob Access Tier

Regardless of other storage account services, blob containers have *access tiers* along with performance tiers, but this is applicable only for the Standard performance tier. Since the Premium performance tier uses SSDs, this kind of tier is not needed. Access tiers include

- Hot: For data that is accessed frequently

- Cool: For data that is not accessed so frequently but must be accessible

- Archive: For data that will be accessed rarely

The *Hot tier* is designed and optimized for data that has to be accessed frequently, and it is the most expensive compared to other tiers. Per TB, we have to pay around $22, but transaction and data retrieval costs are cheap, or there are no costs. Also, there is no limitation on how many days data must retain in the Hot tier. On the other hand, the Cool tier is designed and optimized for data that will not be accessed so frequently but still must be online. Per TB of data in the *Cool tier*, we have to pay between $10 and $15, depending on the location. Transaction and data retrieval costs are still at a low level, but there are some costs. These access tiers could be configured on the account level or blob level. By default, every storage account during creation will get the Hot access tier if we do not configure the Cool access tier. Once the blob is uploaded or copied to the blob container, it will inherit the access tier from the storage account if that is not defined differently in the uploading or copying process. Of course, these access tiers on blobs can be changed later if needed in both directions, but we must know that data in the Cool tier must retain for 30 days. If we change the access tier from Cool to Hot or remove data from the Cool tier, there will be some penalty that we must pay.

The third access tier, which cannot be configured on the account level, is the *Archive tier*. If we move data to the Archive tier, we have to pay between $1 and $3 per TB, depending on the region we select. The incredibly low price for storing data in the Archive tier brings many limitations. The Archive tier is designed and optimized for data that will be accessed rarely, and all data must remain for 180 days in the Archive tier. Also, the pricing scheme for read operations and data retrieval is expensive, mainly because all data in the Archive tier are offline and stored on magnetic tracks. This access tier is ideal for long-term backups for compliance or any other type of data that has to be kept for a long time. Also, data retrieval in the Archive tier can take several hours, especially for large files.

Creating a Blob Container

Once we have created a storage account, creating a blob container is a straightforward process and can be done using all management tools.

Azure Portal

When we are in the desired storage account user interface, in the left pane, we have to find *Containers* under *Blob service*. Then, we have to click **+ Container** and define the container name and public access level if it is needed. These steps are shown in Figure 6-2.

Figure 6-2. *Define the container name and public access level if it is needed*

ARM Template, PowerShell, and Azure CLI

Since the deployment code could be pretty big, all ARM template, Azure PowerShell, and Azure CLI scripts are stored in the Apress GitHub account, available at the following URL:

`https://github.com/Apress/pro-azure-admin-and-automation`

Azure Files

Even though blob containers are widely used and maybe have a better adoption rate, Azure Files is a storage service with its place and customers due to the nature of its service. Unlike blob containers that offer object storage, Azure Files offers fully managed file shares in the cloud accessible via standardized SMB and NFS protocols. Azure Files can be mounted on Windows, Linux, and macOS machines. In addition, Azure Files can be cached in Windows environments by implementing Azure File Sync on Windows Server, so customers will have the same experience as having a local file share while their data are in the cloud.

From a pricing perspective, Azure Files is more expensive than blob containers, and for 1 TB of data in a file share in the Standard tier, we have to pay around $60. A file share in the Premium performance tier is around $180 per TB, but that can vary depending on location. Also, by default, there is a maximum quota of 5 TB per file share, but in the storage account configuration, we can use a large file share and increase the limit to 100 TB per file share.

Azure Files Tiers

Like blob containers, Azure Files also provides tiering, but in a little bit different way. This feature is new and still is not available in all regions, but many regions can leverage its benefits. The Premium tier is available only if the FileStorage account type is deployed, and the price per TB is around $180. All data are stored on high-performant SSD storage. For Azure Files in the Standard performance tier, we can choose one of the three available performance tiers:

- Transaction-optimized

- Hot

- Cool

The *Transaction-optimized* tier is ideal for an application that needs to have Azure Files as back-end storage. This tier does not provide latency as low as what we can get from the Premium tier. The *Hot tier* is designed and optimized for most general workloads, such as company file shares or storing data that are not used frequently. It is a good candidate for Azure File Sync, where caching will occur on the Windows Server side. For 1 TB of data in the Azure Files Hot tier, we have to pay around $30 per month, and in comparison with higher tiers, that is a significant saving. The *Cool tier* is a cost-effective Azure Files offer that could be a good option for Azure File Sync with a nonintensive workload or a SMB or NFS accessible online archive. The Cool tier is twice cheaper than the Hot tier, so $15 per TB of data is an affordable option.

Because this functionality is pretty new, at the time of writing this chapter, there is no option to change tiering on the file level. This is possible only on the file share level, but it will take some costs, depending on the number and size of files and generated transactions.

Creating Azure Files

Once we have created a storage account, creating a file share is a straightforward process and can be done using all management tools. The process is the same, regardless of whether we have deployed a general-purpose or FileStorage account type.

Azure Portal

When we are in the desired storage account user interface, in the left pane, we have to find *File shares* under *File service*. We have to click **+ File Share** and define the file share name, quota in GB, and tier. These steps are shown in Figure 6-3.

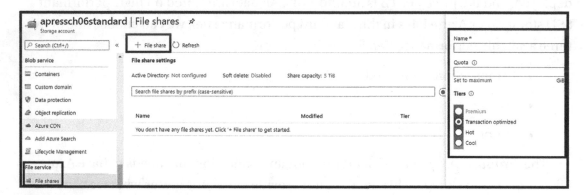

Figure 6-3. *Define the file share name, quota in GB, and tier*

ARM Template, PowerShell, and Azure CLI

Since the deployment code could be pretty big, all ARM template, Azure PowerShell, and Azure CLI scripts are stored in the Apress GitHub account, available at the following URL:

`https://github.com/Apress/pro-azure-admin-and-automation`

Storage Account Security

Even though the storage account is part of the PaaS offering in Microsoft Azure and a bigger part of security is Microsoft's responsibility, there are still many things that we need to think about in terms of security. The *shared responsibility model* that is in use when we talk about security in the cloud provides us with a certain amount of security, but in most cases, there is a need for a "final touch" from our side. For instance, if we share the storage account access key or improperly configure access to the blob containers or blobs, data loss will happen sooner or later. There are a few options that we must analyze and configure based on our needs, so let's start with exploring them.

Storage Access Keys and Shared Access Signature

Storage access keys provide the application with the possibility to authenticate the storage account when making requests. Even though this is not the best idea in a production environment, mainly because the access keys will give the application full access to the whole storage account, sometimes this is the only possible solution. Every storage account has two access keys that can be used for the same level of access. Due to the nature of permissions provided by access keys, storing those keys in the Key Vault *(a resource that will be explained in Chapter 10)* and regenerating the keys regularly is highly recommended. All information about the access keys and connection strings is visible in the storage account pane, under the section **Settings**, as shown in Figure 6-4.

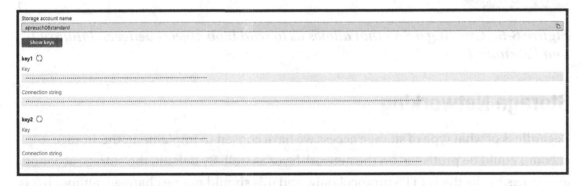

Figure 6-4. *Information about the access keys and connection strings is visible in the storage account pane*

Another option to give someone access to a storage account, which is highly preferable whenever is possible, is the *shared access signature (SAS)*. This option provides us with the ability to define permissions more granularly and avoid unneeded access to our data in the storage account. Using this feature, we can define what services and resource types will be included, the kind of permissions, and start and end times for specific permissions. Additionally, we can define if only HTTPS access will be allowed and if there is any IP-based restriction that will be included in the SAS. If we want to create a shared access signature, we can find this feature under the storage account's **Settings** section. As shown in Figure 6-5, we are creating a SAS that allows us to read blob objects only between January 1 and February 1.

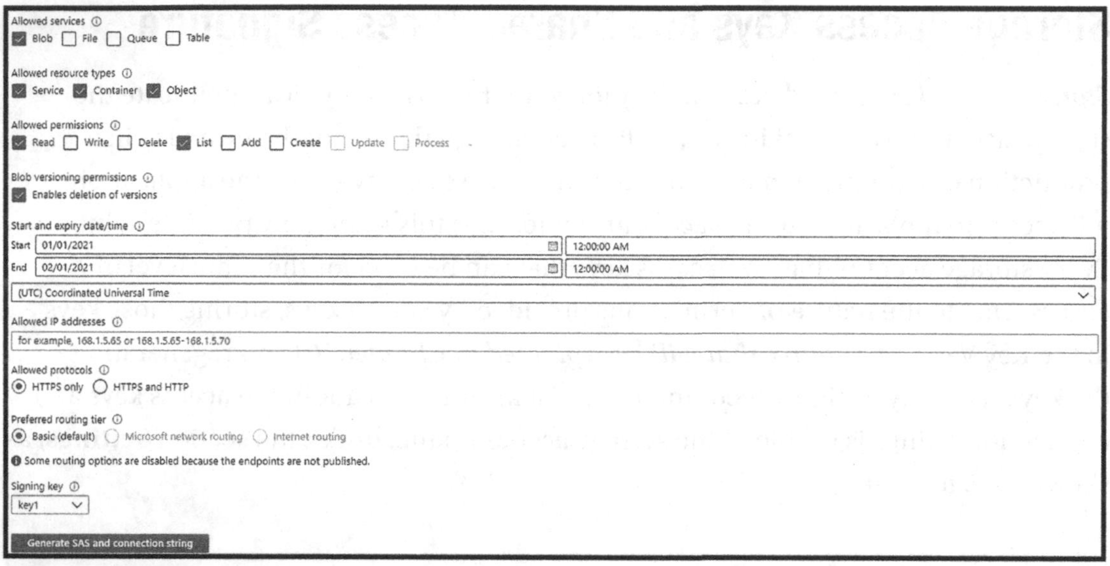

Figure 6-5. *Creating a SAS that allows us to read blob objects between January 1 and February 1*

Storage Networking

Regardless of what type of storage access we have chosen to implement, the storage account could be protected on the network layer as well. By default, the storage accounts are accessible by the HTTPS protocol only, and this should not be changed, although it is possible. Removing a security layer from the HTTP protocol is not the best idea because all data will be transferred without encryption. Also, by default, the storage account allows access from any network. That means every user or application with permissions to access the storage account will be able to make requests to it without any restrictions. In most scenarios, that is not necessary, and network access should be narrowed to specific networks.

In Chapter 3, we explained services and private endpoints for the services. A storage account is one of the services that could leverage these features to provide better network isolation. Once we decide to use these features, we have to navigate to **Networking** under the section **Settings** in the storage account. We can start with configuring network access by switching from *All networks* to *Selected networks*, and more options will be available then, such as connection with specific virtual networks, adding IP address ranges to the firewall, or selecting a specific resource that will have access to the storage account. Additionally, if we block all network traffic to the storage account, we can still make some exceptions and allow trusted Microsoft services access to the storage account or read access for logging and metrics purposes *(see Figure 6-6)*. The private endpoint is also available for the storage account. As for the other resources that support this feature, it provides us with the ability to create a private IP address for communication with other Azure resources in a more secure and isolated manner.

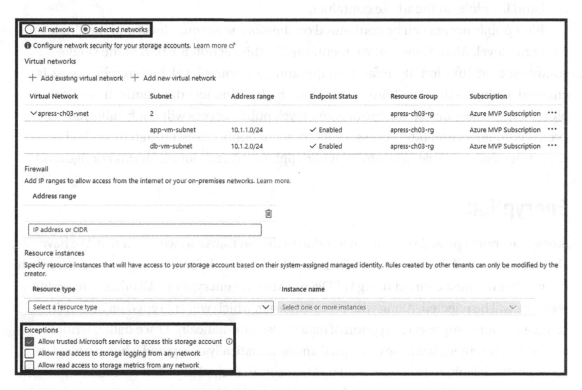

Figure 6-6. *Allow trusted Microsoft services access to the storage account or read access for logging and metrics purposes*

Blob Container Access

Blob containers have their mechanism for controlling public access that could be combined with the aforementioned security methods. When creating a blob container, we have to choose one of the three public access levels: *Private (no anonymous access)*, which is the default option, allows access to data in blob containers only to storage account owners. Of course, if someone has storage account access keys, they will be classified as the owner, and data will be visible, as well as if there is SAS with appropriate permissions. *Blob (anonymous read access for blobs only)* allows anonymous users to have access to blobs only. This option is useful if we want to make data available for access or download without requiring access keys or SAS. In this case, only blobs can be read by anonymous users, whereas container data are not available, and anonymous users cannot enumerate blobs in the container. The third option, *Container (anonymous read access for containers and blobs)*, is the least restrictive and allows the anonymous to read and list blobs in the whole container.

Blob public access can be configured on the storage account level and the single container level. All options that we mentioned in this section are part of the single container configuration. By default, on the storage account level, blob public access is enabled, giving us the possibility to configure blob containers differently. If we disable blob public access on the storage account level, public access will not be allowed, even if containers and blob access levels are set to public. Even though this is highly recommended, we have to ensure that our application can work with this configuration.

Encryption

Storage accounts provide us with encryption of data in transit as well as at rest. We have already mentioned that secure transfer is enabled by default for all storage accounts, which means that we must connect using HTTPS or SMB with encryption. All other connection requests will be rejected. Along with secure transfer, which will encrypt data in transit, storage accounts support encryption of data at rest automatically. Once data is written to Azure datacenters, it will be encrypted and automatically decrypted when we want to access it. By default, data is encrypted by Microsoft-managed keys, but customer-managed keys are also available, but only for blobs and files inside the storage account.

If data encryption on the service level is not something that is enough for specific scenarios, an additional level of encryption can be included. If *infrastructure encryption* is enabled, data will be encrypted twice, once on the service level and another on the storage infrastructure level, but with different keys. This option must be enabled during storage account creation and cannot be added later. To use this feature, we have to register it for our tenant using PowerShell or Azure CLI and then re-register the Azure Storage resource provider.

Azure PowerShell

```
Register-AzProviderFeature -ProviderNamespace Microsoft.Storage
-FeatureName AllowRequireInfraStructureEncryption

Register-AzResourceProvider -ProviderNamespace 'Microsoft.Storage'
```

Azure CLI

```
az feature register --namespace Microsoft.Storage --name
AllowRequireInfraStructureEncryption

az provider register --namespace 'Microsoft.Storage'
```

As we already said, communication between a client and a storage account is encrypted. Transport Layer Security (TLS), as a standard cryptographic protocol, is used to ensure integrity and privacy between parties. Although Azure Storage uses TLS 1.2, it supports backward compatibility with TLS 1.1 and TLS 1.0. If we want to force clients to use the latest version of TLS, we can change a specific configuration setting during the storage account creation process or later at any time. We just have to be careful with this change for the existing storage accounts because a lower TLS version will not be allowed.

Data Transfer

Once we have implemented a storage account, the next logical step is to have some data in that storage account. If the storage account is used programmatically, in most cases, our application will be responsible for the whole process, which includes uploading, downloading, data management, and others. Nevertheless, in some cases, such as storing offsite backup files or using Azure Files, we are responsible for transferring data to Azure. There are many different options to transfer data to the cloud, and choosing the right tool depends on the data amount.

Storage Explorer

Storage Explorer is a standalone GUI-based application that could be installed on Windows, Linux, and macOS operating systems in order to make storage account management more manageable. Using this tool, we can upload/download files to/from blob containers and Azure Files, create/get SAS and access keys, or even copy files between containers or shares. Storage Explorer is designed to analyze storage accounts in the first place, but some of the management tasks, such as uploading data to storage accounts, could be performed by this tool. It is also available as a storage account feature in Azure Portal, but since it is still in preview, there are only specific features, including uploading and downloading blobs and files. We have to keep in mind that transfer will go through the network, and if we have a large amount of data, that will not be the best possible option.

AzCopy

Another tool that allows us to transfer files over the network to Azure is the command-line tool AzCopy. It allows us to copy blobs or files to and from the storage account, with many additional features that give us more possibilities. It also can be installed on Windows, Linux, and macOS operating systems, which gives us the possibility to use it in the same way on various operating systems. AzCopy must be installed on the operating system, and then the first step is to authorize AzCopy to our subscription. That could be done using Azure AD, or we can choose to use a SAS token for transferring data. If we want to use Azure AD, we can use user identity, managed identity, or service principal. Otherwise, the SAS token that we will use for AzCopy must have appropriate permissions for the action that we want to take.

AzCopy gives us the possibility to upload or download data, but also we can use AzCopy for synchronizing our data to the cloud. For example, if we want to upload a local directory to a blob container, we need to run the following command:

```
azcopy.exe copy 'C:\my-data\' https://apressch06standard.blob.core.windows.
net/uploaded-data/SASTOKEN --recursive
```

If our scenario requires us to synchronize blobs or files periodically or constantly from the local directory to Azure or vice versa, we can use the AzCopy functionality *synchronize*. With this functionality, AzCopy will compare the name and last modified values of the files and synchronize only if some of these values are new. By default, AzCopy will not delete files on the destination if they are deleted on the source. In case that we want to enable that option, we have to add the parameter --delete-destination=true, and AzCopy will remove deleted files on the destination automatically, or we can set that parameter to value prompt, and we will be asked to confirm deleting files from a destination:

```
azcopy.exe sync 'C:\my-data\' https://apressch06standard.blob.core.windows.
net/sync-data/SASTOKEN
```

By default, AzCopy will use Internet bandwidth as much as possible, and if we have a large amount of data to transfer, it could be a potential problem. However, if we add the parameter `--cap-mbps`, we can define upload or download bandwidth.

Data Box Gateway and Azure Stack Edge

Azure Stack Edge is a physical network appliance that acts as a storage gateway, creating a link between the on-premises site and Azure Storage. Using this physical device, which provides a local cache and optimizes network traffic, sending data into an Azure storage account and out from it is much more comfortable. AI-enabled computing capabilities included in Stack Edge analyze, process, and transform on-premises data before uploading it to the cloud. On the other hand, Data Box Gateway is a virtual device provisioned in the on-premises virtual environment that enables seamlessly sending data into an Azure storage account. All data will be sent to Data Box Gateway using the NFS or SMB protocol, and cached and processed data will be then transferred to an Azure block blob, a page blob, or Azure Files.

Both solutions are used for continuous ingestion of a large amount of data to an Azure storage account from on-premises networks, where caching and background transfer are essential.

Import/Export Service

If we need to migrate dozens of terabytes of data from an on-premises network to an Azure storage account within a reasonable period, we must use offline methods for transferring data. One of them is Azure Import/Export, which transfers a large amount of data to Azure securely by sending drives to the Azure datacenter. The same service could be used to collect all data from a storage account and send drives to an on-premises datacenter.

The process of sending data to an Azure storage account using the Azure Import service consists of several phases that must be completed in order. We have to provide our driver and comply with the strict procedure before drives are shipped to the Azure datacenter:

- A customer prepares drives using the WAImportExport tool.

- A customer encrypts drives using BitLocker.

- A customer creates an import job in Azure Portal.

- A customer ships drives to the Azure datacenter.

- Drives are processed at the Azure datacenter.

- Data are copied to the storage account.

- Drives are packaged for return shipping.

- Drives are shipped back to the customer.

The process of getting data from a storage account has similar phases but in a reverse way:

- A customer creates an export job in Azure Portal.

- A customer ships drives to the Azure datacenter.

- Drives are processed at the Azure datacenter.

- Data are copied to the drives and encrypted with BitLocker.

- Drives are packaged for return shipping.

- Drives are shipped back to the customer.

The Azure Import/Export service is limited to ten drives, and the time needed to complete this process is between 7 and 10 days. Also, although there is no charge for the data transfer, we need to know that device shipping to the Azure datacenter and back is our expense, as well as the device handling at the Azure datacenter.

Data Box

If we do not buy drives for sending data to Azure or we have more data to transfer, the Import/Export service most probably will not be suitable for us. Fortunately, we can still plan to transfer data to the Azure datacenter offline because Azure can provide us with *Data Box* or *Data Box Disk*. If the amount of our data is not larger than 35 TB, we can order Data Box Disk, and we will get from Microsoft up to five SSD disks of 8 TB. All disks have a USB 3.0 interface, which guarantees that transfer will be quick, and they are secured by AES 128-bit encryption all the time. Once we order Data Box Disk, we will get the key in Azure Portal, which must be used for unlocking disks that we will receive. After transferring data to the storage account, all disks will be wiped to comply with the NIST 800-88r1 standard.

In a scenario where we need to upload more than 35 TB of data, we have to use Azure Data Box. Data Box is an inexpensive and reliable way to transfer a large amount of data to the Azure datacenter by using a proprietary device provided by Microsoft, limited to 80 TB. Data Box is equipped with 1 Gpbs or 10 Gbps network interfaces, allowing fast data transfer to the device. From a security perspective, Data Box comes with AES 256-bit encryption all time. It can be unlocked only with a key provided in Azure Portal during ordering of Data Box. Like Data Box Disk, once data are transferred to the storage account, the device will be wiped to comply with the NIST 800-88r1 standard.

Of course, if we need to transfer more than 80 TB of data, we can order more than one Data Box device or order Data Box Heavy, allowing us to send up to 770 TB of data to the Azure datacenter. The process is pretty much the same as we have for other Data Box options, which includes ordering devices, returning with copied data, and uploading data to a storage account. Like Data Box, the rugged device case is protected by AES 256-bit encryption all the time and can be unlocked only with a key provided in Azure Portal during ordering.

Storage Account Management

Once we have implemented a storage account for any kind of workload, in most scenarios, we can say that we have completed the solution. Nevertheless, in reality, we have to perform the storage account maintenance tasks or even make some reconfiguration. Luckily, some of these actions could be done at any time, without affecting stored data nor causing downtime.

Changing Security Parameters

In every storage account, as we already said in this chapter, there are many security configurations. Almost all of them can be changed at any time if they are not adequately configured, or we need to change them due to new company policies or compliance.

Access Keys and Shared Access Keys

If we suspect that the storage account access keys are compromised, we can regenerate them at any time quickly. Of course, we have to know that all previous connections using these access keys will stop working and we need to replace these keys.

On the other hand, if we use SAS tokens for communication with the storage account and want to block that kind of access, we have two potential options: remove the SAS policy that defines SAS tokens or disable shared access key access.

Storage Networking and Encryption

For networking for storage accounts, we already explained possible options that we can implement. All of those options can be reconfigured quickly, and we can allow additional access to the storage account or even remove unneeded access. We already said that the storage account supports HTTP and HTTPS traffic, but restricting access to HTTPS only is highly recommended. Although allowing HTTP traffic is not the best idea, it is possible if there is a specific need for it. Also, by default the minimum TLS version that is supported is 1.0. At any time, we can change that value to version 1.1 or 1.2 and increase security for the storage account. Of course, if the TLS version is already set to 1.2 and we need to decrease it, it is also possible.

Storage Replication

As we already explained in this chapter, storage accounts can have different types of replication. If we initially set locally redundant replication for our storage account, we can change that at any time and select geo-redundant or read-access geo-redundant replication. At the moment, there is no possibility to switch from locally redundant to zone-redundant if an account is not initially created to support zones.

Lifecycle Management

When we talk about data management in storage accounts, blob containers especially, we have to think about data retention and tiering. For instance, we have a large amount of data on a daily basis sent to the storage account, but we do not need these data after 30 days, or we need to keep these data but only for archiving purposes. Luckily, lifecycle management functionality, which is part of the blob service, provides us with the ability to create specific rules that will manage data based on our plan. Very quickly and easily, we can configure one or more rules, and we do not think about data management. At the time of writing this chapter, only block and append blobs are supported by this functionality. This functionality is based on the *if-then* model. The *If* statement is related to the blob's *Last modified* attribute with the *More than* operator. The *Then* statement gives us three options, as we can see in Figure 6-7, which are more than enough for 99% of cases: Move to cool storage, Move to archive storage, and Delete the blob.

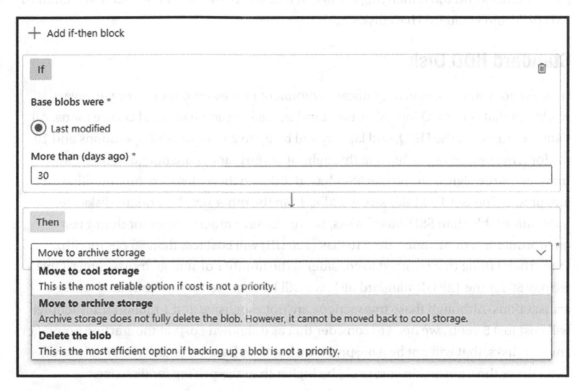

Figure 6-7. The "Then" statement provides a prompt for three options

Managed Disks

A managed disk is another essential service from the storage family, even though it is not directly related to storage accounts from an end user perspective. Since every virtual machine has to be equipped with an OS disk at least, and sometimes with data disks as well, the importance of managed disks is inevitable. Also, a managed disk is not mandatory for virtual machines in Azure because we can use a storage account for storing VHD files that are attached to virtual machines. Nevertheless, performance and management tasks are the most significant advantages from using managed disks because managed disks are block-level storage volumes that Microsoft Azure fully manages with 99.999% of availability.

Types of Managed Disks

If we talk about types of managed disks, we have four categories, based on their performances and the underlying storage in use: ultra disk, premium SSD disk, standard SSD disk, and standard HDD disk.

Standard HDD Disk

If we do not want to spend a significant amount of money on our disks or we have a workload that is not I/O intensive, the standard disk could be an ideal choice for us. All data are stored on the HDD, and latency will be up to 20 ms for read operations and 10 ms for write operations. IOPS and throughput performances are not guaranteed and may vary more significantly than SSD-based disks, so these disks are not intended for any production nor I/O-intensive workload. On the other hand, standard disks are more affordable than SSD-based disks, so we can save much money for dev or test environments. For instance, the S10 disk (128 GB) will cost less than $6 per month. One crucial thing that we need to consider is the number of storage transactions. Once we pay $6 for the 128 GB standard disk, we will be charged for the additional storage transactions. Although these transactions are not expensive and 1 million transactions will cost just 5 cents, we need to consider that as unknown costs at the starting point. For smaller disks, that will not be a big problem, but if we have large disks (1 TB or more), sometimes the transaction cost could be higher than the pricing for disk size.

Standard SSD Disk

If we know that our on-premises workload, which has been or will be moved to Azure, has an issue with disk operations, we maybe need to move that workload to SSD-based disks. Standard SSD disks are cost-effective disks that provide consistent performances on the lower level in terms of IOPS and throughput. For the workloads that are not so intensive, like small websites or blogs, standard SSD disks could be an ideal entry point with a balance between costs and performances. From a pricing perspective, standard SSD disk E10 (128 GB) costs $10, which is more than 50% higher than the cost of the standard HDD disk. Transaction costs apply for the standard SSD disk in the same manner as for the standard HDD disk, but with a different pricing model. For 1 million transactions, we have to pay 20 cents, which is still very cheap, but at the same time is four times expensive than transaction costs for the standard HDD. For smaller disks, that will not be a big deal, but we have to be careful if we have larger disks (1+ TB) with many transactions, such as a SQL Server development environment.

Premium SSD Disk

If a standard SSD disk is not good enough for our workload and we need something better, it is not a problem, because we can use a premium SSD disk. Azure guarantees low latency and high performance for premium SSD disks, so we know what we can expect and whether that will be okay for our workload. This disk type is designed to support mission-critical workloads, such as I/O-intensive applications or SQL Server workloads. Also, with premium SSD disks, we can plan our costs. Although the initial price is higher, almost double that of standard SSD disks, there are no transaction costs. For instance, a P10 disk (128 GB) will cost $20 per month, and there are no additional hidden costs, regardless of the number of transactions.

While performance tiers for standard HDD and SSD disks are defined as "up-to" for IOPS and throughput, premium SSD disks come with guaranteed performances. For example, the aforementioned P10 disk provisions 500 IOPS and 100 MB/sec throughput. In addition, some of the performance tiers have enabled the feature *bursting*, which allows disks to have a much better performance for 30 minutes during the day. That allows us to have a better performance for some spikes without the need to change the performance tier, which could help us to save money. The P10 disk, for instance, can reach 3500 IOPS and 170 MB/sec throughput if there is a need for bursting for specific actions. At the moment, bursting is allowed only for P20 (512 GB) disks and lower.

In contrast, P30 disks (1 TB) and higher can be reserved for 1 year. That option allows us to plan expenses accordingly, especially if we have many big disks. Although the savings with reservation is approximately $7 per month per TB of disk space, let's imagine that we have 50+ TB in provisioned premium SSD disks and calculate what the monthly savings will be. Moreover, there are still no transaction costs.

Ultra Disk

We are still struggling with our workload performance, even though we have implemented the premium SSD disks. For this, the ultra disk should be our choice. The ultra disk is designed to deliver high throughput, high IOPS, and consistently low latency. Also, we can dynamically change disk performance without the need to reboot a virtual machine, which is a mandatory task for all other disk types. Transaction-heavy workloads, such as SAP HANA, SQL, or Oracle, are ideal candidates for ultra disks.

Even though max throughout is more than doubled and max IOPS is eight times higher than the premium SSD disk, the ultra disk pricing plan cannot be declared advantageous. At the same time, the pricing model is pretty complicated, and we need to pay for capacity, IOPS, and throughput in combination. For instance, the P30 disk (1 TB) provisions 5000 IOPS and 200 MB/sec throughput, with a price of $135 per month. If we need higher performance, we can move our disk to a higher performance tier, but performance will not be doubled, and the price will be doubled. Alternatively, we can use the ultra disk and define the performance that we need. For example, if we need a 1 TB disk, with 10000 IOPS and 500 MB/sec throughput, we have to pay approximately $1100 per month. In that case, we must have a perfect reason to use the ultra disk for our workload.

Performance Tiers

All disk types, except ultra disks, have their performance tiers. It is essential to know what that means and how it will affect our billing at the end of the month. We have already said that for standard HDD and SSD disks, we have to pay for the performance tier and the transactions as well, whereas the premium SSD disks do not count transactions as billable. When we select a performance tier, regardless of disk type, we pay for the performance, not for the capacity. That means that if we use the P30 (1 TB) performance tier, we will pay for 5000 IOPS and 200 MB/sec throughput, with a maximum capacity of 1 TB. If we need a disk of 1.5 TB, we need to move our disk to the next performance tier (P40), which will give us 7500 IOPS and 250 MB/sec throughput, with a maximum capacity of 2 TB. Even though we do not use the maximum capacity, we have to pay a full price. In some scenarios, that is not the best possible solution, especially if we do not need better performance or we just need to increase disk capacity for 100 GB or so.

If we are using Windows Server for our workload, we can leverage the feature *Storage Spaces* to increase disk performance for almost the same price. This feature, which is similar to RAID, allows us to group more disks in a pool to get better resilience or performance. For instance, if we add two P30 (1 TB) disks to a virtual machine and configure Storage Spaces to use both disks in the simple mode (similar to striping in RAID), we will get one disk of 2 TB, which is the same as the P40 performance tier. Nevertheless, the maximum IOPS and throughput will be doubled from the P30 performance tier. Our new disk will have 10000 IOPS and 400 MB/sec throughput, which are higher than those of the P40 disk initially, and the price will be almost the same. This could be very useful for bigger disks, P50 (4 TB) and higher, because the performance tiers have a vast discrepancy in capacity, performance, and pricing.

Managed Disk Security

Like storage accounts, a managed disk also has a few security features that could be configured. In the first place, every managed disk is encrypted at rest, and that functionality cannot be disabled. By default, all managed disks are encrypted by the platform-managed key, but there is an option to use a customer-managed key or even combine them to double encryption layers. See Figure 6-8.

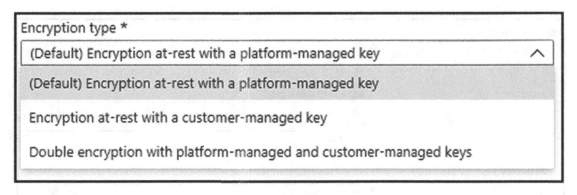

Figure 6-8. *The option to use a customer-managed key or combine them to double encryption layers*

An additional option to secure access to a managed disk is network isolation. By default, the connectivity method is configured to *Public endpoint*, which allows all networks in our subscription to use a managed disk. If we decide to use *Private endpoint*, it will narrow down what virtual networks can access the managed disk. In this case, we have to create *Disc Access*, which will create a private endpoint for the managed disk and allow access to the disk only from specific virtual networks. As a last option, we can select *Deny all* and block access to the managed disk completely.

Creating a Managed Disk

Like almost all Azure services, a managed disk can be created using all management tools, and the process is straightforward.

Azure Portal

If we decide to use Azure Portal to perform this operation, the first step is to click **+ Create a resource**, search for "managed disk" in the *Marketplace*, and click **Create**. As with other Azure resources, we need to define Subscription and Resource group under *Project details*. Under *Instance details,* we will define *Disk name*, which must be unique in the resource group, *Location, Availability Zone* if it is applicable, *Source type,* and *Size*. Once these parameters are filled, click **Review + create** and then **Create** to create a managed disk. All these parameters are shown in Figure 6-9. In this scenario, we will not take care of disk encryption and network isolation.

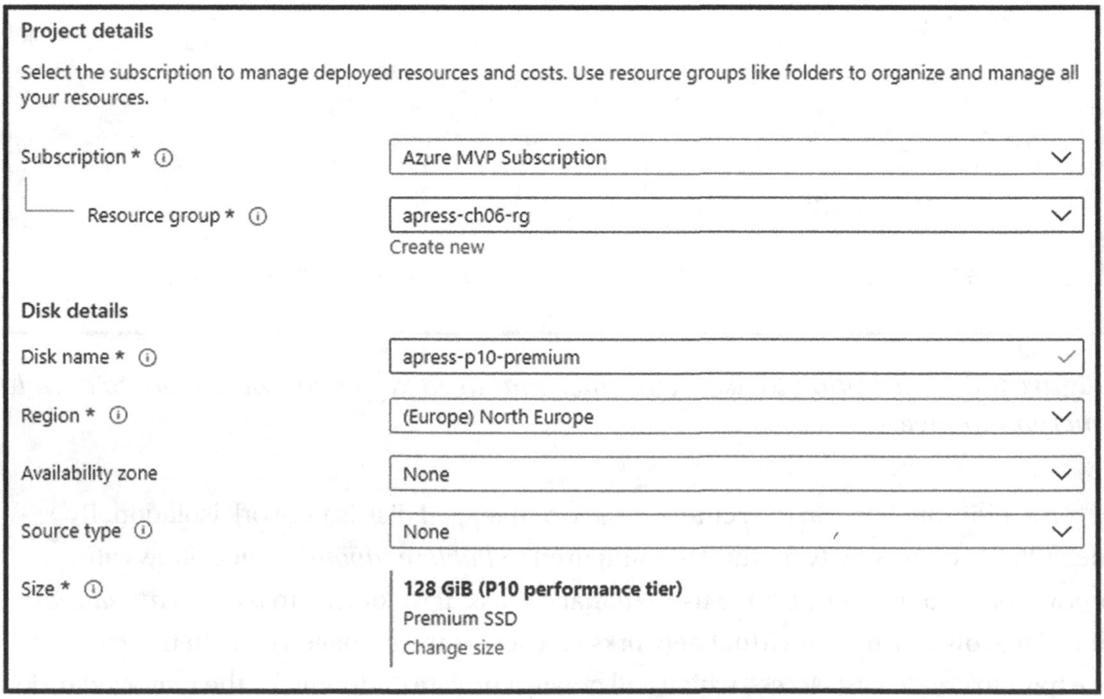

Project details

Select the subscription to manage deployed resources and costs. Use resource groups like folders to organize and manage all your resources.

Subscription * ⓘ	Azure MVP Subscription ⌄
└─ Resource group * ⓘ	apress-ch06-rg ⌄
	Create new

Disk details

Disk name * ⓘ	apress-p10-premium ✓
Region * ⓘ	(Europe) North Europe ⌄
Availability zone ⓘ	None ⌄
Source type ⓘ	None ⌄
Size * ⓘ	**128 GiB (P10 performance tier)** Premium SSD Change size

Figure 6-9. *Enlisting Azure Portal to perform the operation*

In our cases, we will configure parameters just on the *Basics* tab, and all other things we will configure later in this book. As with all other Azure resources, we need to define Subscription and Resource group under *Project details*. Under *Instance details,* we will define *Storage account name*, which must be unique across Azure, *Location*, *Performance tier*, *Account type,* and *Replication* type. Once these parameters are filled, click **Review + create** and then **Create** to create a storage account. All these parameters are shown in Figure 6-1.

ARM Template, PowerShell, and Azure CLI

Since the deployment code could be pretty big, all ARM template, Azure PowerShell, and Azure CLI scripts are stored in the Apress GitHub account, available at the following URL:

```
https://github.com/Apress/pro-azure-admin-and-automation
```

Chapter Recap

In this chapter, we have learned what Azure Storage is and how we can use it, especially because this is one of the most used services in Azure. Even though we can find more storage options in Azure, such as NetApp Files, a storage account will be the first choice for most scenarios, without a doubt. A storage account is suitable for various workloads and types of transfer. Regardless of whether the interaction method is programmatical or in any other way, one storage account can meet all our needs.

In the next chapter, we will learn about advanced networking functionalities in Azure that are important for hybrid environments and intersite connectivity, regardless of whether we need to enable communication between two or more Azure networks or between on-premises and Azure networks.

CHAPTER 7

Advanced Azure Networking

In the previous chapter, we spoke about different types of storage options and how and when we should use them.

This chapter covers the especially important services for more complex architectural designs in Azure. We will cover

- Azure DNS – Private and Public

- Virtual Network Peering

- Intersite connectivity:

    - VNet-to-VNet

    - Site-to-site VPN

    - ExpressRoute

- Azure Firewall

- Azure Bastion

After this chapter and the basics we learned through Chapter 3, we will be able to design and implement the various infrastructure solutions.

Azure DNS

DNS or Domain Name System is a core service on the Internet, in on-premises environments, and, of course, in Azure. This service is responsible for resolving the names of our services to their IP addresses. In Azure, we can differentiate two types of DNS service – Public and Private. Both types are used as SaaS solutions.

© Vladimir Stefanovic and Milos Katinski 2021
V. Stefanovic and M. Katinski, *Pro Azure Administration and Automation*,
https://doi.org/10.1007/978-1-4842-7325-8_7

Public DNS

Azure Public DNS is a service that we could use for a public name resolution by using Azure infrastructure. By using it, we could simplify our infrastructure management by having all services under one portal. Like any other service, Azure DNS offers us the possibility to use specific security features:

- Role-based access control: With using RBAC, we are securing the service from non-authorized access and/or change.

- Activity logs will gather all types of changes on the service.

- Resource locks will secure the service from unwanted modification or even removal.

The process of using Azure DNS for the domain we own is straightforward. We would have to

- Create a DNS zone.

- Gather the list of name servers.

- Delegate the domain.

- Test if the delegation is successful.

We will explain all these steps while creating DNS via the portal.

Creating a Public DNS Zone

As with most of the services in Azure, we can create a DNS zone in different ways. To get acquainted with the service, we will first deploy the zone using the portal.

Azure Portal

From the portal's home view, the first step is to click **+ Create a resource**, search for "DNS zone," and click **Create**. We will notice that there is not much information needed to fill in for this service. We just need to provide the resource group name, where the zone will be deployed, and zone name. Although there is a resource group location to be populated, this will not affect the service. Azure DNS is one of the global services and therefore not affected by the location where the zone resource is. Once these parameters are filled, click **Review + create** and then **Create** to create a DNS zone. All these parameters are shown in Figure 7-1.

Create DNS zone ⋯

Basics   Tags   Review + create

A DNS zone is used to host the DNS records for a particular domain. For example, the domain 'contoso.com' may contain a number of DNS records such as 'mail.contoso.com' (for a mail server) and 'www.contoso.com' (for a web site). Azure DNS allows you to host your DNS zone and manage your DNS records, and provides name servers that will respond to DNS queries from end users with the DNS records that you create. Learn more.

Project details

Subscription * | MVP Visual Studio Subscription   ⌄

    Resource group * | (New) apress-ch07-rg   ⌄
                                                                       Create new

Instance details

☐ This zone is a child of an existing zone already hosted in Azure DNS ⓘ

Name * | designthe.cloud   ✓

Resource group location ⓘ | West Europe   ⌄

Figure 7-1. Create a DNS zone

When the deployment is done, we can go to the resource and, in the Overview pane, gather the list of name servers assigned for our zone.

designthe.cloud ⚲ ⋯
DNS zone

🔍 Search (Ctrl+/)   «   + Record set   + Child zone   → Move ⌄   🗑 Delete zone   ↻ Refresh

⊙ Overview   ⌃ Essentials
📄 Activity log   Resource group (change) : apress-ch07-rg | Name server 1 : ns1-05.azure-dns.com.
👥 Access control (IAM)   Subscription (change)   : MVP Visual Studio Subscription | Name server 2 : ns2-05.azure-dns.net.
🏷 Tags   Subscription ID   : 2348f252-5d66-4ed8-b6b3-86b9a5825ba7 | Name server 3 : ns3-05.azure-dns.org.
                                                                                          | Name server 4 : ns4-05.azure-dns.info.
✎ Diagnose and solve problems
                            Tags (change)   : Click here to add tags

Figure 7-2. A view of the Overview pane and the list of name servers assigned for our zone

Now we can go back to our domain registrar and change the default name servers. When the propagation is done, we could quickly test it by using the command *nslookup -type=SOA domainname.com*.

ARM Template, PowerShell, and Azure CLI

Since the deployment code could be pretty big, all ARM template, Azure PowerShell, and Azure CLI scripts are stored in the Apress GitHub account, available at the following URL:

```
https://github.com/Apress/pro-azure-admin-and-automation
```

Private DNS

Azure Private DNS is used to manage and resolve names within a virtual network. It eliminates the need for a custom DNS solution. With Private DNS, we can use custom domain names, which helps us design the Azure infrastructure the way we need it. From the moment we link the virtual network with the zone, we will be able to resolve records created for services inside that VNet. Also, it is possible to enable auto-registration, which means that the record will be created for the virtual machine from the moment we deploy it within the VNet.

The private DNS zone gives us an option to use standard record types: A, CNAME, PTR, MX, SOA, TXT, and SRV. Also, by connecting multiple VNets to the zone, we enable resolution between virtual networks. The most used case for Private DNS is the private link endpoint, which we discussed in Chapter 3. So, besides just using private IP, the private link endpoint can be registered in a dedicated private DNS zone. That way, it can be accessed by the registered name.

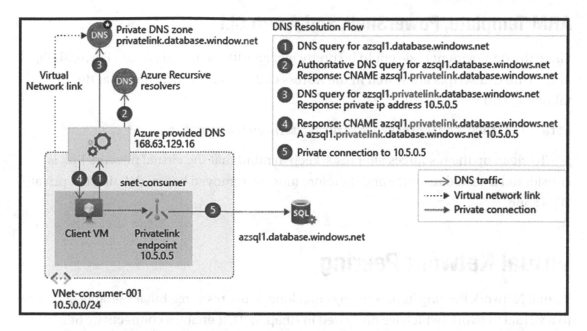

Figure 7-3. *Azure Private DNS (courtesy of Microsoft)(Source:* `https://docs.`
`microsoft.com/en-us/azure/private-link/private-endpoint-dns)`

Creating a Private DNS Zone

While creating an architecture for infrastructure, keep in mind that DNS is usually a
centralized solution. Considering that, we should probably create as few as possible
zones (especially for private link endpoints). In the next couple of pages, we will cover
possible deployment methods for Azure Private DNS.

Azure Portal

First, we need to click **+ Create a resource**, search for "private DNS zone," and click
Create. On the next page, we need to populate Resource Group, Location (will be
automatically filled if we choose the existing resource group), and Name (for the zone).
If we are creating the zone for one of the private link–enabled services, have in mind
that Microsoft proposes a specific naming convention for that. It can be found on this
link – `https://docs.microsoft.com/en-us/azure/private-link/private-endpoint-`
`dns#azure-services-dns-zone-configuration`.

ARM Template, PowerShell, and Azure CLI

Since the deployment code could be pretty big, all ARM template, Azure PowerShell, and Azure CLI scripts are stored in the Apress GitHub account, available at the following URL:

`https://github.com/Apress/pro-azure-admin-and-automation`

To clean up the resources after tests, keep in mind that the virtual network link is considered a nested resource and therefore must be removed before deleting the private DNS zone.

Virtual Network Peering

Virtual Network Peering itself is not a standalone Azure resource but a valuable addition to a virtual network (which we discussed in Chapter 3). It enables connectivity between two or more virtual networks. The peering relies on a private network and is routed via the Azure backbone.

There are two possible types of peering – one connecting virtual networks in the same Azure region and the other creating the connection across regions (known as a global peering). Since it uses the Azure backbone, the peering connection has low latency and very high bandwidth. The peering is not limited to virtual networks only within one subscription but can be created between virtual networks from different subscriptions, tenants, and, as mentioned, regions.

During the peering creation, there is no downtime, but if we are to make any change to a VNet IP address space (add/remove/change), the peering must be removed and re-established after the change. (At the time of writing this book, Microsoft is working on a solution that will enable IP address space change without the need to remove peerings.)

Implementation of Virtual Network Peering is one more important situation where our infrastructure's good design comes into play. To peer two VNets, there must not be any IP space overlap between them. So the good vision of what workloads will be hosted in Azure and their networking demands will shape our future options in connectivity. Later, we will talk about connectivity with on-premises, emphasizing the importance of IP address management even more.

Creating Virtual Network Peering

For a start, we will go with basic peering between two virtual networks in the same region, and based on this, we will explain different options within peering and other connectivity types.

Azure Portal

We will assume that, based on Chapter 3, we are now able to deploy two virtual networks. Keep in mind to use different IP spaces. Choose one of the deployed VNets, and under the *Settings* pane in the virtual network, we will find *Peerings*. Click *Add*. Populating the required parameters in Portal in only one VNet is enough, as it will initiate the creation of both connections (source and destination VNets), as shown in Figure 7-4.

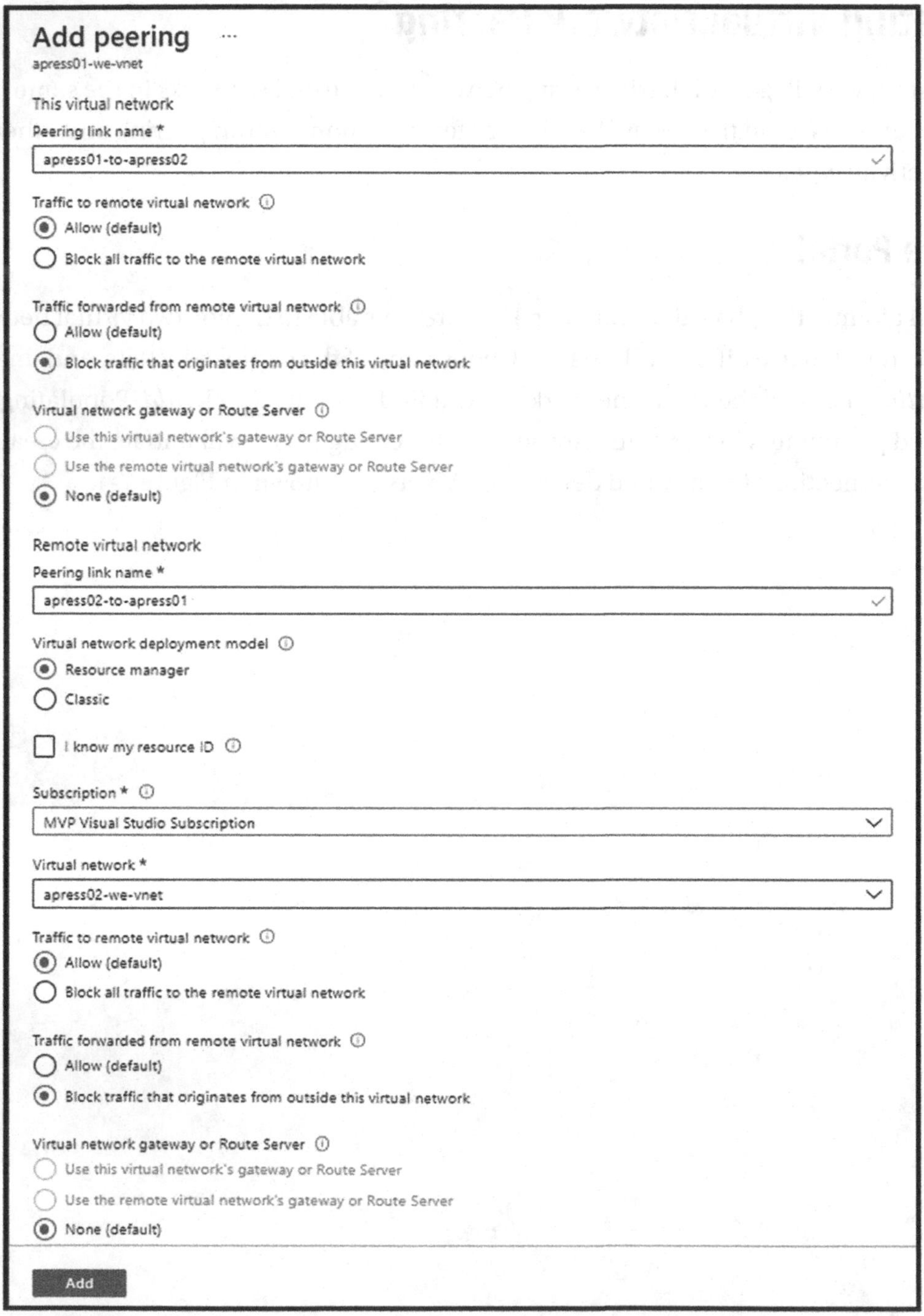

Add peering ⋯
apress01-we-vnet

This virtual network
Peering link name *

| apress01-to-apress02 | ✓ |

Traffic to remote virtual network ⓘ
◉ Allow (default)
◯ Block all traffic to the remote virtual network

Traffic forwarded from remote virtual network ⓘ
◯ Allow (default)
◉ Block traffic that originates from outside this virtual network

Virtual network gateway or Route Server ⓘ
◯ Use this virtual network's gateway or Route Server
◯ Use the remote virtual network's gateway or Route Server
◉ None (default)

Remote virtual network
Peering link name *

| apress02-to-apress01 | ✓ |

Virtual network deployment model ⓘ
◉ Resource manager
◯ Classic

☐ I know my resource ID ⓘ

Subscription * ⓘ

| MVP Visual Studio Subscription | ∨ |

Virtual network *

| apress02-we-vnet | ∨ |

Traffic to remote virtual network ⓘ
◉ Allow (default)
◯ Block all traffic to the remote virtual network

Traffic forwarded from remote virtual network ⓘ
◯ Allow (default)
◉ Block traffic that originates from outside this virtual network

Virtual network gateway or Route Server ⓘ
◯ Use this virtual network's gateway or Route Server
◯ Use the remote virtual network's gateway or Route Server
◉ None (default)

Add

Figure 7-4. *Populating the required parameters in Portal in one VNet will initiate the creation of both connections (source and destination VNets)*

Let us now go through the different options for setting up the peering. When we deep-dive into an Azure architectural design, we will see that, when it comes to peering, hub-to-spoke and spoke-to-spoke are mentioned. Spoke virtual networks are usually considered the ones where we are keeping our application workloads. Hub virtual networks are used for connectivity between Azure and on-premises or as a centralized point of communication. For now, we will talk about spoke-to-spoke connectivity and will explain hub-to-spoke more later:

- Peering link name: Placeholder for a link name – in Figure 7-4, we see that we are using direction for clarity.

- Traffic to remote virtual network: This will allow traffic toward a peered network (peering with this setting set to **Block** does not have many use cases).

- Traffic forwarded from remote virtual network: This option allows/ blocks traffic originating from an outside source (destination) peered network. Usually used in hub-to-spoke topologies with network virtual appliance in HUB.

- Virtual network gateway: This option becomes available when we create a virtual network gateway within the mentioned virtual network (networks of this type are usually considered HUBs).

- Virtual network deployment model: Since it is still possible to have a Classic type of Vnet deployment (before ARM was introduced in Azure), this option allows us to make that selection.

- I know my resource ID: This gives us an option to manually enter the destination Vnet resource ID (helpful in making a connection toward a VNet in a different subscription – the user initiating peering must have the Network Contributor role in the destination subscription).

- Virtual network: Destination VNet with which we want to achieve peering.

ARM Template, PowerShell, and Azure CLI

Since the deployment code could be pretty big, all ARM template, Azure PowerShell, and Azure CLI scripts are stored in the Apress GitHub account, available at the following URL:

https://github.com/Apress/pro-azure-admin-and-automation

Intersite Connectivity

In this part of the chapter, we will explain an additional way of connecting two or more virtual networks and expanding connectivity toward on-premises environments.

VNet-to-VNet Connection

Besides direct Virtual Network Peering, we can achieve connectivity between two or more VNets using VPN Gateways. This solution introduces encrypted connection but also has a limited bandwidth and a higher latency. As we will see, besides virtual networks, we need to deploy an additional Azure service (per VNet) – virtual network gateway. Based on virtual network gateway usage, we must choose the type – VPN or ExpressRoute.

A prerequisite for deploying a virtual network gateway is to have a subnet precreated for it. The subnet name must be "*GatewaySubnet*," and the recommended size is "/27." To create this subnet, we need to have enough space in the VNet IP address space, and then we can, in the *Subnets* panel, click "+ *Gateway subnet*" (as shown in Figure 7-5).

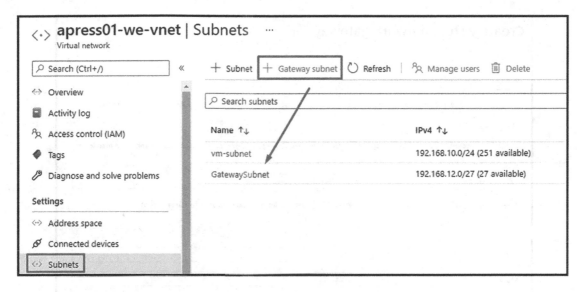

Figure 7-5. *A prerequisite for deploying a virtual network gateway is to have a subnet pre-created for it*

Creating a Virtual Network Gateway

If we have decided to use virtual network gateways to connect our VNets, we can deploy them (at least two) in different ways in ~30 minutes (check in the portal!).

Azure Portal

If we decide to use Azure Portal to perform this operation, the first step is to click **+ Create a resource**, search for "virtual network gateway" in the *Marketplace*, and click **Create**. As with other Azure resources, we need to define some basic parameters. In this case, Gateway type should be *VPN*. SKU and Generation should be chosen based on the needs. Keep in mind that the deployment via Portal takes approximately 30 minutes.

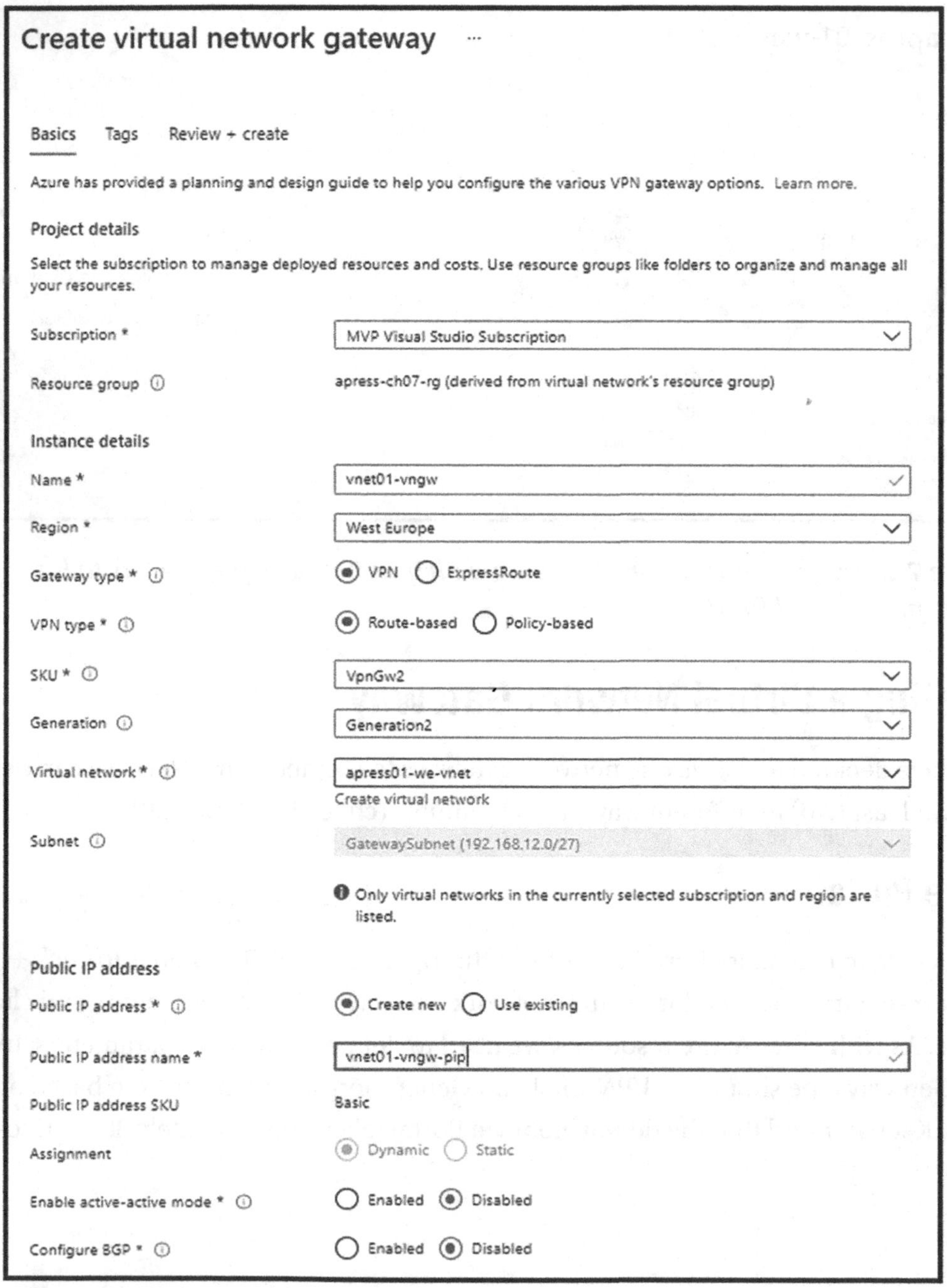

Figure 7-6. *Defining basic parameters in Azure Portal*

ARM Template, PowerShell, and Azure CLI

Since the deployment code could be pretty big, all ARM template, Azure PowerShell, and Azure CLI scripts are stored in the Apress GitHub account, available at the following URL:

APRESS GITHUB REPOSITORY URL

Point-to-Site VPN

One more connection type that can be achieved by using virtual network gateways is point-to-site VPN. This means that we can connect the individual client to an Azure virtual network.

During point-to-site configuration, we need to define

- Address pool: Clients will be getting IPs from here.

- Tunnel type: Currently, five types of protocol can be used.

- Authentication type (Azure certificate, Radius, AAD)

This type of connection is supported on Windows systems from Windows 7 onward, on Mac OS X version 10.11 or above, and on Linux (using the strongSwan open source VPN solution).

An important notice is that TLS 1.2 is now only supported, so we would have to enable it on a client system.

Site-to-Site VPN

A bit more complicated version of the previously mentioned connection is site-to-site VPN. Besides all the network components we have deployed till now, we have to add one more – *local network gateway*. It can be found in the *Marketplace* as any other (Figure 7-7). One prerequisite for deploying a local network gateway is that we know the public IP of the on-premises VPN device we want to connect to.

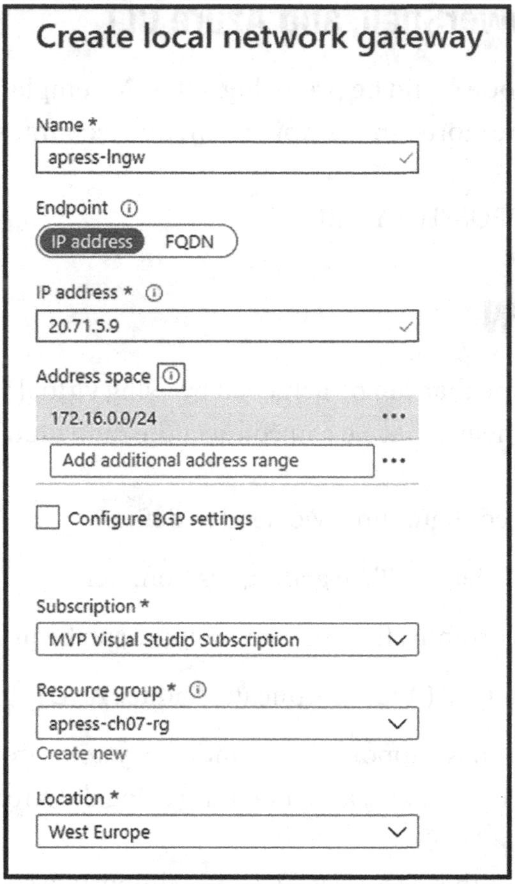

Figure 7-7. Locating the site-to-site VPN in the Marketplace

To configure on-premises VPN devices, Microsoft is offering configuration scripts for all compatible devices. All that is left now is to create a connection from our virtual network gateway (as shown in Figure 7-8) using the previously deployed local network gateway.

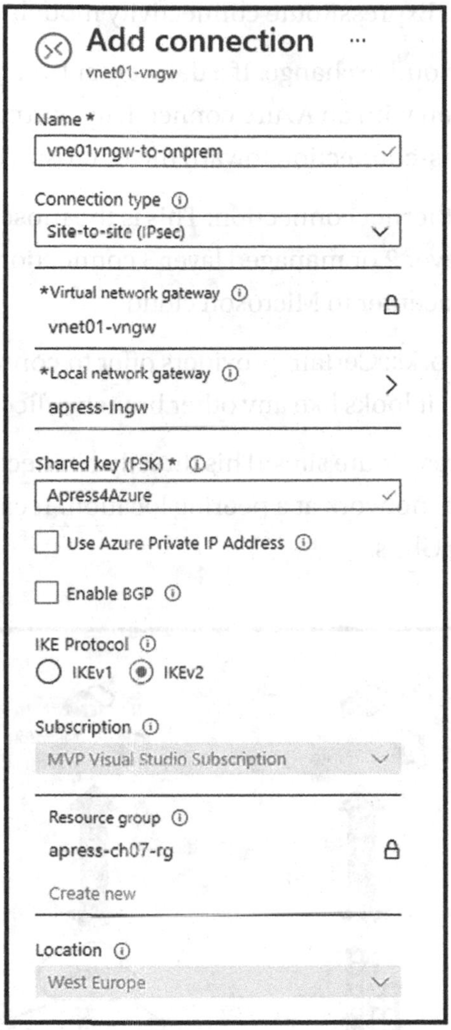

Figure 7-8. *Create a connection from the virtual network gateway*

ExpressRoute

ExpressRoute is a service that connects the on-premises network with the Microsoft cloud. It is provided by Microsoft connectivity partners and can be offered as a layer 2 or a layer 3 connection. ExpressRoute connections are not using the public Internet and therefore are more reliable, can offer faster speeds, and have consistent latency compared to connections established via the Internet (e.g., point-to-site and site-to-site VPN).

There are four different ExpressRoute connectivity models:

1. Co-located at a cloud exchange: If a datacenter (or a part of it) shares the location with an Azure connectivity partner, you may order virtual cross-connection toward the Microsoft cloud.

2. Point-to-point Ethernet connection: This is the most used type. Providers offer layer 2 or managed layer 3 connections from the on-premises datacenter to Microsoft cloud.

3. Any-to-any networks: Certain providers offer to connect Microsoft cloud to WAN, so it looks like any other branch office.

4. Direct from ExpressRoute sites: This directly connects to Microsoft's global network at a peering location. It can offer speeds up to 100 Gbps.

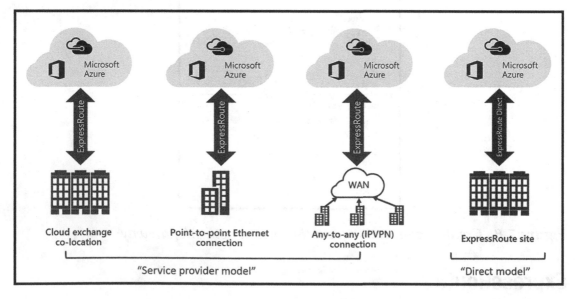

Figure 7-9. *ExpressRoute connectivity models (courtesy of Microsoft)(Source: https://docs.microsoft.com/en-us/azure/expressroute/expressroute-connectivity-models)*

One special option of the point-to-point Ethernet connection model is ExpressRoute Global Reach. If we, for example, have multiple locations across the world, each with its point-to-point ExpressRoute connection, we can use Microsoft's backbone. By linking ExpressRoute circuits, we make a private network between our on-premises networks (as shown in Figure 7-10).

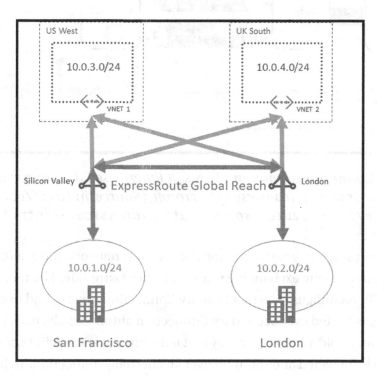

Figure 7-10. *ExpressRoute Global Reach (courtesy of Microsoft)(Source: https://docs.microsoft.com/en-us/azure/expressroute/expressroute-global-reach)*

Each ExpressRoute circuit has two connections between Microsoft Enterprise Edge routers and connectivity partner edge. From partner edge towards our side, we may choose to terminate both connections on the same device (which would then break the high availability chain).

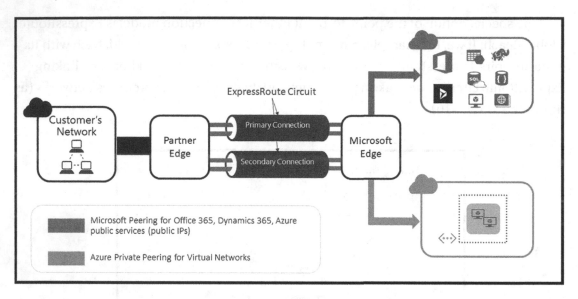

Figure 7-11. *Connections between Microsoft Enterprise Edge routers and connectivity partner edge (courtesy of Microsoft)(Source:* `https://docs.microsoft.com/en-us/azure/expressroute/expressroute-introduction`*)*

The protocol used for dynamic routing between our network and Microsoft is BGP. By using it, our devices are exchanging routes with the Azure side. The most common setup is that BGP is configured so that Primary Connection is used, and in case of failure, traffic gets routed over Secondary Connection automatically. BGP, by default, has keep-alive and hold-time set in a way that if it comes to a link failure, it can take up to 3 minutes to be detected and rerouted over an alternate connection. To lower that time, Microsoft recommends enabling BFD (Bidirectional Forwarding Detection).

ExpressRoute circuits offer different bandwidths that we may purchase – from 50 Mbps up to 10 Gbps. This bandwidth is not shared between two connections within the circuit but is guaranteed per connection. That means that we could set up our routing to use both connections and make use of double bandwidth. However, this should not be used constantly because we would lose redundancy, but it is helpful if we require additional traffic for a specified time.

Besides bandwidth, ExpressRoute has other limits and quotas. One limit that we need to keep in mind is the number of advertised prefixes – 1000 on a single connection. Why this one is so important is because if we exceed the limit, the connection between the ExpressRoute circuit and the gateway will go down. The connection will be re-established when the limit is no more exceeded.

Since it is a specific service, we will not deep-dive into various deployment options. However, it is good to know that besides Classic deployment via Azure Portal, we can automate it using ARM templates, Azure PowerShell, or CLI. A prerequisite for an ExpressRoute connection is to have a virtual network gateway deployed as an ExpressRoute type.

Azure Firewall

Azure Firewall is one of the SaaS network security services. It is a stateful firewall (able to monitor the state of all traffic going through and defend the network based on traffic patterns and flows), which is highly available and can scale automatically based on monitored metrics. It offers protection on both Layer 3 (network) and Layer 7 (application).

Azure Firewall is built based on virtual machine scale set logic. By default, we always have at least two instances in the back end. Enabling Availability Zones during Firewall deployment, we gain higher availability (99.99%) because new instances will spin up in different zones.

Other features offered by Azure Firewall Standard are

- Network traffic filtering rules (Layer 3 security).

- Application FQDN filtering rules (Layer 7 security).

- Use of FQDN and service tags:

  - To ease the implementation, Microsoft has grouped specific Azure IP address prefixes behind service tags that can be used in network security group rules.

  - FQDN tags are used within application rules and represent groups of specific Microsoft online services (e.g., Azure Backup, Windows Update, etc.).

- Threat intelligence: This option has three operational levels (Off, Alert only, Alert and Deny) and can help in blocking traffic to or from known malicious IP addresses and domains.

- Inbound DNAT (Destination Network Address Translation): Traffic coming from outside our protected network over a specific IP/port/protocol can be translated to an internal IP/port combination.

- Outbound SNAT (Source NAT): Traffic originating from our Azure private network toward an Azure public resource or the Internet is being translated to use Azure Firewall public IP.

- Multiple public IP addresses: Azure Firewall has its limitations (e.g., number of available SNAT ports per IP), which can be extended by using multiple assigned public IPs.

- Full integration with Azure Monitor.

- DNS: Azure Firewall (since November 2020) has an option to use custom DNS and to act as a DNS proxy.

- Forced tunneling: Azure Firewall can route Internet-based traffic toward other devices (e.g., on-premises edge firewall) for enhanced security and filtering.

At the time of writing this book, Azure Firewall Premium is in *Public Preview*. Additional options offered in this SKU are

- TLS inspection

- IDPS (Intrusion Detection and Prevention System)

- URL filtering (more granular)

- Web categories (e.g., gambling, news, social media, etc.)

Creating Azure Firewall
Azure Portal

We click + **Create a resource**, search for "firewall," and click **Create**. On the next page, we need to populate Resource group for the deployment, Name, Region for the Firewall, and Availability zone we want to use (if possible). After that, we need to choose a tier and the way we want to manage our Firewall. Then we need to place the Firewall in a virtual network (new or existing). If we pre-created the VNet, we also had to create an AzureFirewallSubnet. Finally, we will assign a public IP for the Firewall.

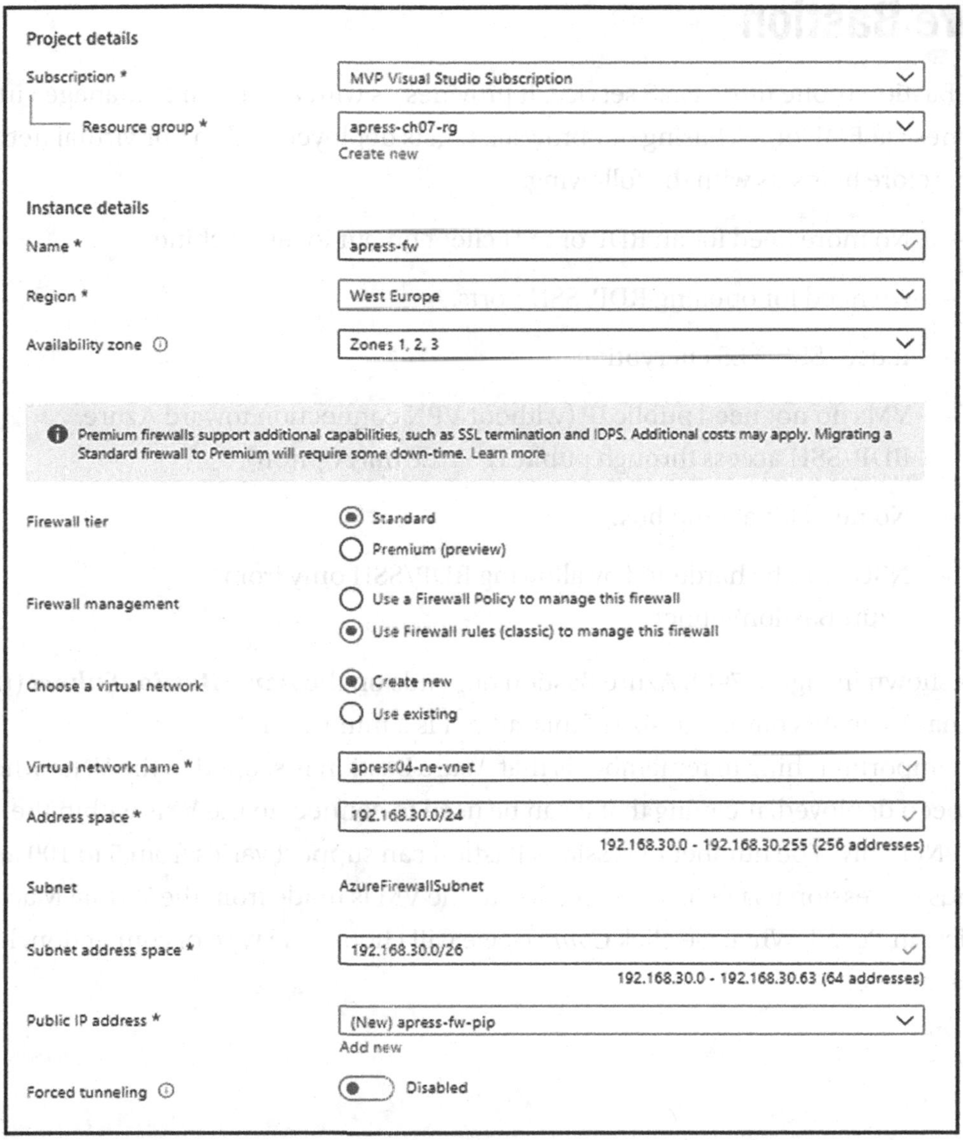

Project details

Subscription *	MVP Visual Studio Subscription
└── Resource group *	apress-ch07-rg
	Create new

Instance details

Name *	apress-fw
Region *	West Europe
Availability zone ⓘ	Zones 1, 2, 3

> ⓘ Premium firewalls support additional capabilities, such as SSL termination and IDPS. Additional costs may apply. Migrating a Standard firewall to Premium will require some down-time. Learn more

Firewall tier	⦿ Standard
	○ Premium (preview)
Firewall management	○ Use a Firewall Policy to manage this firewall
	⦿ Use Firewall rules (classic) to manage this firewall
Choose a virtual network	⦿ Create new
	○ Use existing
Virtual network name *	apress04-ne-vnet
Address space *	192.168.30.0/24
	192.168.30.0 - 192.168.30.255 (256 addresses)
Subnet	AzureFirewallSubnet
Subnet address space *	192.168.30.0/26
	192.168.30.0 - 192.168.30.63 (64 addresses)
Public IP address *	(New) apress-fw-pip
	Add new
Forced tunneling ⓘ	⦿ Disabled

Figure 7-12. *Populate Resource group for the deployment, Name, Region for the Firewall, and Availability zone (if possible)*

ARM Template, PowerShell, and Azure CLI

Since the deployment code could be pretty big, all ARM template, Azure PowerShell, and Azure CLI scripts are stored in the Apress GitHub account, available at the following URL:

https://github.com/Apress/pro-azure-admin-and-automation

Azure Bastion

Azure Bastion is one more PaaS service. It provides us with an option to manage virtual machines via RDP or SSH using our browser. It gets deployed within our virtual network and therefore helps us with the following:

- No more need for an RDP or SSH client on our local machine.

- No need for opening RDP/SSH ports.

- It uses SSL/TLS encryption.

- VMs do not need public IP (without VPN connection toward Azure, RDP/SSH access through public IP is the only option).

- No need for a jump box.

- NSGs can be hardened by allowing RDP/SSH only from AzureBastionSubnet.

As shown in Figure 7-13, Azure Bastion depends on the *AzureBastionSubnet* (the name has to be this one). The size of this subnet is a minimum /27.

An important thing to remember is that Azure Bastion is scoped to the VNet where it has been deployed, meaning that it can be used to connect to the VMs within the same VNet only. The number of sessions Bastion can support varies from 5 to 100 and depends on session usage. The connection to the VM is made from the Virtual Machine overview in Portal. When we click *Connect,* we will choose the type of connection, having Bastion as one.

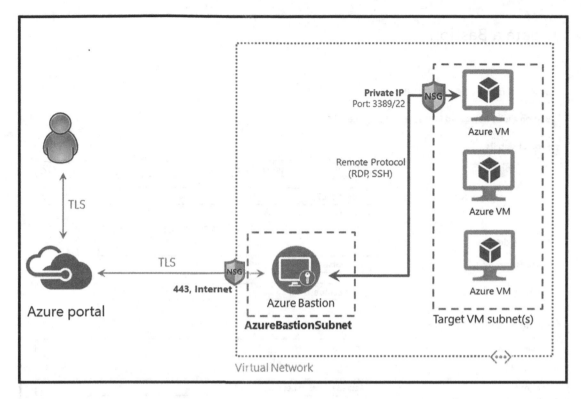

Figure 7-13. *Azure Bastion depends on the AzureBastionSubnet (courtesy of Microsoft)*

Creating Azure Bastion

Here, I will assume that you know how to create a virtual network subnet, so creating the one for Azure Bastion will not be covered. For the service itself, we will, as always, cover all four ways of possible deployment.

Azure Portal

For deploying Azure Bastion, the first step is to click **+ Create a resource**, search for "bastion" in the *Marketplace*, and click **Create**. As with other Azure resources, we need to define some basic parameters. Like Firewall deployment, if we have pre-created VNet, we also had to create a subnet with a specific name – *AzureBastionSubnet*.

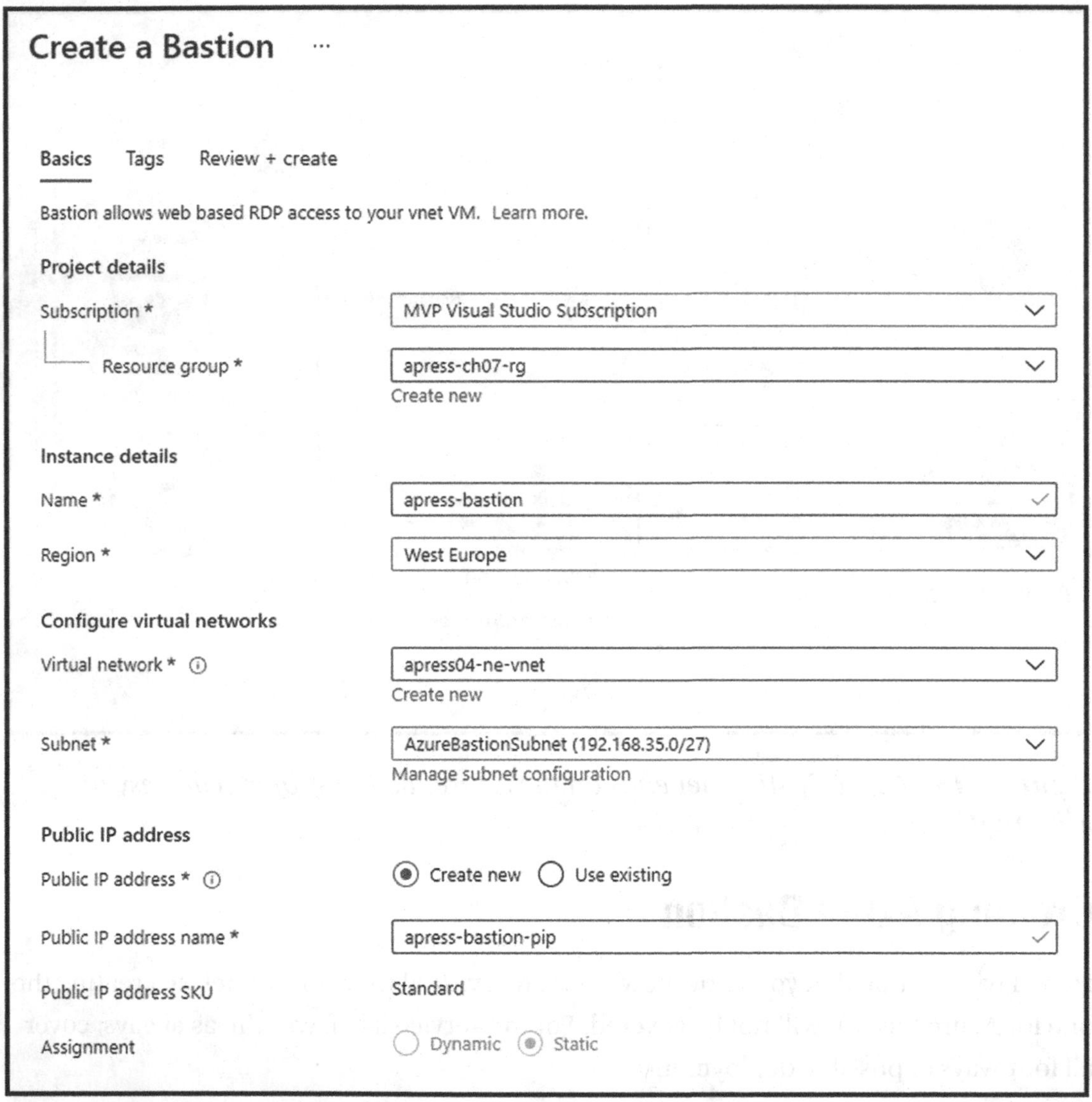

Figure 7-14. *Like other Azure resources, define the basic parameters*

ARM Template, PowerShell, and Azure CLI

Since the deployment code could be pretty big, all ARM template, Azure PowerShell, and Azure CLI scripts are stored in the Apress GitHub account, available at the following URL:

`https://github.com/Apress/pro-azure-admin-and-automation`

Chapter Recap

In this chapter, we have learned more about networking components that can be used in environments of different types – from a single subnet to hub-and-spoke topologies, from only Azure-based to Hybrid environments, with additional security on top.

In the next chapter, we will learn about services that will help us to log metrics and diagnostic settings. We will learn how to use them for troubleshooting issues with our services. Also, we will learn how to ensure we can recover from data loss or IaaS failure.

## CHAPTER 8

Monitoring and Data Protection

In the previous chapter, we have discussed and explained advanced networking features in Microsoft Azure, such as intersite connectivity, Virtual Network Peering, and Public and Private DNS, and learned how to use them. Also, we have talked about Azure Firewall, which is essential for network security, and in this chapter, we will continue to talk about security-related features. Please keep in mind that Chapter 10 will be dedicated to security services and features in Azure.

In this chapter, we will pay attention to services that are essential and have to be included in every environment, but, on the other hand, in many scenarios are forgotten. This chapter covers the following topics that are important for the monitoring and protection of data:

- Monitors and alerts

- Log Analytics

- Application Insights

- Network Watcher

- Azure Backup

- Disaster recovery

After this chapter, we will be able to design and implement a data protection solution in Azure and monitor deployed resources.

© Vladimir Stefanovic and Milos Katinski 2021
V. Stefanovic and M. Katinski, *Pro Azure Administration and Automation*,
https://doi.org/10.1007/978-1-4842-7325-8_8

Azure Monitors and Alerts

For every production environment, regardless of platform type, operating system, or industry, monitoring is essential. Without an appropriate monitoring system implemented, we will not be able to track system performances in real time or be informed of something unusual, such as high CPU load, running out of disk space, a high number of application connections, and many others. Nowadays, on the market, we can find dozens of high-quality monitoring solutions, which can be integrated with Azure infrastructure, and monitor services in real time with alerting functionality. Luckily, we do not need to rely on third-party tools for monitoring since we can leverage Azure Monitor as a native solution for monitoring.

Collecting Data

If we want to realize what is happening in the Azure infrastructure, including a tenant and subscriptions, Azure Monitor will be the central point for getting information. The very first step in this process is collecting data from sources, which could be applications, operating systems, Azure resources, subscriptions, tenants, or any other custom sources. Once data is collected, which is the automated process in many scenarios, it will be divided into *metrics* and *logs*. Metrics are values that describe a specific aspect of the resource, such as CPU load or network traffic, and, in most scenarios, represent real-time statistics, with the possibility to check metrics historically. Logs are data organized into records with different sets of properties for each type, and it fits perfectly for telemetry or analysis, especially for applications. Another difference between metrics and logs is that metrics are represented as graphs, whereas logs need to be queried by KQL (Kusto query language) to get desired data. KQL can organize gathered results in a chart or pie and make a graphical representation, but it is not a default output.

Analyzing and Processing Data

Most Azure infrastructure collected data are part of a fully automated process, and we do not need to do anything. If we want to collect data from operating systems or applications, we need to install additional agents or Software Development Kits (SDKs), but in some scenarios, that also could be a one-click action. Once all needed data are there, now is time to see what kind of information we can get from Azure Monitor and what we can do with it.

Insights

Infrastructure monitoring is helpful and more than enough in many scenarios. However, there are situations where we want to know what is happening "under the hood" and find out why our application has a memory leak or what URL is most popular or what is happening inside of the operating system and how much RAM is available. In this case, we need to leverage *Insight Analytics*, which is one of the components of Azure Monitor. As shown in Figure 8-1, Insight Analytics is available for the most important resources. That list will grow in the forthcoming period, as we can see that SQL Insights is currently in the preview stage. If we talk about applications and virtual machines, there is an option to send insight data from the on-premises application and operating systems.

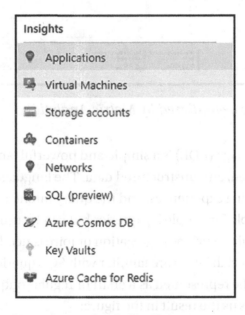

Figure 8-1. *Insight Analytics is available for the most important resources*

Visualize

In case that we need to have a graphical representation of specific resources and their metrics and statistics, that is possible to implement in different ways. We can create a custom dashboard in Azure Portal, create custom views, or even use Power BI for advanced views. Of course, we can use many third-party tools for parsing and visualizing collected logs, but that will cost additional money.

Analyze

As we already said, all data that arrive at Azure Monitor will fit into metrics or logs. Based on that, metrics can be analyzed by Metric Analytics (see Figure 8-2), whereas log results could be found in the Log Analytics workspace and analyzed by running the Kusto query language (KQL) queries.

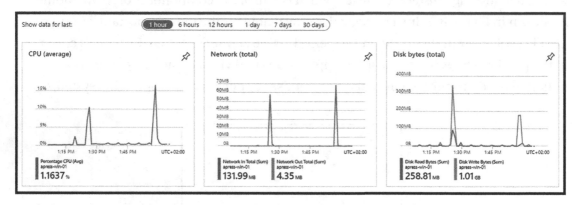

Figure 8-2. *Metrics can be analyzed by Metric Analytics*

The Kusto query language (KQL) is a simple and powerful language to query structured, semi-structured, and unstructured data. The language is very expressive and optimized for authoring experiences, and the query intent is easy to read and understand. KQL is suitable for simple log queries but can be used for advanced analytics where functionality, such as aggregation or join, is needed. It is not so complicated to learn, especially if we are familiar with SQL queries. As we can see in Figure 8-3, results can be represented as a chart or regular output table, and the following KQL query gives us the result in the figure:

```
requests
    | summarize CountByCountry=count() by client_CountryOrRegion
    | top 10 by CountByCountry
    | render piechart
```

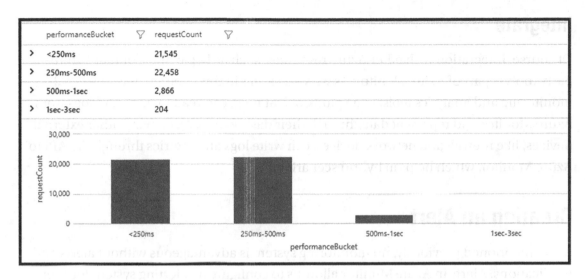

Figure 8-3.   Results are visualized as a chart or output table

Respond

In addition to interactively analyzing data using Metric or Log Analytics, we have an option to configure an alerting mechanism in case if something is not as expected. This is a crucial part of monitoring infrastructure and applications because we could be proactive with specific actions or long-term decisions. In Azure Monitor, we have many options to configure alerts, and they consist of scope, condition, and action. Under *Scope*, we need to define what resources will be tracked for the alerts. In most cases, we can select a whole resource group or subscription for a specific resource (i.e., virtual machines), which means that all resources will be tracked. Under *Condition*, we need to define what signal will be tracked and what the threshold will be. Under *Action*, we need to define who will be notified if an alert is fired and optionally what kind of action will be triggered, such as Logic Apps, Azure Functions, or Azure Automation.

Auto-scaling, which was explained in Chapter 4, is also part of the response process triggered by Azure Monitor. For instance, the auto-scaling rule is configured to add one more instance to the virtual machine scale set if the CPU load is higher than 70% in a duration of 5 minutes or decrease the number of instances if the CPU load is lower than 40% in a duration of 10 minutes.

Integrate

Of course, integration with other Azure resources, such as Logic Apps, or many third-party tools is part of Azure Monitor. As we said earlier in this chapter, many external monitoring and analytics tools, like Splunk or Datadog, can read metrics and logs from Azure Monitor and represent data through their dashboards. Also, many other external devices, like firewall and network devices, can write logs and metrics through the API to Azure Monitor, which helps in hybrid scenarios.

Creating an Alert

As we mentioned previously, no monitoring system is advantageous without alerts and notifications. Alerts in Azure Monitor allow us to configure an alerting system for every metric or log that is important for the infrastructure. Once we navigate the Overview page of Azure Monitor and click Create Alert, we are just a few configuration parameters away from setting up the alert.

Scope

Under Scope, we need to define what resource we want to track. For instance, if we select virtual machines as a resource, we can define a level of placement this tracking and alerts. We can select one or more virtual machines, or we can configure this on the resource group or even subscription level. This is very helpful because one alert covers all virtual machines in the subscription or resource group so that we do not need to create the same alert for each virtual machine (see Figure 8-4).

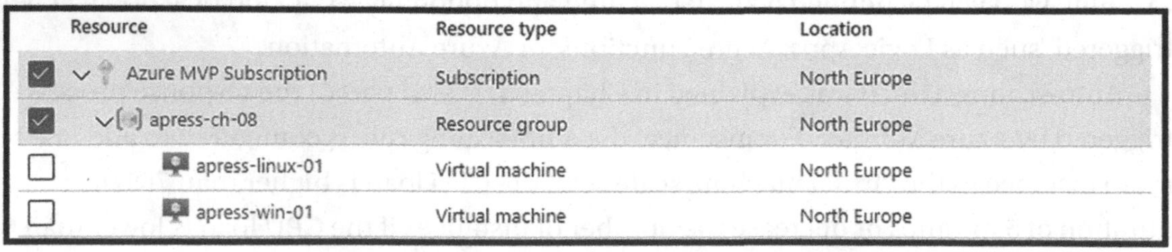

	Resource	Resource type	Location
☑	∨ 🜲 Azure MVP Subscription	Subscription	North Europe
☑	∨ [≡] apress-ch-08	Resource group	North Europe
☐	🖥 apress-linux-01	Virtual machine	North Europe
☐	🖥 apress-win-01	Virtual machine	North Europe

Figure 8-4. *One alert covers all virtual machines in the subscription or resource group*

If we configure the scope in this way, the option "*Include all future resources*" is automatically checked, which could be found on the main page for creating an alert rule once you confirm selecting a scope.

Condition

The next step in configuring an alert rule is defining one or more conditions for this alert. First, we need to choose a signal type for alerting, activity logs or metrics, and that depends on our needs. For this scenario, we will select metrics and choose percentage CPU as a signal for alerting. Then we need to create alert logic and configure in what circumstances we will be alerted. As shown in Figure 8-5, the threshold for a trigger is average CPU consumption above 80% in a duration of 5 minutes, and the frequency of evaluation is 1 minute.

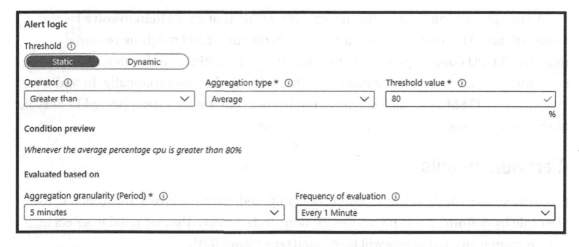

Figure 8-5. *Average CPU consumption above 80% in a duration of 5 minutes, and the frequency of evaluation is 1 minute*

Actions

Before we create any action that the previously configured condition will trigger, we need to create an action group. If there is no one action group already configured, we need to create one. An action group is a collection of notification preferences defined for notifications and actions. Along with the name, we need to configure *Notifications*. We can choose between two possible notification types: *Email Azure Resource Manager*

Role and *Email/SMS Message/Push/Voice*. The first one will notify one of the predefined roles for monitored resources, whereas the other allows us to configure direct messaging to a person or a group. Also, we can configure more than one notification type if that is needed. Also, we can configure *Actions*, where we can choose to use one of the following action types:

- Automation Runbook

- Azure Functions

- ITSM

- Logic Apps

- Secure Webhook

- Webhook

All of these action types can run a specific action that could help to solve issues automatically. For instance, if we know that IIS on our virtual machine requires to restart if CPU consumption is higher than the value defined in the alert, we can configure Azure Functions or Automation Runbook to do it automatically. In addition, we can select ITSM as an action type to open a ticket in any of the supported IT Service Management tools.

Alert Rule Details

Once the scope, condition, and action are configured, we must give a final touch to the alert rule by defining a rule name, description, and severity. Also, we need to select in what resource group this rule will be created (see Figure 8-6).

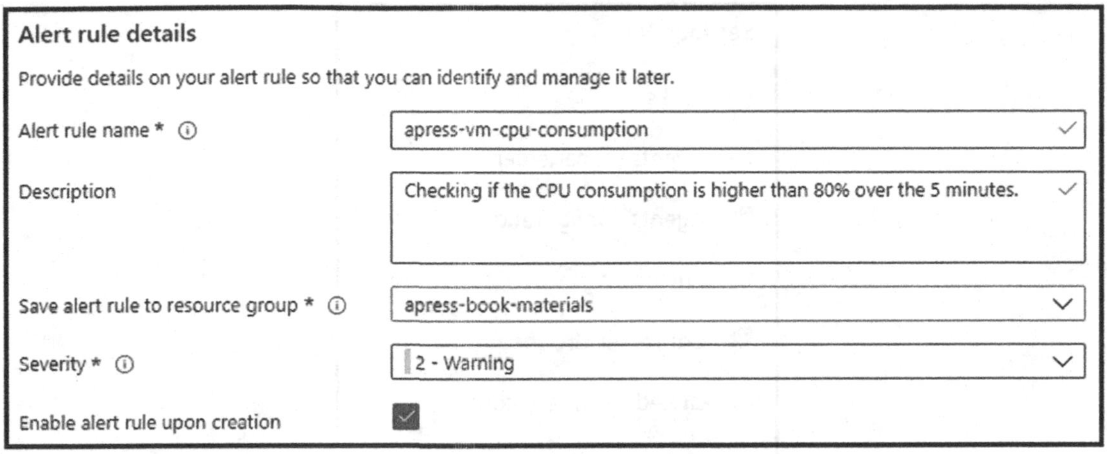

Alert rule details

Provide details on your alert rule so that you can identify and manage it later.

Alert rule name * ⓘ	apress-vm-cpu-consumption ✓
Description	Checking if the CPU consumption is higher than 80% over the 5 minutes. ✓
Save alert rule to resource group * ⓘ	apress-book-materials ⌄
Severity * ⓘ	2 - Warning ⌄
Enable alert rule upon creation	☑

Figure 8-6. Select the resource group in which the rule will be created

Log Analytics

Log Analytics is an Azure resource that is there for a long time and has undergone many changes over time. We will not cover its history, because that is not so relevant today, and we will stay focused on today's Log Analytics functionalities. Log Analytics allows us to run predefined or custom queries on data that the aforementioned Azure Monitor collects. As we mentioned earlier, Log Analytics uses the Kusto query language (KQL), which is similar to SQL, and that is the first step if we decide to use Log Analytics. Although there are a solid number of predefined queries, in many cases, they will not be appropriate for our analysis.

Log Analytics is divided into workspaces, which is, in general, a single Azure resource. Since the pricing was moved to the per-GB model a few years ago, we can create more than one Log Analytics workspace and organize our logs per source. Since the one Log Analytics workspace could be a landing zone for many different log sources, many configuration parameters are not applicable for every scenario. For instance, if we want to send logs from on-premises virtual machines, we will work with agents and related configurations in the workspace, as shown in Figure 8-7.

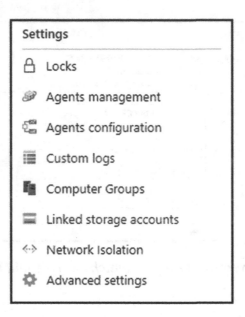

Figure 8-7. *To send logs from on-premises virtual machines, work with agents and related configurations in the workspace*

Under *Agents management,* we can find instructions on configuring the agent on the on-premises virtual machines. Under *Agents configuration,* we can define what kind of logs will be sent to the Log Analytics workspace. *Custom logs* and *Computer Groups* allow us to define custom log tables and fields in the workspace and group computers by their purpose. A *linked storage account* gives us the possibility to define what storage account will be used to store queries and some type of ingested data if we do not want to use storage managed by Azure Monitor. Suppose we want to configure network restriction for data ingestion or querying, or even both, that needs to be done under *Network Isolation.* Of course, at any moment, we can see data sources linked to a specific Log Analytics workspace under *Workspace Data Sources*, as shown in Figure 8-8.

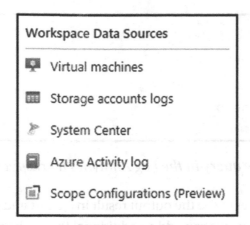

Workspace Data Sources

🖥 Virtual machines

⊞ Storage accounts logs

⚐ System Center

🗋 Azure Activity log

🖵 Scope Configurations (Preview)

Figure 8-8. See data sources linked to a specific Log Analytics workspace under Workspace Data Sources

KQL (Kusto Query Language) Queries

As we already said, Log Analytics and many other Azure resources, such as Application Insights or Resource Graph, can execute queries to get results regarding infrastructure and logs using KQL. If we want to leverage the full capabilities of resources that use KQL, we need to become familiar with this language. However, because it is not the main topic of this book, we will just show some examples of how we can get some results and what we can do with them. For instance, we want to know how much available memory is on the virtual machines in our environment in the last 5 minutes. The following query will give us that information:

```
InsightsMetrics
| where TimeGenerated > ago(5m)
| where Origin == "vm.azm.ms"
| where Namespace == "Memory" and Name == "AvailableMB"
| summarize AvailableMB = percentile(Val, 90) by Computer
```

Once we execute this query in the Log Analytics workspace, where our virtual machines send data, the result will look like that in Figure 8-9.

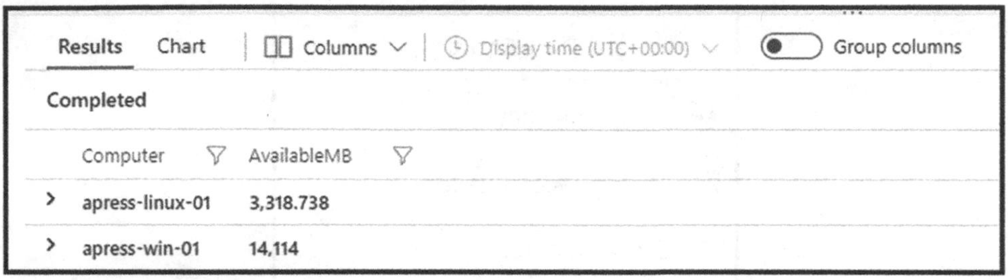

Figure 8-9. *Execute the query in the Log Analytics workspace. See the result*

Although we can select to see the output result in a chart and get some graphical representation of the query, we can add an additional line with the `render` command in the query and force it to give us a graphical output as a pie chart or bar chart, for instance:

```
InsightsMetrics
| where TimeGenerated > ago(5m)
| where Origin == "vm.azm.ms"
| where Namespace == "Memory" and Name == "AvailableMB"
| summarize AvailableMB = percentile(Val, 90) by Computer
| render piechart;
```

Once we have created an appropriate query and want to track the result, we can easily create a new alert rule by clicking **+ New alert rule**. That query will be loaded into the alert rule configurator, and we just need to complete the alert rule configuration in the similar way we did it already.

Application Insights

Application Insights is just one part of the whole Azure monitoring stack, and it is designed to give us an insight into application functionality, like many third-party APM *(Application Performance Management)* tools. Although its primary purpose is to provide application analytics for App Service, it also could be integrated with IIS on Azure virtual machines and virtual machine scale sets, as well as with IIS on on-premises machines. Application Insights could be implemented in two modes: Server and Code. The first one is available for ASP.NET applications on Web Apps in Azure and IIS and ASP.NET Core apps on Web Apps in Azure. For both scenarios, the process of configuring is straightforward, and in most scenarios, the amount of information we can collect is more than enough. Conversely, if we want to have deep insight and track applications from the development stage, we need to integrate Application Insights into the application code by implementing SDK (Software Development Kit). Once one of these methods is implemented, telemetry will be sent to Application Insights.

Application Insights monitors and gives us detailed information about requests and dependency rates, response times, failure rates, exceptions, page views and load performances, user and session counts, and many others. In addition, if we configure Application Insights to track applications hosted on virtual machines, specific performance counters for CPU and memory will be tracked as well. Once logs and metrics land on Application Insights, many out-of-the-box features give us a graphical representation of these data, as shown in Figure 8-10.

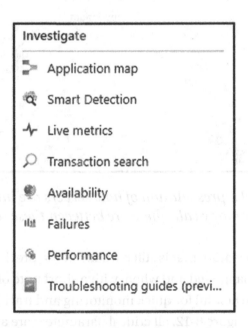

Figure 8-10. Out-of-the-box features offer a graphical representation of data

If we have a complex application, which is more than a two-layer design, and have many external dependencies, an *application map* can give us a great graphical representation of how servers or services are interconnected, what the response time is, and how many calls are between these services (see Figure 8-11). This type of view can help us to identify bottlenecks quickly, which has a direct impact on how quickly a specific problem could be solved.

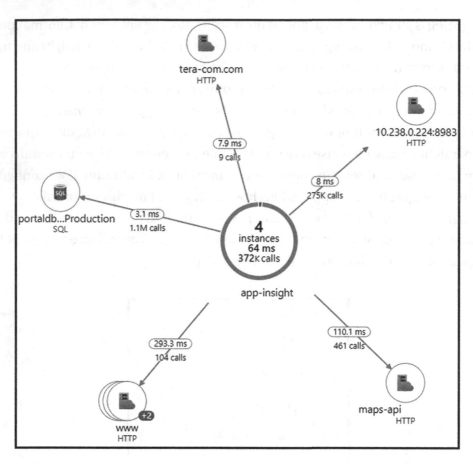

Figure 8-11. *Graphical representation of how servers are interconnected, the response time, and how many calls there are between these services*

A *smart detection* is a feature that is still partially in the preview phase but can give us information on what happened and when, with a short note of why that could be a problem. Live metrics are helpful for quick monitoring and tracking of application data in real time. As shown in Figure 8-12, all critical parameters are added to this dashboard for tracking by default, but we can make changes if needed.

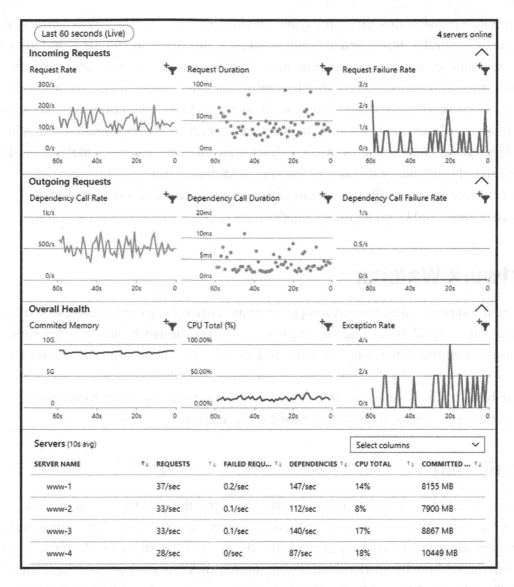

Figure 8-12. *Critical parameters are included in the dashboard for tracking by default, but can be changed*

Transaction search is a feature that will allow us to track all transactions in detail, regardless of whether that was a connection to the database or complex interaction between many external services. We will get end-to-end transaction details, which can help us to identify where the problem is so that we can focus on fixing it. The *failures* feature gives us information only on failures that happened in an application and provides us with a timeline of errors and a list of the top ten errors, as well as the

195

top three response codes, exception types, and failed dependencies. The *performance* feature has a similar dashboard as failures, but presented data are different, and there we can see details on application performances. That also could be useful for application optimization and improvement, although we do not have a list of errors. For instance, on this dashboard, we can quickly identify what operation takes much time and why, which can help us to focus our development on improving performances instead of fixing bugs.

Application Insights allows us to configure many of these features and dashboards appropriately and makes it easier for tracking. Additional configurations, such as network isolation or continuous export to the storage account, are similar to Log Analytics and could be configured if needed.

Network Watcher

One of the very important monitoring features in Azure is Network Watcher, which can help us with helpful information during troubleshooting network connectivity issues. It can also monitor network connectivity and, in some scenarios, could initiate repair of network connectivity. Network Watcher comes as a regional service and needs to be enabled in the region we want to use. Its features are separated into three main categories: monitoring, network diagnostic tools, and logs.

Monitoring

If we look at Network Watcher's monitoring features, the first thing that we can see is *topology*. As we can see in Figure 8-13, we can see and download a graphical representation of the topology of a specific virtual network in Azure. That can help us to understand how network resources are interconnected, especially if there are a lot of them.

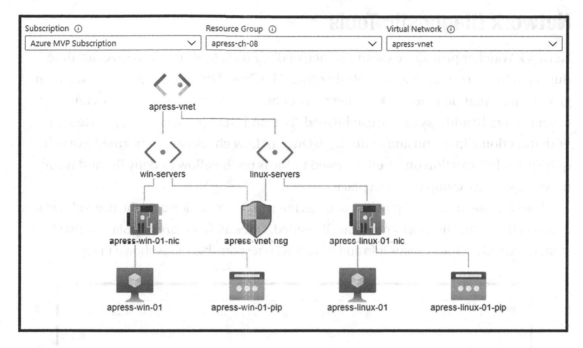

Figure 8-13. *A graphical representation of the topology of a specific virtual network in Azure*

Under the monitoring features, we can also find a Connection Monitor that allows us to monitor connectivity in Azure and hybrid networks as well. Monitoring data must be stored in the Log Analytics workspace, which can be analyzed at any time. A Connection Monitor provides end-to-end connection monitoring in different scenarios, such as communication between front-end and database virtual machines in Azure or an on-premises workload with Azure services or applications. Configuration of this functionality is pretty straightforward, and we need to create a source, destination, and type of check. In addition, the alert will be prepared automatically, and we just accept it if we want to be informed in case of a network issue. The frequency for the network connectivity test could be between 30 seconds and 1800 seconds.

Along with a Connection Monitor, we can find a Network Performance Monitor (NPM) under Network Watcher monitoring. Keep in mind that starting July 1, 2021, NPM will not accept a new connection test for existing workspaces, nor can new workspaces be added. Previously added tests would continue to work until February 2024, but it is recommended to migrate all tests from Connection Monitor (Classic) and Network Performance Monitor to the Connection Monitor.

Network Diagnostic Tools

Network Watcher provides us with a bunch of diagnostic tools that can save our time during network connectivity troubleshooting. The first of them is *IP Flow Verify*, which gives us information if network connectivity between virtual network devices and any other remote IP address can be established. TCP and UDP packets are supported, in both directions: Inbound and Outbound. Once IP flow checks are performed, we will quickly get information on whether tested traffic is on the allow or deny list and what network security group rule is in place.

The NSG diagnostic tool provides detailed information to understand the network security group in the virtual network and debug if needed. Once all fields are populated and check started, we will get traffic status info and what NSG is responsible for, as shown in Figure 8-14.

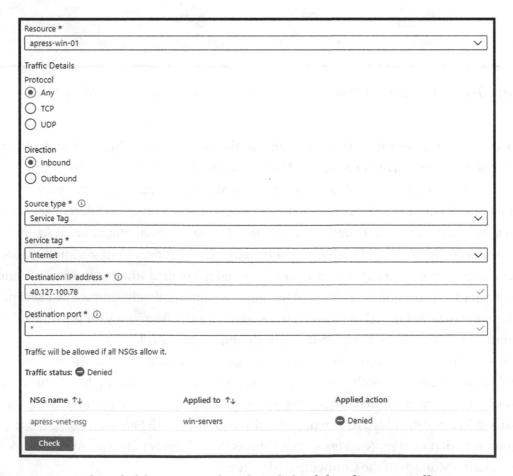

Figure 8-14. *When fields are populated and check has begun, traffic status information is provided*

The *next hop* tool could help a complex network environment, where many routing tables are implemented and we want to know what the next hop address is. Once we define source and destination IP addresses, the result will be given in seconds. *Effective security rules* is one of the tools that must be used in a complex network environment, where more than one network security group is assigned to the virtual machine. In specific cases, we can find that network security groups are assigned on the subnet level and on the NIC level as well, which could lead to connectivity issues if it is not configured correctly. In this scenario, this tool will evaluate all network security groups processing network traffic for the affected virtual machine and give us the result of where the problem is.

If the VPN Gateway is implemented to provide communication with the on-premises location or between two virtual networks, in specific scenarios, we need to have more detailed troubleshooting than restarting the VPN Gateway service or tunnels. In this case, we can run the *VPN troubleshooter*, a functionality of Network Watcher, analyzing the health of the gateway or connection. A long-running transaction will give us results of one or more troubleshooting sessions once the diagnosis is complete.

A *Packet Capture* is one beneficial functionality of Network Watcher, which provides us with the ability to capture traffic that comes into the virtual machine, as we did it with Wireshark or similar tools in on-premises environments. There are a few filtering options that we could include in capturing, which are crucial if we want to have a long-running capture because capturing is limited to 5 hours and a 1 GB file. A created capture file is in the .pcap format, and it will be stored in a storage account or local file to analyze the file using any popular network analyzer tools.

Last but not the least diagnostic tool in Network Watcher is *Connection troubleshoot*, which can check a direct TCP connection from a virtual machine to a virtual machine, FQDN, URI, or IPv4 address. Once we populate all needed fields and click "Check," the result will be displayed in a few seconds in two graphical representations: grid view and topology view (see Figure 8-15).

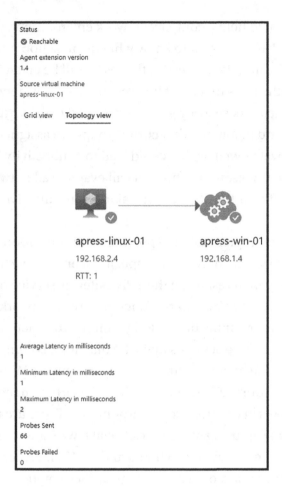

Figure 8-15. *Grid view and topology view*

Logs

Logs in Network Watcher are essential for detailed analysis and analytics and, by default, are not enabled. They are separated into *NSG flow logs* and *diagnostic logs*, and before using them, we need to enable them. NSG flow logs allow us to view information about ingress and egress IP traffic through NSG. All information will be stored in a storage account, with the possibility to set retention. Diagnostic logs give us the ability to define what kind of metrics or logs will be tracked and where the diagnostic data will be sent. Destination options are Log Analytics, storage account, or Event Hub.

If we decide to enable NSG flow logs, which is recommended for analytics and analysis, we could enable *Traffic Analytics*. Traffic Analytics provides rich analytics and visualization derived from NSG flow logs and other Azure resources' data. Log Analytics is mandatory for this feature, which provides us with the ability to make additional queries to get details about NSG flows that Traffic Analytics does not cover by default. Also, we can choose how much time for the traffic analysis processing interval, but at the moment, there are only two possible options: every 10 minutes and every 1 hour.

Azure Backup and Disaster Recovery

When we talk about security, numerous topics need to be discussed and planned to protect infrastructure and data. Backup is one of the essential things in design, regardless of infrastructure size and the amount of data; mainly small businesses need to be protected as well as enterprise companies. Over the last few years, with an expansion of ransomware attacks around the world, where no one is safe, awareness of having a valid backup has become an inevitable part of infrastructure design. Thousands of companies worldwide that were ransomware victims were paid much money for data decryption or lost their data entirely because they did not have implemented a proper backup procedure.

If our infrastructure is in Microsoft Azure, we can freely say that we are lucky because implementing a backup procedure is easier than ever. Moreover, some Azure resources, such as Azure SQL, have implemented a backup by default that cannot be disabled. An Azure resource responsible for virtual machine and data backup is the Recovery Service vault, which is also responsible for implementing a disaster recovery plan for infrastructure. Once we have deployed the recovery vault, we can start configuring backup policies for our workload, but first, we need to select one of the possible workloads and what we want to back up.

Backup Types and Workloads

As we already mentioned, a recovery vault is a one-stop shop for all backup types for all supported workloads. Supported workloads are Azure, Azure Stack, and On-Premises, and all of these workloads have supported backup types:

Azure

- Virtual machine

- Azure file share

- Azure blobs (preview)

- SQL Server in Azure VM

- SAP HANA in Azure VM

- Azure Database for PostgreSQL servers (preview)

Azure Stack

- Files and folders

- Microsoft SQL Server

- Microsoft SharePoint

- System state

On-Premises

- Files and folders

- Hyper-V virtual machines

- VMware virtual machines

- Microsoft SQL Server

- Microsoft SharePoint

- Microsoft Exchange

- System state

- Bare-metal recovery

Configuring a backup for an Azure workload is a straightforward process since Azure Backup is fully integrated with supported Azure resources. On the other hand, backing up Azure Stack and On-Premises workloads requires installation and configuration of Azure Backup Server, which will be responsible for backing up the workload and interacting with Azure. Since this resource is extensive and we cannot cover every configuration, we will focus on the Azure workload.

Azure Virtual Machine

Azure Backup provides an independent system to protect Azure virtual machine data from unexpected failures. All virtual machine backups are stored in the recovery vault with a built-in mechanism implemented for recovery points, fully managed by Azure. A backup process consists of two steps: taking a virtual machine snapshot and transferring it to the vault, without affecting production workload and with an optimized process for backing up more virtual machine disks in parallel. Backing up the Windows virtual machines uses VSS to take an app-consistent backup, but if that is not possible, it will take a file-consistent backup. For the Linux virtual machines, the default state for taking backups is file-consistent, while if app-consistent is needed, customized scripts from OS need to be written.

In the backup process, we can find three different snapshot consistency types:

- App-consistent: Capture memory and pending I/O operations to ensure consistency of application data before a backup is taken. In case of virtual machine recovery, there will be no data loss or corruption, and the virtual machine will boot up.

- File-consistent: Providing consistency by taking a backup of all files at the same time. When recovery is needed, virtual machines will boot up, and there will be no data loss or corruption. There is a possibility that the application needs additional restores to put data in a consistent state.

- Crash-consistent: Typically occurs if virtual machines are turned off or failed during the backup process. Only data that were already on disk at the backup time are backed up. In the case of virtual machine restore, additional disk checks will occur, and all in-memory data and I/O operations are lost.

Azure Backup fully supports most operating system versions, but there could be some specific Linux distributions, mainly used by virtual appliances, that are still not supported.

Azure File Share

Although Azure Files, as a service of the storage account, can have up to six copies of data globally distributed through the zones, that is a mechanism for data replication that ensures data access in case of Azure region or datacenter failure. If that data needs to be backed up, we must implement and configure Azure Backup for Azure Files. In just a few seconds, as shown in Figure 8-16, we can enable backup for Azure Files by selecting one or more file shares and setting a backup policy.

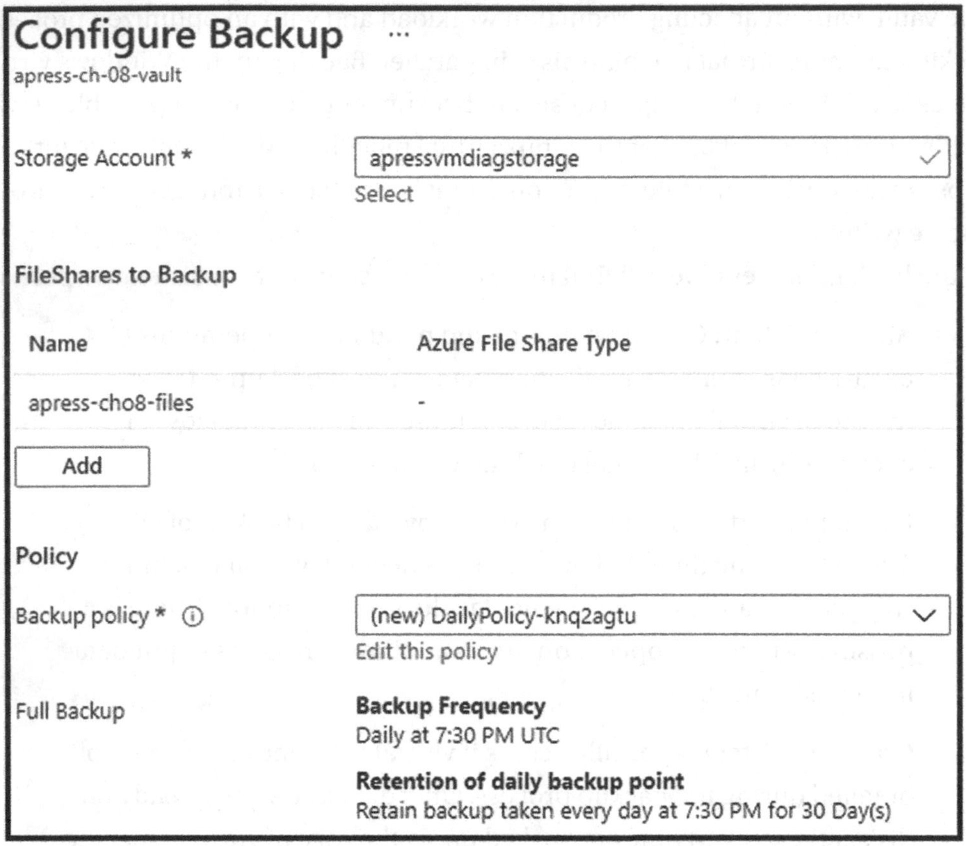

Configure Backup ···
apress-ch-08-vault

Storage Account *
> apressvmdiagstorage   ✓

Select

FileShares to Backup

Name	Azure File Share Type
apress-cho8-files	-

[Add]

Policy

Backup policy * ⓘ
> (new) DailyPolicy-knq2agtu   ∨

Edit this policy

Full Backup

Backup Frequency
Daily at 7:30 PM UTC

Retention of daily backup point
Retain backup taken every day at 7:30 PM for 30 Day(s)

Figure 8-16. *Enable backup for Azure Files by selecting one or more file shares and setting a backup policy*

Since both resources, the storage account and Azure Backup, are Azure services, a complete process occurs in the Azure backbone, and there is no adverse effect on data nor production workload.

SQL Server/SAP HANA in Azure VM

Backing up SQL Server hosted on an Azure virtual machine is a bit more challenging since there are active transactions that need to be handled adequately during backup. Although that is one of the essential tasks when we have SQL workload in the environment, that is not a "new feature" since SQL Server has built-in mechanics responsible for backing up SQL databases. That backup plan is trendy in many environments. One product is responsible for backups on the virtual machine level, and SQL Server is responsible for the database backups, using one of few potential built-in backup methods.

If we are running SQL Server in Azure VM and at the same time we are not familiar with the mechanisms for the SQL database backup, we can configure Azure Backup to do that for us. By selecting an option in Azure Backup to back up *SQL Server in Azure VM,"* the system will discover all virtual machines. When we check desired SQL Server(s), a backup agent on the virtual machine will start registration and database discovery. Once the discovery phase is completed and SQL Server is registered, we can start configuring a backup plan for SQL databases by adding databases and backup frequency, as shown in Figure 8-17. Additionally, we can enable auto-protect mode, which will by default include all SQL databases to the backup plan and every new database, so that we do not need to pay attention to this process.

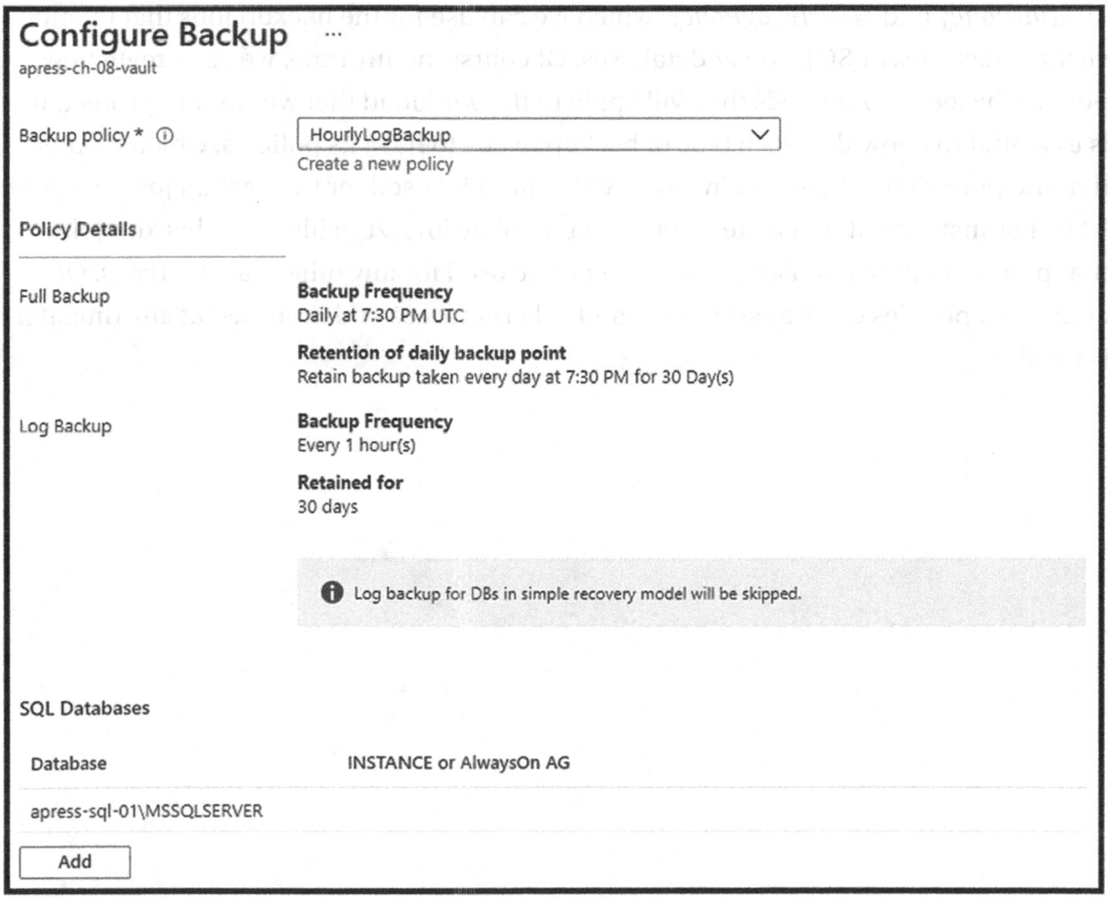

Figure 8-17. *Once the discovery phase is completed and SQL Server is registered, it is possible to begin configuring a backup plan for SQL databases by adding databases and backup frequency*

A backup policy for this type of backup is very flexible so that we can combine fill, differential, and transaction log backups based on needs. The lowest frequency for transaction log backup is 15 minutes, which is more than enough for most environments.

Once we become familiar with the SQL Server in Azure VM backup process and procedure, the same can be used to configure SAP HANA database backup if hosted on an Azure virtual machine.

Backup Policies

As we mentioned earlier, the backup policy is an inevitable part of configuring backup jobs, regardless of backup type. By default, we can find two backup policies, *DefaultPolicy* and *HourlyLogPolicy*, which we can use for the backup jobs that include virtual machines or SQL Server databases. Of course, at any time, we can create new policies based on our needs that will apply to the workload that we want to protect. It is essential to know that each type of backup needs to have its policies, which means that the policy for SQL Server in Azure VM cannot be used for the backup job for Azure VMs. For instance, if we create a new backup policy for Azure file share backup jobs, that policy, as shown in Figure 8-18, can not be used for any other backup types. Of course, all policies can be assigned to multiple resources and modified at any time if it is needed.

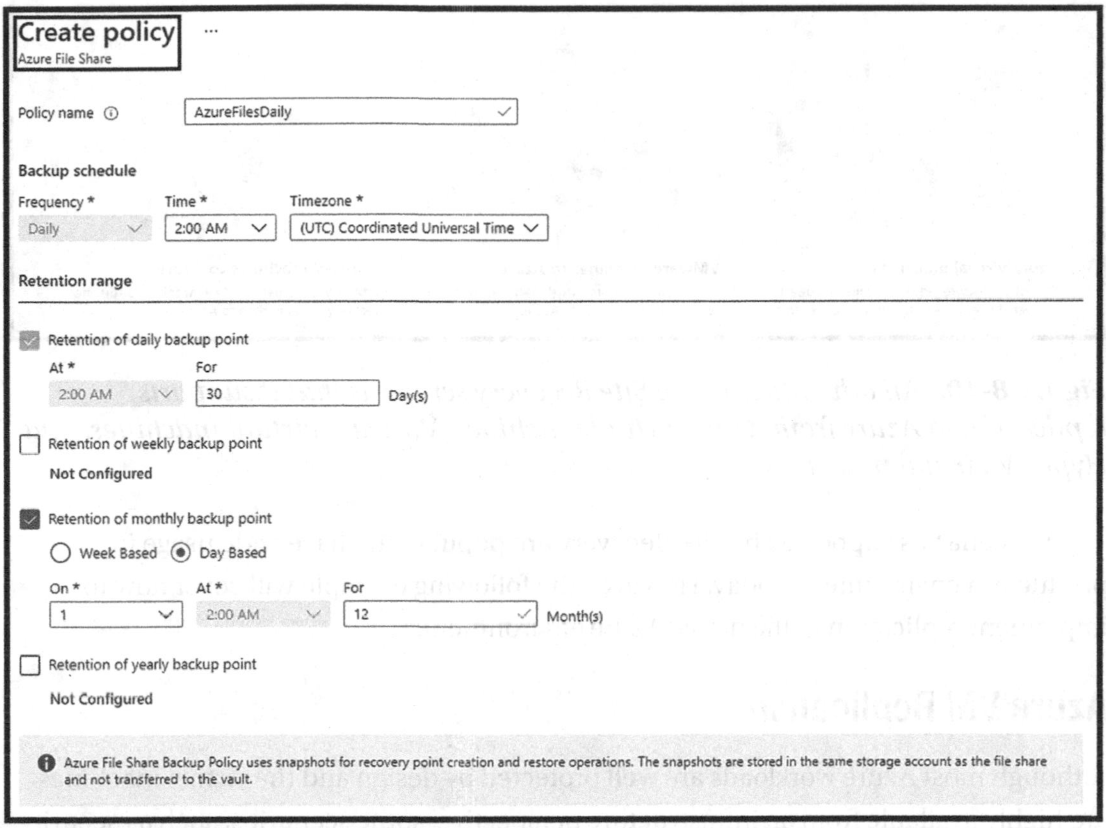

Create policy
Azure File Share

Policy name ⓘ   AzureFilesDaily   ✓

Backup schedule
Frequency *   Time *   Timezone *
Daily   ∨   2:00 AM   ∨   (UTC) Coordinated Universal Time ∨

Retention range

☑ Retention of daily backup point
  At *   For
  2:00 AM   ∨   30   Day(s)

☐ Retention of weekly backup point
  Not Configured

☑ Retention of monthly backup point
  ○ Week Based   ◉ Day Based
  On *   At *   For
  1   ∨   2:00 AM   ∨   12   ✓   Month(s)

☐ Retention of yearly backup point
  Not Configured

ⓘ Azure File Share Backup Policy uses snapshots for recovery point creation and restore operations. The snapshots are stored in the same storage account as the file share and not transferred to the vault.

Figure 8-18. *If a new backup policy for Azure file share backup jobs is created, it cannot be used for any other backup types*

Site Recovery

Another service that can help us to protect our data, but in a different way, is *Site Recovery*. Along with Backup, Site Recovery is a service under the Recovery Service vault resource, and it is responsible for creating a replica of virtual machines, also known as a disaster recovery site. A significant advantage of this service, as shown in Figure 8-19, is that it supports replication to Azure from Azure virtual machines, VMware virtual machines, and Hyper-V virtual machines. Also, this service is responsible if we want to migrate virtual machines to Azure from on-premises infrastructure.

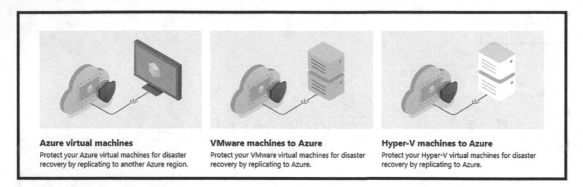

Figure 8-19. *An advantage of the Site Recovery service is that it supports replication to Azure from Azure virtual machines, VMware virtual machines, and Hyper-V virtual machines*

All scenarios supported by Site Recovery are popular and have wide usage in production environments today. However, the following example will cover how to implement replication in the native Azure environment.

Azure VM Replication

Although most Azure workloads are well protected by design and the virtual machines are highly available from an infrastructure perspective, some scenarios, such as security compliance or protection from a regional outage, require a disaster recovery site. If our workload is in Azure, implementation is not a complicated process because Site Recovery fully supports Azure workloads.

Once we decide to enable Azure virtual machine replication, the very first step is creating a new recovery vault in the region, which will be used as a destination for replicated virtual machines. When a Recovery Service vault is created, we can enable replication for Azure virtual machines by selecting source location, resource group, and virtual machines. The last step is the configuration of replication settings, which include defining a target location and specific resources on the target side, as shown in Figure 8-20.

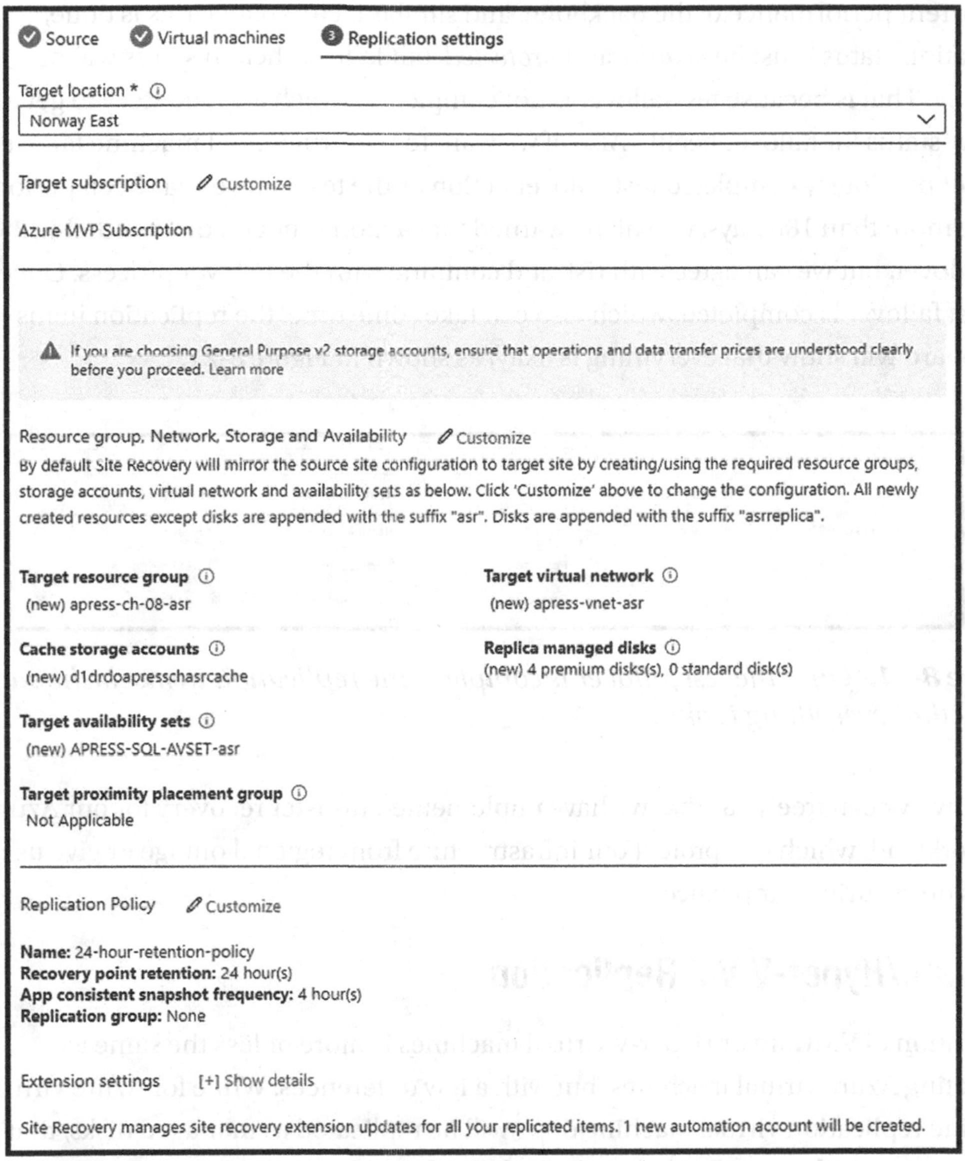

Figure 8-20. *The last step is the configuration of replication settings, which include defining a target location and specific resources on the target side*

Of course, many of these configuration parameters can be customized and configured based on our needs. For instance, the default replication policy for Site Recovery is configured with a retention of 24 hours, while the application-consistent snapshot frequency is 4 hours. Initial replication and synchronization will take some time to complete, and that depends on virtual machine size, distance to the destination, the current performance of the backbone, and similar factors. Once this is done, replication status must be *healthy* and *protected*, but failover health status will be *warning*. That is because test failover is not completed, which is mandatory to get a *healthy* status for failover health. Also, if we want to perform virtual machine failover without previously completed test failover action or the test failover has been performed before more than 180 days, we will be warned that action is not recommended without test failover, but we can agree with risk and continue with the failover process. Once the test failover is completed, which also can take some time, the replication items dashboard will show that everything is okay, as shown in Figure 8-21.

Name	Replication Health	Status	Active location	Failover Health	
apress-sql-01	✅ Healthy	Protected	North Europe	✅ Healthy	...
apress-win-01	✅ Healthy	Protected	North Europe	✅ Healthy	...
apress-linux-01	✅ Healthy	Protected	North Europe	✅ Healthy	...

Figure 8-21.   Once the test failover is complete, the replication items dashboard shows that everything is okay

Now, we can freely say that we have implemented disaster recovery for our Azure VM workload, which can protect our infrastructure from regional outage or give us more points on security compliance.

VMware/Hyper-V VM Replication

Replication of VMware or Hyper-V virtual machines is more or less the same as replicating Azure virtual machines, but with a few differences. While for Azure virtual machine replication virtual machine disks will be replicated as managed disks, that option comes with some limitations in the hybrid site recovery scenario. If we select that scenario for replication from on-premises to Azure and perform a failover at some time, there is no possibility of replicating virtual machines in a different direction, from Azure to on-premises infrastructure. That option is suitable only in scenarios where we want to migrate on-premises virtual machines to Azure and, after the completed failover, we do not need to replicate virtual machines back to the on-premises environment. If we want a fully functional disaster recovery, virtual machine disk replication needs to be configured to use a storage account instead of managed disks.

Another difference in infrastructure requirements for creating a replication of an on-premises VMware virtual machine to Azure is installing and configuring a configuration server. That virtual machine will host all site replication components needed for the successful implementation of disaster recovery. It consists of three components:

- Configuration server: Coordinates communications between on-premises and Azure and manages data replication.

- Process server: Works as a replication gateway. It optimizes, compresses, and encrypts received data before being sent to the Azure storage account.

- Master target server: Handles replication data during failback from Azure.

The easiest way to have this server up and running is to download a prepared template and import the template into VMware to create the VM. If we want to replicate Hyper-V virtual machines, we need to register a Hyper-V server to the Hyper-V site in Azure.

All of these configurations are very well explained through the process of configuring. All needed information, such as download links for VMware OVA template or agent for Hyper-V host registration, will be provided during the configuration process.

Failover and Recovery Plans

Although all of us would like to use only test failover periodically to check the health of replication, in reality, production failover will happen at some time. Once that is needed, Site Recovery allows us to fail over one or more of our replicated virtual machines in a few clicks. We just need to select what recovery point will be used, as shown in Figure 8-22, and replication will start. Recovery points that we can choose are

- Latest app-consistent: A period of creating an app-consistent snapshot is defined in replication settings and provides us with the ability to have app-consistent data in a replicated virtual machine.

- Latest processed (low RTO): Since the data replication is almost real time, received data are processed every 5 minutes. This recovery point will activate a replicated virtual machine with the latest processed data, which is more or less 5 minutes old.

211

- Latest (lower RPO): This recovery point will process all received data once the primary virtual machine is shut down. In theory, potential data loss is minimal, but recovery time is a bit longer since data need to be processed first.

- Custom: This allows us to select any processed snapshot from the last 24 hours, defined by a default policy.

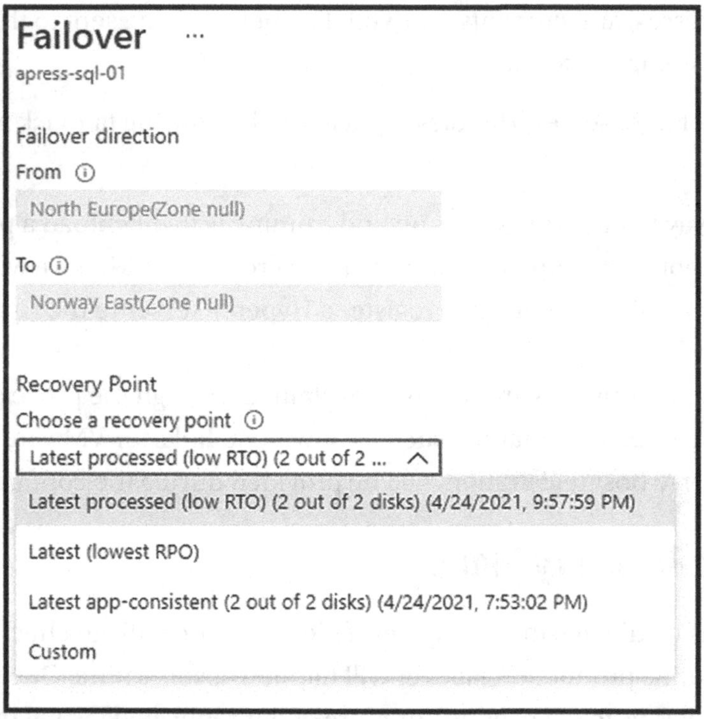

Figure 8-22. *Select the recovery point to be used*

In a scenario where we need to replicate more than one virtual machine simultaneously, such as clustered virtual machines or virtual machines in the Active Directory environment, we need to create a *Recovery Plan*. The Recovery Plan will group virtual machines that are selected, and these virtual machines cannot be replicated as a single anymore. Once the Recovery Plan is created, we can do initial failover for this plan in the same way as we do it for a single virtual machine, and the same recovery point options are available.

Once the failover is completed and we can confirm that everything is okay and there is no need to change the recovery point, we need to commit a failover action, and after that, the recovery point cannot be changed. After failover is committed, we need to re-protect virtual machines, which means that virtual machine replication will continue, but in a different direction.

Chapter Recap

In this chapter, we have learned the principles that we need to follow to monitor and protect Azure workloads. Although Azure Monitor allows us to deep-dive into the analytics of Azure resources, many of these resources are not fully covered in detail with needed metrics for detailed analysis. However, this service is constantly updating since all services need to be monitored well, and Microsoft wants to be in a good position against its competitors. Also, we have covered Azure Backup and Site Recovery and shown what can be backed up and how we can configure virtual machine replication, regardless of whether they are located in other Azure regions or on-premises environments.

In the next chapter, we will learn about Azure resources responsible for traffic management at a regional level or globally and how to choose the best one for our needs. We will learn what the differences between Load Balancer, Application Gateway, and Front Door are and when we need to use any of them.

## CHAPTER 9

Network Traffic Management

In the previous chapter, we talked about the essential components of each service – monitoring and logging. We also learned how to troubleshoot the network and how to protect our IaaS environment.

This chapter covers the services providing additional network security, high availability for PaaS services, and generally network traffic flow management. We will cover

- Network routing

- Azure Load Balancer

- Application Gateway

- Traffic Manager

- Azure Front Door

- Content Delivery Network (CDN)

Virtual Network Routing

Routing tables are automatically generated when we create a virtual network. They are created for each subnet. Within them, it is defined how the traffic flow within and from our virtual network will look like. On top of this, we can create "*user-defined routes*" and override the default ones that way.

© Vladimir Stefanovic and Milos Katinski 2021
V. Stefanovic and M. Katinski, *Pro Azure Administration and Automation*,
https://doi.org/10.1007/978-1-4842-7325-8_9

Default (System) Routes

In the following table, the default routes are listed:

Source	Address prefixes	Next hop type
Default	Unique to the virtual network	Virtual network
Default	0.0.0.0/0	Internet
Default	10.0.0.0/8	None
Default	192.168.0.0/16	None
Default	100.64.0.0/10	None

The first one routes traffic inside the virtual network, between address ranges assigned to the VNet. Traffic between subnets is automatically routed. The second one is called the *default route* (0.0.0.0/0) and is routing all traffic not defined by the VNet address space to the Internet. If the public destination belongs to one of the Azure services, the traffic will be routed over the Azure backbone network and not toward the Internet.

For the rest of the routes in the table, we can see that the next hop is *None*. That means that the traffic will be dropped. If we assign mentioned address prefixes to our virtual network, the next hop will be changed to *virtual network*. Depending on the services we add to our virtual network, Azure will assign additional default routes.

Source	Address prefixes	Next hop type	Subnet within the virtual network the route is added to
Default	Unique to the virtual network, for example, 10.10.0.0/24	VNet peering	All
Virtual network gateway	Prefixes advertised from on-premises via BGP or configured in the local network gateway	Virtual network gateway	All
Default	Multiple	VirtualNetwork ServiceEndpoint	Only the subnet a service endpoint is enabled for

Custom Routes

Besides having the default routes within our subnets, we can define our own. These are known as user-defined routes (UDRs). When we create a user-defined route, we can override an existing one (by specifying the same address prefix) or add additional ones. For a UDR to become active, we must assign it to a specific subnet. Only then it affects the default routing table. For example, we could create a UDR that would point 0.0.0.0/0 toward a network virtual appliance (e.g., Azure Firewall mentioned in Chapter 7).

This is also a moment when we must have in mind certain service limits. Per subscription, it is possible to create up to 200 user-defined route tables and 400 routes per table. Based on this, we must make a good design decision for our company's cloud environment. If we foresee that we will have more virtual networks (or subnets) than 200 and want to control routing, we must consider splitting our environment into multiple subscriptions (enterprise-scale landing zones architecture). We will now cover all possible options for creating user-defined routes (manually and using Infrastructure as Code).

Creating a Route Table

Azure Portal

From the home view in the portal, the first step is to click **+ Create a resource**, search for "route table," and click **Create**. We will notice that there is not much information needed to fill in for this service. We just need to provide the resource group name, where the routing table will be deployed, and a name. One more available parameter is "*Propagate gateway routes*" – in case the subnet we are preparing a UDR for is within the VNet where we have virtual network gateway connectivity toward on-premises, we can choose to prevent propagations of those routes. Once these parameters are filled, click **Review + create** and then **Create**. All these parameters are shown in Figure 9-1.

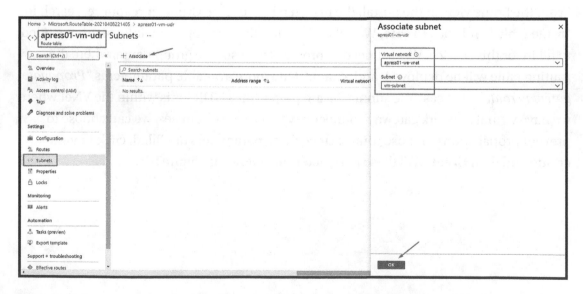

Figure 9-1. *Parameters for creating a route table*

The next step would be to associate the newly created UDR with the desired subnet, as shown in Figure 9-2.

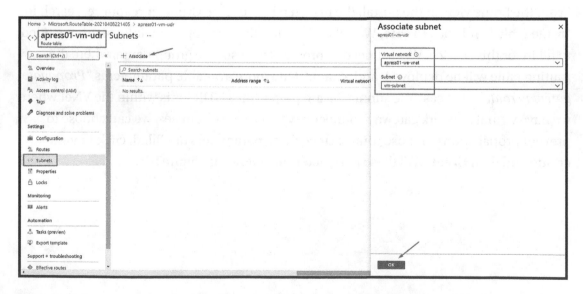

Figure 9-2. *Associate the newly created UDR with the desired subnet*

ARM Template, PowerShell, and Azure CLI

Since the deployment code could be pretty big, all ARM template, Azure PowerShell, and Azure CLI scripts are stored in the Apress GitHub account, available at the following URL:

https://github.com/Apress/pro-azure-admin-and-automation

Load Balancing

Azure offers multiple solutions for load balancing the traffic. They are all used in a certain way to optimize back-end resource use, minimize response time, and help us achieve high availability for our application. They can be categorized as global or regional and HTTP(S) or non-HTTP(S):

- Global ones can control traffic toward systems in different regions, while regional services are used to load balance traffic within one region.

- HTTP(S) services are considered Layer 7 types of balancers that can accept only HTTP(S) traffic. They are to be used mainly for web applications or other HTTP(s) endpoints. Non-HTTP(S) load balancers are recommended for non-web workloads.

Azure services that we will cover within this chapter are described in the following table.

Service	Global/regional	Recommended traffic
Azure Front Door	Global	HTTP(S)
Traffic Manager	Global	non-HTTP(S)
Application Gateway	Regional	HTTP(S)
Azure Load Balancer	Global	non-HTTP(S)

Microsoft offers guidance in Azure Portal to help us choose the best option for our solution. In *Search resources*, when we type *Load balancing*, we will be able to choose *Load balancing – help me choose* (as shown in Figure 9-3). This option is still in preview (at the time of writing this book), but I am satisfied with the functionality.

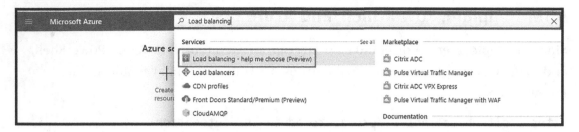

Figure 9-3. *In Search resources, type Load balancing, and choose Load balancing – help me choose*

The first question is to choose whether our application uses HTTP(S) or not. The next question is if the application is an Internet-facing one. Depending on the choice, the next possible question is if our application is deployed in multiple regions or not. Then we will have to answer if we need performance acceleration and if we want to use SSL offloading or application layer processing. The last possible question that we will come to is if our application is hosted on PaaS.

Answering some or all of these (depending on choices, we could have more or fewer questions), Azure will filter possible services for our solution with an additional explanation of the recommended one. Besides the tab for this kind of help, there is a *Service comparison* tab where we will see the four most important services with their options in a table so we could also decide based on them (Figure 9-4).

Help me choose Service comparison Tutorial	Application Gateway	Front Door	Load Balancer	Traffic Manager
	Optimize delivery from application server farms while increasing application security with web application firewall.	Scalable, security-enhanced delivery point for global, micro service-based web applications.	Balance inbound and outbound connections and requests to your applications or server endpoints.	Distribute traffic optimally to services across global Azure regions, while providing high availability and responsiveness.
	Create	Create	Create	Create
Supported protocols	HTTP, HTTPS, HTTP2	HTTP, HTTPS, HTTP2	TCP, UDP	Any
Private load balancing	✓		✓	
Global load balancing		✓		✓
Routing Policies	Round robin	Latency, priority, round robin, weighted round robin	Round robin	Geographical, latency, weighted, priority, subnet, multi-value
Supported environments	Azure, non-Azure cloud, on prem	Azure, non-Azure cloud, on prem	Azure	Azure, non-Azure cloud, on prem
Connection draining	✓			
Session affinity	✓	✓	✓	
Host and path based load balancing	✓	✓		
TLS offloading	✓	✓		
Site acceleration		✓		
Security	WAF, NSG	WAF	NSG	
Caching and compression		✓		

Figure 9-4. *The Service comparison tab shows the four most important services in a table*

Azure Load Balancer

Azure Load Balancer is a service that is functioning on layer 4 of the OSI model (Transport layer). It distributes inbound traffic from its front end to the back-end pool (Azure virtual machine or virtual machine scale set described in Chapter 4). Based on the use case, we can differentiate two scenarios:

1. Public Load Balancer: It provides us with an outbound connection for our VMs, by translating their internal private IP addresses to a public one. From the other side, it balances the traffic originating from the Internet toward our VMs.

2. Internal (Private) Load Balancer: It is used inside the virtual network when we need only private IPs at the front end.

Example for the case where we can use both types:

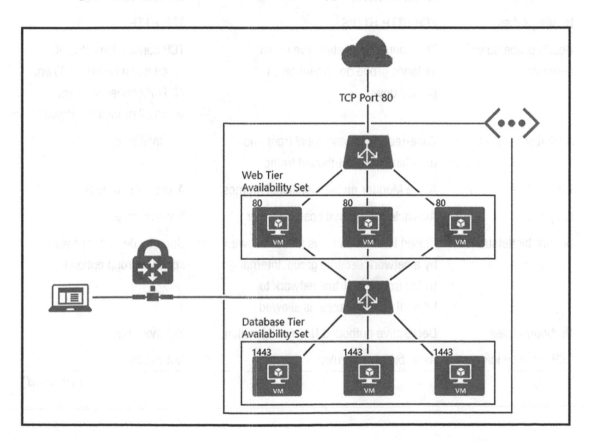

Figure 9-5. *Azure Load Balancer scenario where both types are used*

When it comes to pricing and the SKU of Load Balancer, there are two types:

1. Basic Load Balancer: This is a free option offered by Microsoft.

2. Standard Load Balancer: A service that is charged by the number of rules and data processed.

The following table shows all the differences between mentioned SKUs.

	Standard Load Balancer	Basic Load Balancer
Back-end pool size	Supports up to 1000 instances.	Supports up to 300 instances.
Back-end pool endpoints	Any virtual machines or virtual machine scale sets in a single virtual network.	Virtual machines in a single Availability Set or virtual machine scale set.
Health probes	TCP, HTTP, HTTPS.	TCP, HTTP.
Health probe down behavior	TCP connections stay alive on an instance probe down **and** on all probes down.	TCP connections stay alive on an instance probe down. All TCP connections end when all probes are down.
Availability Zones	Zone-redundant and zonal front ends for inbound and outbound traffic.	Not available.
Diagnostics	Azure Monitor multidimensional metrics.	Azure Monitor logs.
HA ports	Available for Internal Load Balancer.	Not available.
Secure by default	Closed to inbound flows unless allowed by a network security group. Internal traffic from the virtual network to Internal Load Balancer is allowed.	Open by default. Network security group optional.
Outbound rules	Declarative outbound NAT configuration.	Not available.
TCP reset on idle	Available on any rule.	Not available.

(continued)

	Standard Load Balancer	Basic Load Balancer
Multiple front ends	Inbound and outbound.	Inbound only.
Management operations	Most operations < 30 seconds.	60–90+ seconds typical.
SLA	99.99%.	Not available.

Source: https://docs.microsoft.com/en-us/azure/load-balancer/skus#skus

What we might point out from the table is that Standard Load Balancer is designed on a zero-trust model – it is closed for inbound traffic unless explicitly allowed via a network security group, and it offers high SLA serving two or more healthy virtual machine instances. The algorithm used by default for balancing the traffic is the five-tuple hash. That includes

- Source IP address

- Source port

- Destination IP address

- Destination port

- Protocol

Creating Azure Load Balancer

As it is offering more options, we will base our deployments on a Standard Load Balancer. Keep in mind that it is a paid service and that we should remove it after the exercise.

Azure Portal

When we click **+ Create a resource** and choose the *Networking* submenu, we will find *Load Balancer*. Click **Create**. On the next page, we need to populate Resource group, Location, and Name for the zone. If we are creating a Public type, we will have to create a new public IP address or choose an existing public IP address (as shown in Figure 9-6), and if we are creating an Internal one, we would have to choose a virtual network from which we would like to assign the IP to Load Balancer.

The process of deploying Load Balancer is speedy. By going to the deployed service, we will be able to set further options:

- Back-end pools

- Balancing rules

- Inbound NAT rules

- Outbound rules

Front-end IP configuration will be preset with the public IP we choose to create during the deployment process.

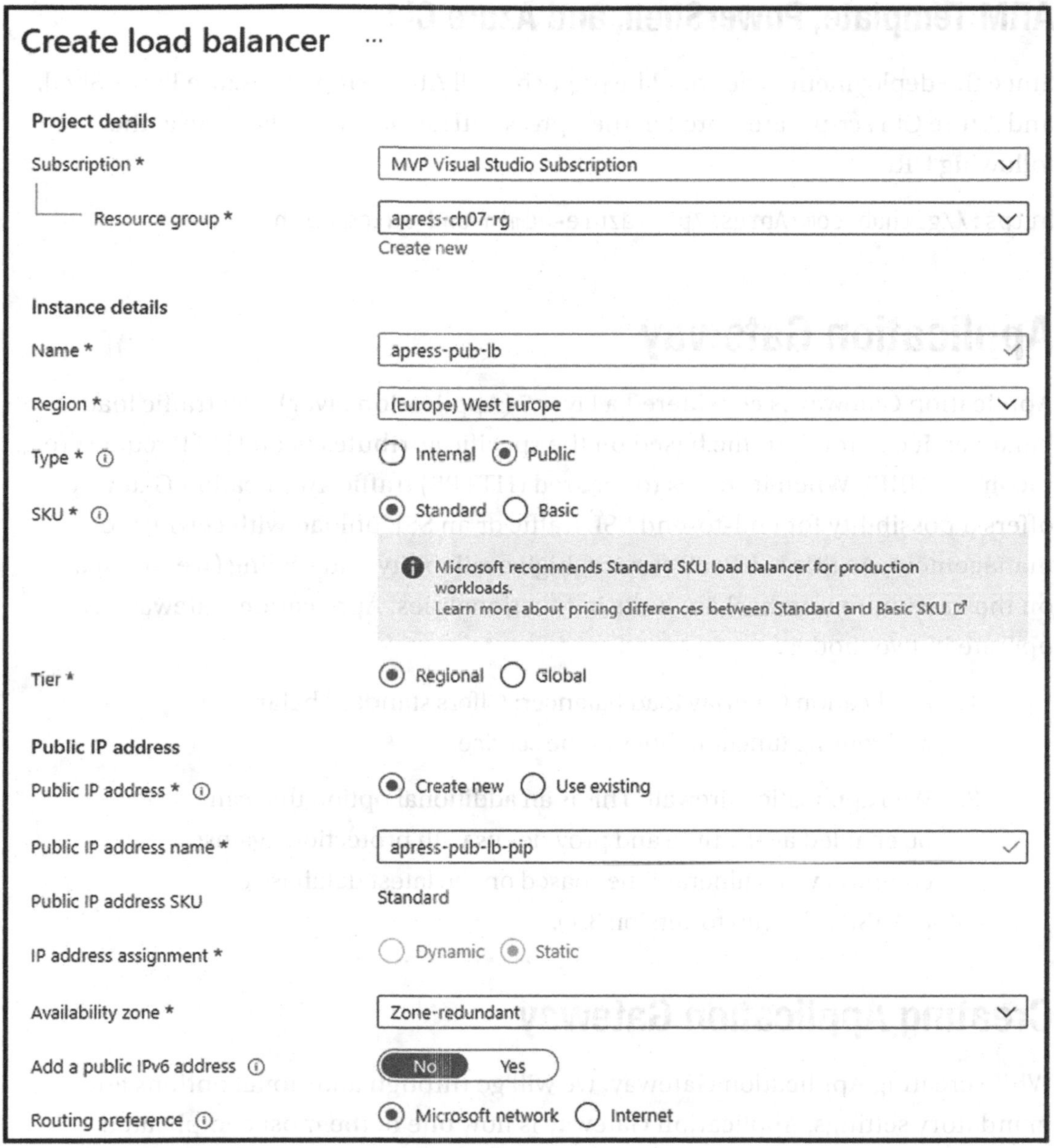

Create load balancer ···

Project details

Subscription *

MVP Visual Studio Subscription ⌄

Resource group *

apress-ch07-rg ⌄
Create new

Instance details

Name *

apress-pub-lb ✓

Region *

(Europe) West Europe ⌄

Type * ⓘ

◯ Internal ⦿ Public

SKU * ⓘ

⦿ Standard ◯ Basic

> ⓘ Microsoft recommends Standard SKU load balancer for production workloads.
> Learn more about pricing differences between Standard and Basic SKU ⎘

Tier *

⦿ Regional ◯ Global

Public IP address

Public IP address * ⓘ

⦿ Create new ◯ Use existing

Public IP address name *

apress-pub-lb-pip ✓

Public IP address SKU

Standard

IP address assignment *

◯ Dynamic ⦿ Static

Availability zone *

Zone-redundant ⌄

Add a public IPv6 address ⓘ

(No) Yes

Routing preference ⓘ

⦿ Microsoft network ◯ Internet

Figure 9-6. *When creating a Public type, it is necessary to create a new public IP address or choose an existing public IP address*

ARM Template, PowerShell, and Azure CLI

Since the deployment code could be pretty big, all ARM template, Azure PowerShell, and Azure CLI scripts are stored in the Apress GitHub account, available at the following URL:

```
https://github.com/Apress/pro-azure-admin-and-automation
```

Application Gateway

Application Gateway is considered a layer 7 (Application layer) web traffic load balancer. It can route traffic based on the specific attributes of an HTTP request (e.g., incoming URL). When it comes to secured (HTTPS) traffic, Application Gateway offers a possibility for end-to-end SSL traffic or an SSL offload with certificate management. As this is a PaaS service, high availability and scaling (we can decide on the maximum number) are built-in functionalities. Application Gateway can operate in two modes:

1. Application Gateway load balancer: Offers standard balancing and routing functionalities of the service.

2. Web application firewall: This is an additional option that can be enabled at any time and provides us with protection against common web vulnerabilities based on the latest database of OWASP rules (up to version 3.1).

Creating Application Gateway

While creating Application Gateway, we will go through additional options and mandatory settings. Application Gateway is now one of the most complicated services for deployment. There are many options and possible ways of setup. Some cannot be changed after the deployment, so we have to make a good plan at the start (deployment takes 20–40 minutes, so we will save much time if we make it right from the beginning).

Azure Portal

As with previous services, we can click **+ Create a resource** and type *Application Gateway*. Then, click **Create**. On the first screen (Figure 9-7), we must populate some standard parameters like **Resource group**, **Name**, **Region**, and **Tier**.

From this point, things are specific to Application Gateway. We need to decide if we want to use auto-scaling and, if yes, the minimum and the maximum number of instances. This option is great when we want the high traffic load on our website to be automatically handled by Azure. However, it also could cause a high bill if we do not monitor the traffic that overloads our Application Gateway (e.g., DDOS attack can also initiate auto-scaling).

Support for HTTP2 is there, but only for traffic from the client to Application Gateway. The traffic toward the back-end pool is still using HTTP 1.1. We need to assign a dedicated virtual network subnet for Application Gateway. Addresses from this subnet will be used for Application Gateway instances that are running. This means that the size of the subnet directly depends on the maximum number of allowed auto-scaling instances.

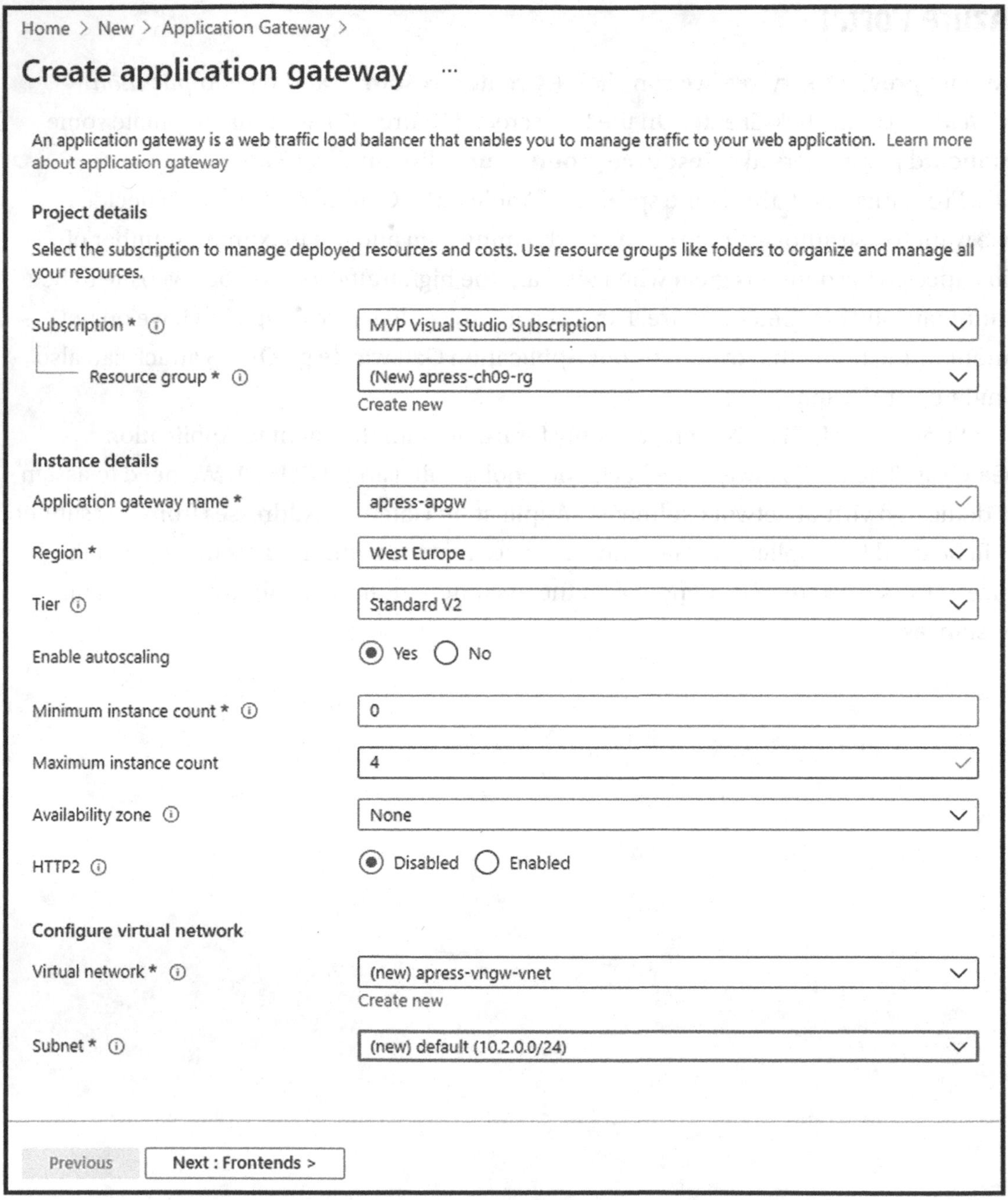

Home > New > Application Gateway >

Create application gateway   ···

An application gateway is a web traffic load balancer that enables you to manage traffic to your web application. Learn more about application gateway

Project details

Select the subscription to manage deployed resources and costs. Use resource groups like folders to organize and manage all your resources.

Subscription * ⓘ	MVP Visual Studio Subscription ⌄
⌐ Resource group * ⓘ	(New) apress-ch09-rg ⌄
	Create new

Instance details

Application gateway name *	apress-apgw ✓
Region *	West Europe ⌄
Tier ⓘ	Standard V2 ⌄
Enable autoscaling	● Yes ○ No
Minimum instance count * ⓘ	0
Maximum instance count	4 ✓
Availability zone ⓘ	None ⌄
HTTP2 ⓘ	● Disabled ○ Enabled

Configure virtual network

Virtual network * ⓘ	(new) apress-vngw-vnet ⌄
	Create new
Subnet * ⓘ	(new) default (10.2.0.0/24) ⌄

Previous	**Next : Frontends >**

Figure 9-7. *Populate standard parameters like **Resource group**, **Name**, **Region**, and **Tier***

The next step is to configure the front end of Application Gateway (Figure 9-8). This is the address that will be accessible to the clients. Like Azure Load Balancer, we can set Application Gateway to have a public or private front end (or both in this case).

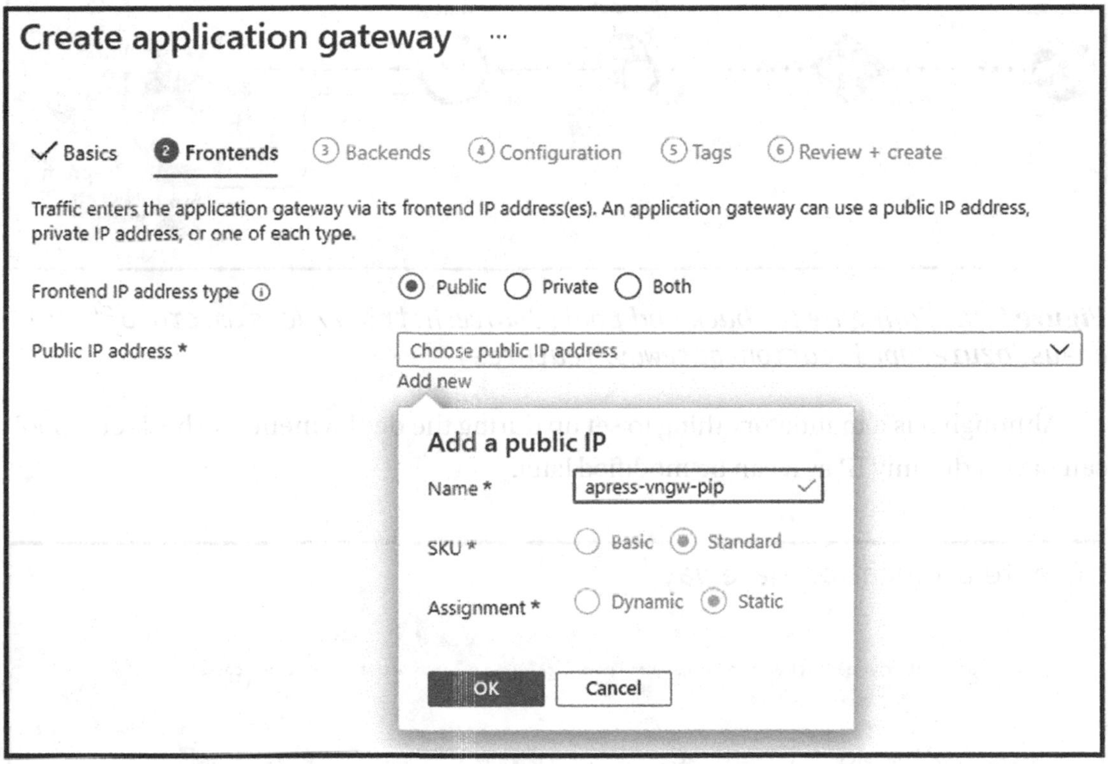

Figure 9-8. *Configure the front end of Application Gateway*

Now we must configure the back-end pool (Figure 9-10). As we can see, Application Gateway supports more options than Azure Load Balancer. We can choose virtual machines, virtual machine scale sets, and app services, plain IPs, or service FQDNs. The possibility to set IP or FQDN as a back-end target gives us an option to set not only Azure services as a back-end target but also some that can reside in our on-premises environment (Figure 9-9).

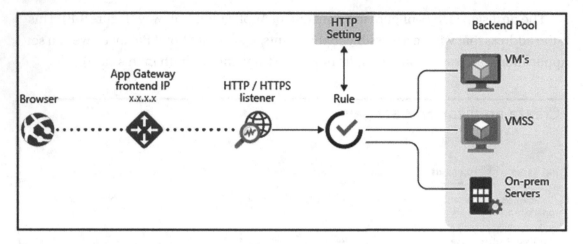

Figure 9-9. *Configure the back-end pool.(Source: https://docs.microsoft.com/ en-us/azure/application-gateway/features)*

Although it is a mandatory thing to set up during the deployment, the back-end pool can have a dummy IP as it can be modified later.

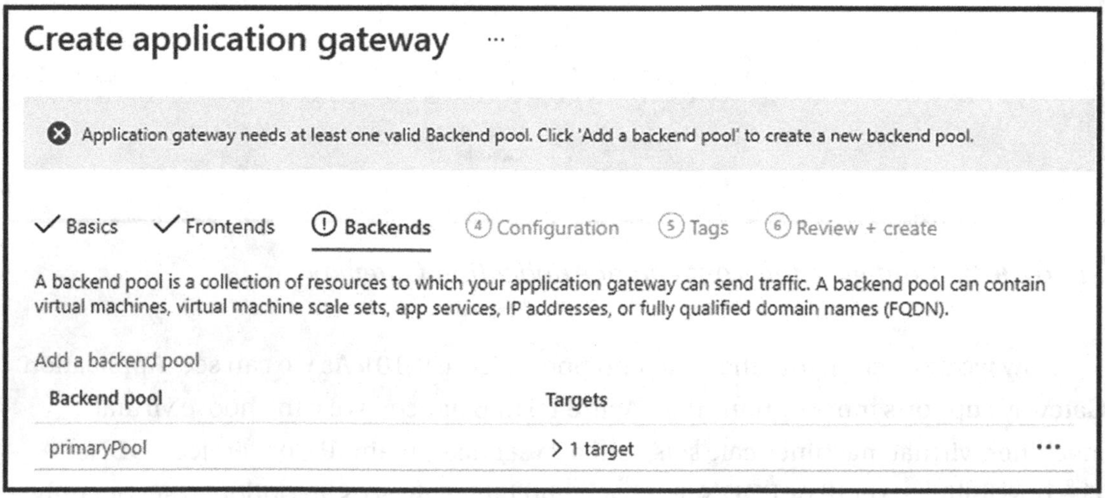

Create application gateway ...

❌ Application gateway needs at least one valid Backend pool. Click 'Add a backend pool' to create a new backend pool.

✓ Basics   ✓ Frontends   ⓘ **Backends**   ④ Configuration   ⑤ Tags   ⑥ Review + create

A backend pool is a collection of resources to which your application gateway can send traffic. A backend pool can contain virtual machines, virtual machine scale sets, app services, IP addresses, or fully qualified domain names (FQDN).

Add a backend pool

Backend pool	Targets
primaryPool	› 1 target ...

Figure 9-10. *Application Gateway supports more options than Azure Load Balancer*

The next option to set is a routing rule (Figure 9-11). Here, things become a bit complicated, as there are many options to configure:

1. Listener: This is a part of Application Gateway that serves client requests (it "listens" for queries on front-end IP). It can use the HTTP or HTTPS protocol. The port used for listener does not have to be 80 or 443, but keep in mind that we can have only one HTTP using port 80 (multiple HTTPS using 443 is allowed).

    a. Basic listener: It is used when we host a single site behind Application Gateway.

    b. Multi-site listener: We should use this option in case we host more web applications or have multiple subdomains. In that case, we define the hostname for the listener.

If we are configuring the HTTPS listener, we must upload a pfx certificate file (domain name must match the hostname we specify or the one the back-end target serves). Error pages can be customized, but only for 502 and 403 errors. We can, for example, use the Static website option in Azure Blob storage for hosting custom error pages.

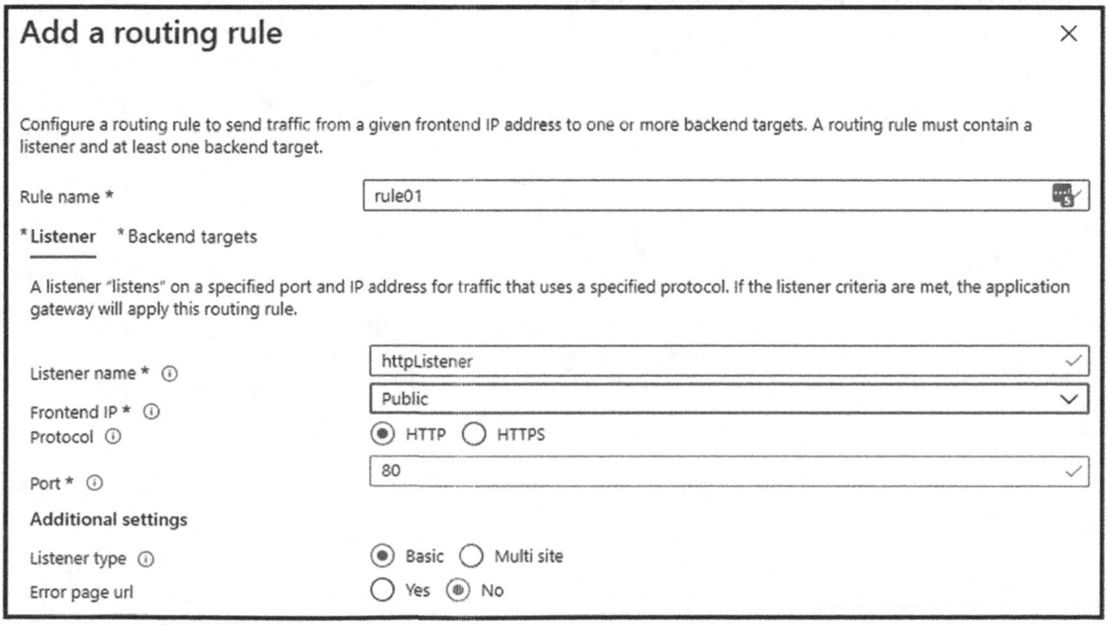

Add a routing rule   ✕

Configure a routing rule to send traffic from a given frontend IP address to one or more backend targets. A routing rule must contain a listener and at least one backend target.

Rule name * | rule01 |

*Listener   *Backend targets

A listener "listens" on a specified port and IP address for traffic that uses a specified protocol. If the listener criteria are met, the application gateway will apply this routing rule.

Listener name * ⓘ | httpListener   ✓ |
Frontend IP * ⓘ | Public   ⌄ |
Protocol ⓘ   ⦿ HTTP ◯ HTTPS
Port * ⓘ | 80   ✓ |

Additional settings

Listener type ⓘ   ⦿ Basic ◯ Multi site
Error page url   ◯ Yes ⦿ No

Figure 9-11. Set a routing rule

The second part of setting the routing rule is to choose a back-end target for the specified listener and to set HTTP settings (Figures 9-12 and 9-13). Besides choosing the back-end target we previously created, we can also use the redirection option. So, for example, if we create the listener on port 80, we may choose to redirect traffic to the listener that uses port 443 (that way, we force secured traffic toward our application).

HTTP setting is a back-end-oriented one. There we set the port and the protocol that our application listens to. This is the moment when we are deciding whether to use end-to-end SSL or to offload the SSL on Application Gateway. If we are using HTTPS, we must upload a CER certificate. We would recommend creating a certificate that consists of a complete chain (Root ➤ Intermediate ➤ Application) because some of the web servers have that requirement in order to return the correct response to Application Gateway. Otherwise, the back end might end up in an unhealthy state.

Probes are an Application Gateway way to check the health of the back end. If we do not specify our check (custom probe), the default one will be used – HTTP GET request toward the IP or FQDN of the back-end pool. Custom probes give us more control over how we want to determine if our application is healthy. We can specify the protocol, hostname, path, and port we want to check.

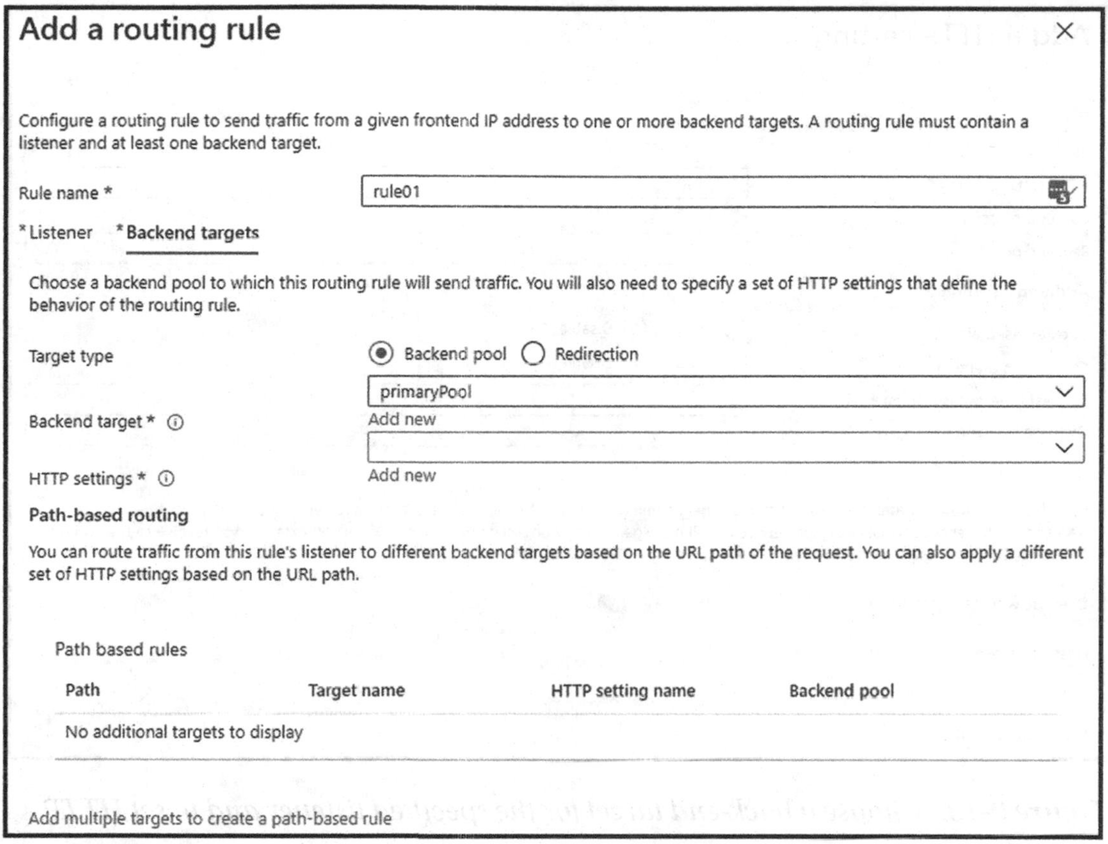

Add a routing rule   ✕

Configure a routing rule to send traffic from a given frontend IP address to one or more backend targets. A routing rule must contain a listener and at least one backend target.

Rule name * | rule01 |

*Listener   *Backend targets

Choose a backend pool to which this routing rule will send traffic. You will also need to specify a set of HTTP settings that define the behavior of the routing rule.

Target type   ◉ Backend pool ○ Redirection

                               | primaryPool   ∨ |
Backend target * ⓘ   Add new
                               | ∨ |
HTTP settings * ⓘ   Add new

Path-based routing

You can route traffic from this rule's listener to different backend targets based on the URL path of the request. You can also apply a different set of HTTP settings based on the URL path.

Path based rules

Path	Target name	HTTP setting name	Backend pool
No additional targets to display			

Add multiple targets to create a path-based rule

Figure 9-12. *Choose a back-end target for the specified listener*

233

```
Add a HTTP setting                                                    ✕

← Discard changes and go back to routing rules

HTTP settings name *            │ httpSettings01                        ✓│
Backend protocol                ● HTTP  ○ HTTPS
Backend port *                  │ 80                                    ✓│

Additional settings

Cookie-based affinity ⓘ         ○ Enable  ● Disable
Connection draining ⓘ           ○ Enable  ● Disable
Request time-out (seconds) * ⓘ  │ 20                                    ✓│
Override backend path ⓘ         │                                       ✓│

Host name

By default, Application Gateway does not change the incoming HTTP host header from the client and sends the header unaltered to the
backend. Multi-tenant services like App service or API management rely on a specific host header or SNI extension to resolve to the correct
endpoint. Change these settings to overwrite the incoming HTTP host header.

Override with new host name     ( Yes    No )
                                ○ Pick host name from backend target
Host name override              ● Override with specific domain name
                                  e.g. contoso.com
Create custom probes            ( Yes    No )
```

Figure 9-13. *Choose a back-end target for the specified listener and to set HTTP settings*

Deployment of Application Gateway requires a lot of preparations and a good design decision. Nevertheless, once deployed and configured, it offers us a great service. Now that we have deployed Application Gateway, let us tweak a few more things about security. On the *Settings – Listener tab*, we will see that the default minimum protocol version used is set to TLSv1.0 and that all available cipher suites are enabled. By security recommended practice, these settings need to be changed. It is possible to customize mentioned options fully. TLS should be set to version 1.2, and cipher suites to be used are

- TLS_ECDHE_RSA_WITH_AES_256_CBC_SHA384

- TLS_ECDHE_RSA_WITH_AES_128_GCM_SHA256

- TLS_ECDHE_RSA_WITH_AES_128_CBC_SHA256

- TLS_ECDHE_RSA_WITH_AES_256_GCM_SHA384

ARM Template, PowerShell, and Azure CLI

Since the deployment code could be pretty big, all ARM template, Azure PowerShell, and Azure CLI scripts are stored in the Apress GitHub account, available at the following URL:

`https://github.com/Apress/pro-azure-admin-and-automation`

Traffic Manager

Azure Traffic Manager is used for controlling incoming DNS requests toward our public-facing applications based on the routing method (profile) we choose. There are six available options for routing:

- Priority: It is used when we choose to set one service endpoint as a primary one. In this case, we can have multiple backup endpoints.

- Performance: In this case, routing will choose the endpoint with the lowest latency from the end user.

- Geographic: Based on the origin of the DNS queries, we can point the users to a specific endpoint.

- Weighted round-robin: We can set weight on endpoints based on which traffic will be routed. If we set the same value, traffic will be evenly distributed.

- Subnet: Based on the request source IP, we can set which endpoint to be routed.

- Multi-value: This option can be used only when the endpoint is set with IPv4 or IPv6 addresses. On the incoming request, all healthy endpoints will respond.

With Traffic Manager, we can increase our application availability as it offers health monitoring of endpoints and automated failover in case the endpoint is not reachable. With specific routing options (performance), it can improve our application responsiveness. Traffic Manager gives us an option to use hybrid application deployment as it can have non-Azure endpoints set in the configuration. This means that we can, with no pain, move our application from on-premises into cloud iterations.

We can start with creating the one that we have on-prem, also in Azure, and by putting Traffic Manager in front, we can test an app before we decide to decommission the on-prem one. The subnet routing method can be advantageous in this situation.

One more great option in using Traffic Manager is that we are not limited to only one routing profile, but we could set *nested profiles* to get the best out of different types. When we create a routing profile, we define the method we want to use. A great option is that we can change the method at any time, with no downtime. The back-end transition time of the change is approximately 60 seconds. An important thing to know is that after successful DNS resolution (Traffic Manager returns endpoint IP to the end user), a connection from the end user is established directly to the selected endpoint and not through Traffic Manager.

Traffic Manager can use three types of endpoints:

- Azure endpoints

  - PaaS services

  - Web Apps

  - Web app slots

  - Public IP resources (must have DNS name assigned on the IP)

- External endpoints

- Nested endpoints

Within one profile, we can have a mix of endpoint types. Endpoint monitoring is an essential part of the Traffic Manager configuration. There we need to choose

- Protocol

  - HTTP/HTTPS: Probing agent sends the GET request toward the endpoint.

  - TCP: TCP connection is created using the specified port.

- Port: Used for the connection request.

- Path: Only used with the HTTP/HTTPS protocol – the page from which we require an OK response.

- Custom header settings

- Expected status code ranges: We can specify more than the default 200 as acceptable app responses.

- Probing interval: Time that defines how often the probing agent sends a request to the endpoint.

- Tolerated number of failures

- Probe timeout: The value of this property must be lower than the probing interval one.

Creating Traffic Manager

In the case of Traffic Manager, different deployment options come with different base results. We will describe it in detail.

Azure Portal

If we decide to use Azure Portal to perform this operation, the first step is to click + **Create a resource**, search for "Traffic Manager profile" in the *Marketplace*, and click **Create**. In this case, we have only a few things to populate to deploy the base profile with no additional settings (Figure 9-14). Only after the initial deployment can we configure endpoints and other needed options.

Figure 9-14. *Populate to deploy the base profile with no additional settings (Figure 9-14)*

ARM Template, PowerShell, and Azure CLI

Since the deployment code could be pretty big, all ARM template, Azure PowerShell, and Azure CLI scripts are stored in the Apress GitHub account, available at the following URL:

```
https://github.com/Apress/pro-azure-admin-and-automation
```

Azure Front Door

Azure Front Door is a global service that operates on layer 7. It uses Microsoft's global network, thus improving global connectivity toward our Internet-facing application, and (with new versions) is considered a modern Content Delivery Network service. As previously described for Traffic Manager, Azure Front Door can also use different routing policy types:

- Latency

- Priority

- Weighted round-robin

- Session affinity

As it is a global service, it can continue to operate even if a complete Azure region is down. Like Application Gateway, we can use SSL offloading and enable a web application firewall. Things specific to Azure Front Door are that we can set geo-filtering policies and caching options. It has built-in DDOS protection (the basic tier is free). It supports three different SKUs:

- Basic SKU (created as Azure Front Door)

- Standard SKU (created under Azure Front Door Standard/Premium (Preview)):

  - Content delivery optimized

  - Offering both static and dynamic content acceleration

  - Global load balancing

  - SSL offloading

  - Domain and certificate management

  - Enhanced traffic analytics

  - Basic security capabilities

- Premium SKU (created under Azure Front Door Standard/Premium (Preview)) (additional options):

  - Extensive security capabilities across WAF

  - BOT protection

  - Private link support

  - Integration with Microsoft threat intelligence and security analytics

Azure Front Door is a complex service that offers many different settings and customizations, with which we can secure high availability, responsiveness, and security for our application. From the Premium SKU, we would like to single out one option, and that is private link support. When enabled, it allows us to securely connect using a private link endpoint to Internal Load Balancer, a storage account, or a web app. In each case, a connection must be approved on the mentioned service's side.

Creating Azure Front Door

We might notice that under SKUs, we have mentioned two different things:

- Azure Front Door *(*/providers/Microsoft.Network/frontdoors/*)*

- Azure Front Door Standard/Premium (Preview) *(*/providers/ Microsoft.Cdn/profiles/*)*

With new options available, Microsoft decided to move Front Door under a different provider, which might be a bit confusing at the start. The thing is that the second one is still in *Preview mode* and, therefore, not considered to be used in production environments. We will focus on Azure Front Door, and while creating it, we will go through mandatory settings. There are many options and possible ways of setup, so it must be explored and planned well for our needs.

Azure Portal

We click + **Create a resource**, search for "front door," and click **Create**. On the next page, we need to populate Resource Group for the deployment. After that, there is an excellent Configuration overview that guides us in setting specific parts of the service (Figure 9-15):

- Front ends

- Back-end pools

- Routing rules

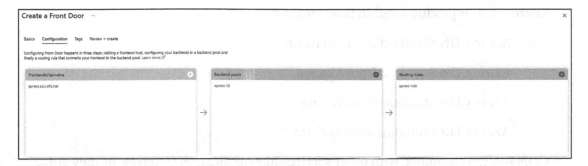

Figure 9-15. *Configuration overview offers guidance in setting specific parts of the service*

Once deployed, we can access the same Configuration overview from the *Front Door designer* settings. An important thing to mention is that not all options can be set through the portal. Geo-filtering policy and web application firewall policy must be configured via PowerShell or AzCli.

ARM Template, PowerShell, and Azure CLI

Since the deployment code could be pretty big, all ARM template, Azure PowerShell, and Azure CLI scripts are stored in the Apress GitHub account, available at the following URL:

APRESS GITHUB REPOSITORY URL

Content Delivery Network (CDN)

CDN is a global service specialized in helping us in reducing load times of our application, saving bandwidth by caching content, and accelerating other content by using network and routing optimizations. The main features of the service are

- Dynamic site acceleration

- CDN caching rules

- HTTPS custom domain support

- Azure diagnostic logs

- File compression

- Geo-filtering

There are four products within this category:

- Azure CDN Standard from Microsoft

- Azure CDN Standard from Akamai

- Azure CDN Standard from Verizon

- Azure CDN Premium from Verizon

CDN is often combined with other services like Application Gateway, as they are offering some different and valuable functionalities. If we would like to protect access toward our application fully, we could filter incoming traffic based on the IP segment of the CDN. For Akamai and Verizon, this can be obtained via API calls (e.g., Akamai might change public IPs of some servers once in a month), and for Microsoft, it is documented (IPv4 IP space used is 147.243.0.0/16). We would then put these ranges as a source in the *Incoming NSG rule*. If we choose to use Azure CDN from Microsoft, we additionally get Azure basic DDOS protection. Other products have their DDOS protection systems.

Creating Content Delivery Network

The deployment of CDN consists of two parts – profile and endpoint. No matter which product we choose, the procedure is the same.

Azure Portal

For deploying CDN via the portal, the first step is to click **+ Create a resource**, search for "CDN" in the *Marketplace*, and click **Create**. Besides defining *Resource group* and *Name* for the service, we must choose a pricing tier (Figure 9-16). Here we would strongly recommend to explore the *View full pricing details* option to get familiar with the differences between products. The mentioned key features are identical, but some specifics might guide us to choose one over the other.

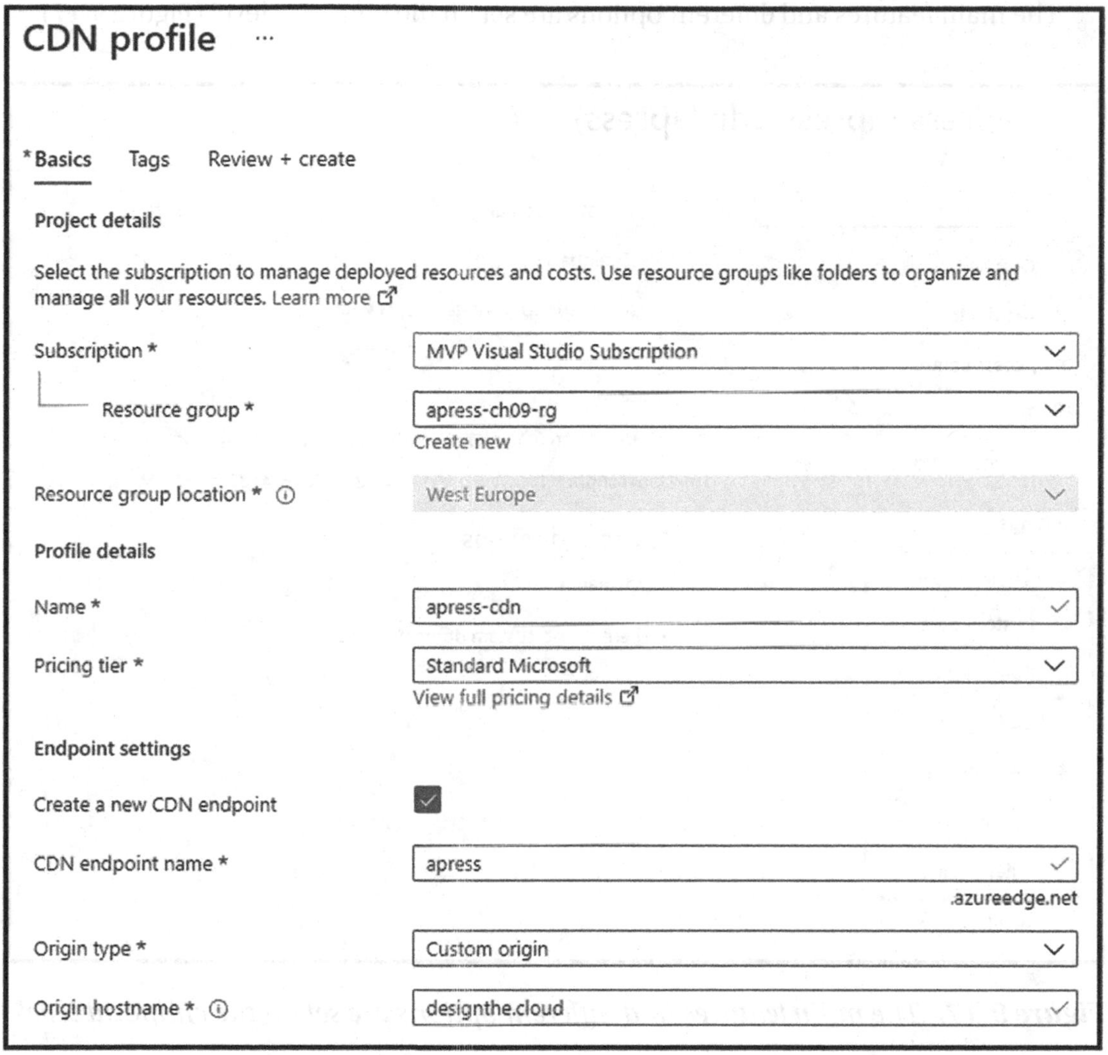

CDN profile   ···

*Basics   Tags   Review + create

Project details

Select the subscription to manage deployed resources and costs. Use resource groups like folders to organize and manage all your resources. Learn more ☐

| Subscription * | MVP Visual Studio Subscription | ⌄ |

| Resource group * | apress-ch09-rg | ⌄ |

Create new

| Resource group location * ⓘ | West Europe | ⌄ |

Profile details

| Name * | apress-cdn | ✓ |

| Pricing tier * | Standard Microsoft | ⌄ |

View full pricing details ☐

Endpoint settings

| Create a new CDN endpoint | ☑ |

| CDN endpoint name * | apress | ✓ |

.azureedge.net

| Origin type * | Custom origin | ⌄ |

| Origin hostname * ⓘ | designthe.cloud | ✓ |

Figure 9-16. *Choose a pricing tier*

The main features and different options are set on the endpoint level (Figure 9-17).

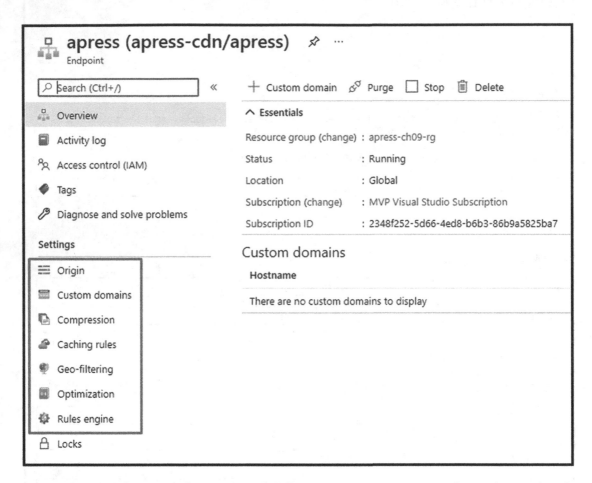

Figure 9-17.   *The main features and different options are set on the endpoint level*

ARM Template, PowerShell, and Azure CLI

Since the deployment code could be pretty big, all ARM template, Azure PowerShell, and Azure CLI scripts are stored in the Apress GitHub account, available at the following URL:

https://github.com/Apress/pro-azure-admin-and-automation

Chapter Recap

In this chapter, we have learned more about services that can be used in front of our applications – to use load balancing and achieve high availability and high responsiveness.

In the next chapter, we will learn more about what Azure offers "out of the box" and what we need to do to gain more out of it.

CHAPTER 10

Azure Security and Compliance

In the previous chapter, we talked about the services that offer more security and high availability by "standing" between clients and our applications.

This chapter covers the core of Azure infrastructure – Azure AD. We will learn what Azure has to offer for securing identity and our IaaS/PaaS environments. We will cover

- Azure AD
- RBAC
- Multi-factor authentication (MFA)
- Identity Protection
- Azure Security Center
- Azure Policy

Azure AD

There is no better and simpler definition than the one Microsoft provided – "Azure Active Directory (Azure AD) is a multi-tenant, cloud-based identity and access management service." Our users get authenticated with Azure AD not just when accessing Azure Portal but also when using Microsoft 365 applications or any other SaaS application.

Azure AD has integrated tools that help us to protect user identities and to achieve specific governance requirements. An important thing to mention is that Azure AD has different licensing tiers:

- Free
- Office 365 Apps

247

- Premium P1

- Premium P2

An excellent comparison overview is made on this link – `https://azure.microsoft.`
`com/en-us/pricing/details/active-directory/`. Based on the needs and the level of
protection we want to achieve, we should move from the Free tier toward premium ones.
There is a 30-day Premium Trial that can be used for testing different functionalities.

Microsoft is constantly working on improving the offer of Azure AD and the level
of security that can be set. As the complete setup of Azure AD (with all protections,
policies, etc.) is very complex, Microsoft has offered an Azure Security Benchmark –
`https://docs.microsoft.com/en-us/security/benchmark/azure/`. This is a set
of Security Controls that will guide us in setting up the different parts of AAD in the
recommended way.

An option that can help us start securely using Azure AD is *Enable Security defaults*.
With just one click, we can safely start our journey (Figure 10-1).

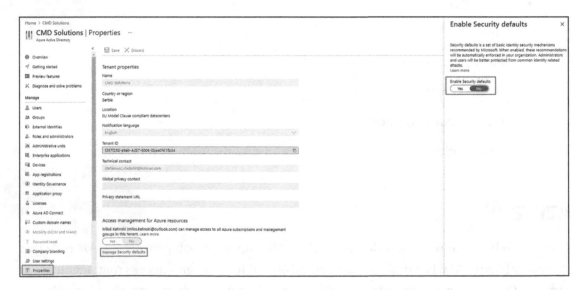

Figure 10-1. *Enable Security defaults is an option that can help users start
securely using Azure AD*

By enabling this option, we will start using preconfigured security settings:

- Require MFA registration for all users.

- Require MFA to be used for all users when necessary.

- Require MFA to be used by administrators (always).

- Block legacy authentication protocols.

- Protect privileged activities (e.g., accessing Azure Portal).

Role-Based Access Control (RBAC)

Azure role-based access control is a system that authorizes Azure AD identities to access specific resources and defines the level of access they can have.

Azure RBAC is based on the Azure roles. Three elements that make the role assignment are

- Security principal: An object that represents a *user, group, service principal, or managed identity*. We assign roles to one of them.

- Role definition: It represents the collection of permissions (e.g., read, write, delete). There are two base types of roles: *built-in and custom ones.*

- Scope: This defines the level on which we will assign the role to a security principal. There are four levels on which we can define a scope: *Management group, Subscription, Resource group, Resource.*

Roles assigned are inherited on lower levels, which means that if we assign the user a role on the subscription level, the user will have the same rights across all resource groups. If there is an overlap of multiple role assignments, the result will be the sum of all (if one assignment gives us higher rights over specific resources than the other, those higher rights will be applied – Figure 10-2).

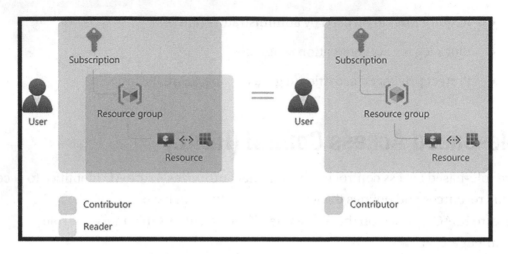

Figure 10-2. *If one assignment gives us higher rights over specific resources than the other, those higher rights will be applied (courtesy of Microsoft).(Image source:* `https://docs.microsoft.com/en-us/azure/role-based-access-control/` `overview#multiple-role-assignments`*)*

The flow of the role assignment process is as shown in Figure 10-3.

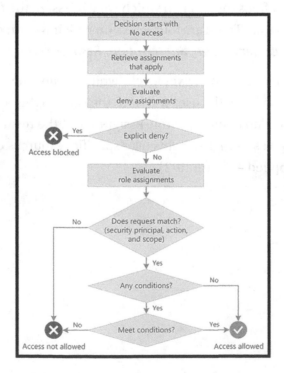

Figure 10-3. *The flow of the role assignment process*

To provide more fine-grained access control, Microsoft has introduced the preview of ABAC – attribute-based access control. Currently, the only built-in roles that can be edited and used with ABAC are

- Storage Blob Data Contributor

- Storage Blob Data Owner

- Storage Blob Data Reader

For example, ABAC could provide access based on the storage account tag value. Azure RBAC includes more than 70 built-in roles, but four can be considered base ones:

- Owner: Has full access to all resources under the assigned scope and can delegate access

- Contributor: Can create and manage resources but cannot grant access to others

- Reader: Has only the option to view resources

- User Access Administrator: Manages user access to resources in Azure

The rest of the roles are resource-based ones (e.g., Virtual Machine Contributor).

Assigning a Role to a Security Principal

Like most other services, we can assign roles by using Azure Portal, Azure PowerShell, Azure CLI, and ARM templates. There is a limit on the number of roles that can be assigned: 500 on a management group scope and 2000 on a subscription (and lower) scope.

Azure Portal

To be able to assign a role, there is a prerequisite that our user has *Microsoft. Authorization/roleAssignments/write* permissions (e.g., Owner or User Access Administrator).

When we have defined the scope for the assignment, we can access RBAC by going to *Access control (IAM)*, which can be found in the menu of almost all Azure resources. In Figure 10-4, we can see the different roles assigned on different scopes and being inherited.

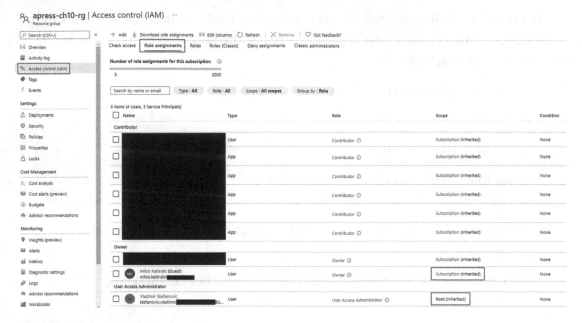

Figure 10-4. *Different roles assigned on different scopes*

By clicking the **Add** button, we can assign an additional role to a security principal. When we click **Add,** we may notice two options for adding a role, of which one is in preview. We strongly recommend the one in preview as we will be able to see the fine-grained options that built-in roles are covering (Figure 10-5).

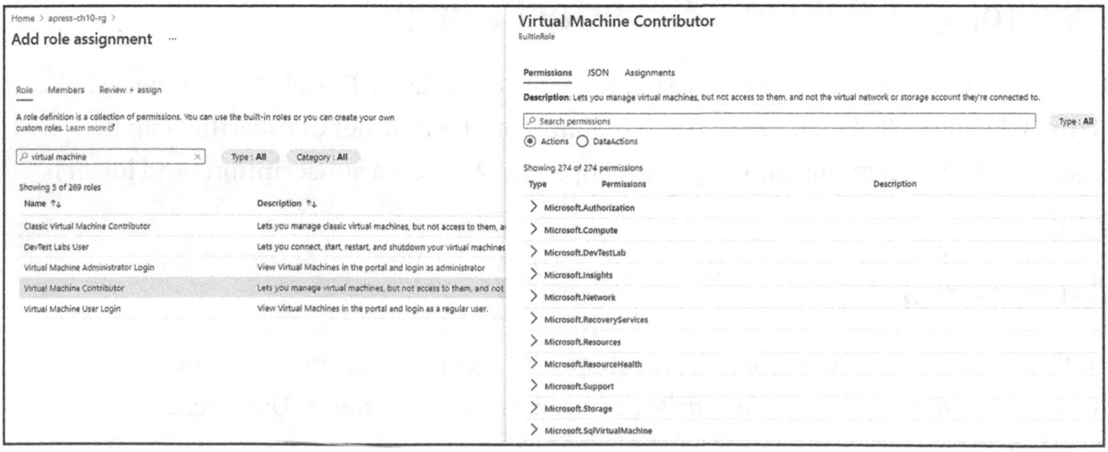

Figure 10-5. *Selecting Preview enables the user to see the fine-grained options*

We will also be able to see the *JSON* representation of the role assignment, based on which we may create an ARM template later on to automate certain deployments.

ARM Template, PowerShell, and Azure CLI

Since the deployment code could be pretty big, all ARM template, Azure PowerShell, and Azure CLI scripts are stored in the Apress GitHub account, available at the following URL:

APRESS GITHUB REPOSITORY URL

Custom Roles

Sometimes we may end up in a situation where built-in roles are not giving us all the rights that we need or, more frequently, they allow us more than we need. In that case, we must create a custom role.

Let us, for example, look at the "*Network Contributor*" role. By running the following command, we will get role definition as output:

```
Get-AzRoleDefinition -Name 'Network Contributor' | ConvertTo-Json
{
  "Name": "Network Contributor",
  "Id": "4d97b98b-1d4f-4787-a291-c67834d212e7",
  "IsCustom": false,
  "Description": "Lets you manage networks, but not access to them.",
  "Actions": [
    "Microsoft.Authorization/*/read",
    "Microsoft.Insights/alertRules/*",
    "Microsoft.Network/*",
    "Microsoft.ResourceHealth/availabilityStatuses/read",
    "Microsoft.Resources/deployments/*",
    "Microsoft.Resources/subscriptions/resourceGroups/read",
    "Microsoft.Support/*"
  ],
  "NotActions": [],
  "DataActions": [],
  "NotDataActions": [],
  "AssignableScopes": [
    "/"
  ]
}
```

If our goal is to allow certain service principal rights just to initiate VNet peering, actions within this built-in role will allow us too much access. A custom role for this case would look like this:

```
{
  "properties": {
    "roleName": "InitiateVnetPeering",
    "description": "Allowed to write Vnet Peerings and read resources",
    "assignableScopes": [],
    "permissions": [
      {
        "actions": [
          "Microsoft.Network/virtualNetworks/peer/action",
          "Microsoft.Network/virtualNetworks/read"
        ],
        "notActions": [],
        "dataActions": [],
        "notDataActions": []
      }
    ]
  }
}
```

By working with custom roles, we can make our environment more secure.

Multi-factor Authentication

Today MFA has become a standard process for accessing different services. Besides entering the username and password, we require additional identification (verification code from a mobile app, SMS, etc.).

Depending on the user role and level of access to our Azure environment, not using MFA could expose us to a threat of being compromised and hacked.

Currently available options for MFA verification are

- Microsoft authenticator app

- OATH hardware token

- SMS

- Voice call

Setting up MFA within Azure AD could be as easy as enabling one additional option for users, up to a complicated setup with conditional access policies.

At the beginning of this chapter, we mentioned *security defaults* – they provide us with the option to enable the use of MFA for all users quickly. However, to have more granular control, we should be using *conditional access policies*. By setting up *conditional access policies,* we define events or applications that require MFA. That means that in case a user is compliant with a certain policy, they will not be asked to use MFA, but if there is a non-compliance situation, the user might be forced to activate/use MFA.

Important to mention is that the use of *conditional access policies* depends on the license we have within our AD. Only Premium P1 (partially) and P2 (fully) support it. In the case of Azure AD Free, we may use only the *security defaults* setup (`https://docs.microsoft.com/en-us/azure/active-directory/authentication/concept-mfa-howitworks`).

Identity Protection

Microsoft is leveraging the power of machine learning with Azure AD to provide us with the tool with which we can

- Automate the detection of identity risks.

- Investigate risks by using collected data from the portal.

- Export the data to third-party applications for additional analysis.

The tool currently uses ten risk detection types (e.g., anonymous IP address, leaked credentials, etc.). When the risk signal is triggered, it can further trigger the remediation task (e.g. requirement for activating MFA, resetting the password, etc.). All the detections can be manually reviewed in the portal, and admins can take further actions based on the risk. Exporting the data toward one of the SIEM solutions is available through Microsoft Graph-based API (Azure native solution for Sentinel).

To use all the identity protection options available, we would need to upgrade to the Azure AD Premium P2 license. The three main policies within identity protection are

- Multi-factor authentication registration policy: A self-remediation-type policy that will allow users to take needed steps to secure their account if needed.

- User risk remediation policy: Identity protection traces user's behaviors and calculates the possible risk of the identity being compromised.

- Sign-in risk remediation policy: Identity protection assigns a risk score, based on which admins may choose for users if they want to allow access, block access, or allow access with activating MFA.

Azure Security Center

Azure Security Center is a management system that helps us better understand the security status of our complete infrastructure (not just Azure, but also on-premises workloads). It provides us with different tools to harden our environment, both infrastructure and services.

The IaaS part of our environment (VMs) requires onboarding to Security Center by installing a Log Analytics agent, while Azure PaaS services are monitored out of the box. Security Center provides us with recommendations based on the built-in security policies. It will not just provide us with guidance on what should be done and how, but it will also offer a remediation task that can automatically bring our resources to the recommended state.

When we open the Azure Security Center blade, we will be offered to upgrade from the free plan and start with a 30-day trial. In case we do not want to upgrade just yet, scroll to the bottom of the page, and we will find a small blue *Skip* button. Now we may explore what the Free tier has to offer. The *starting page* for our exploration should be the **Recommendations** blade (Figure 10-6).

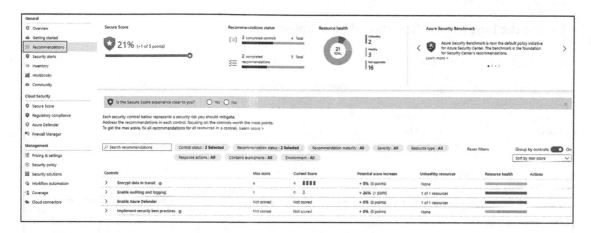

Figure 10-6. *The starting page for exploration should be the **Recommendations** blade*

We can see our current secure score, the resource health diagram, and details for each currently active control (which controls we see depends on the resources we have deployed within our environment). Each control sub-bullet is clickable and will take us further to a detailed reporting for our resources (Figure 10-7).

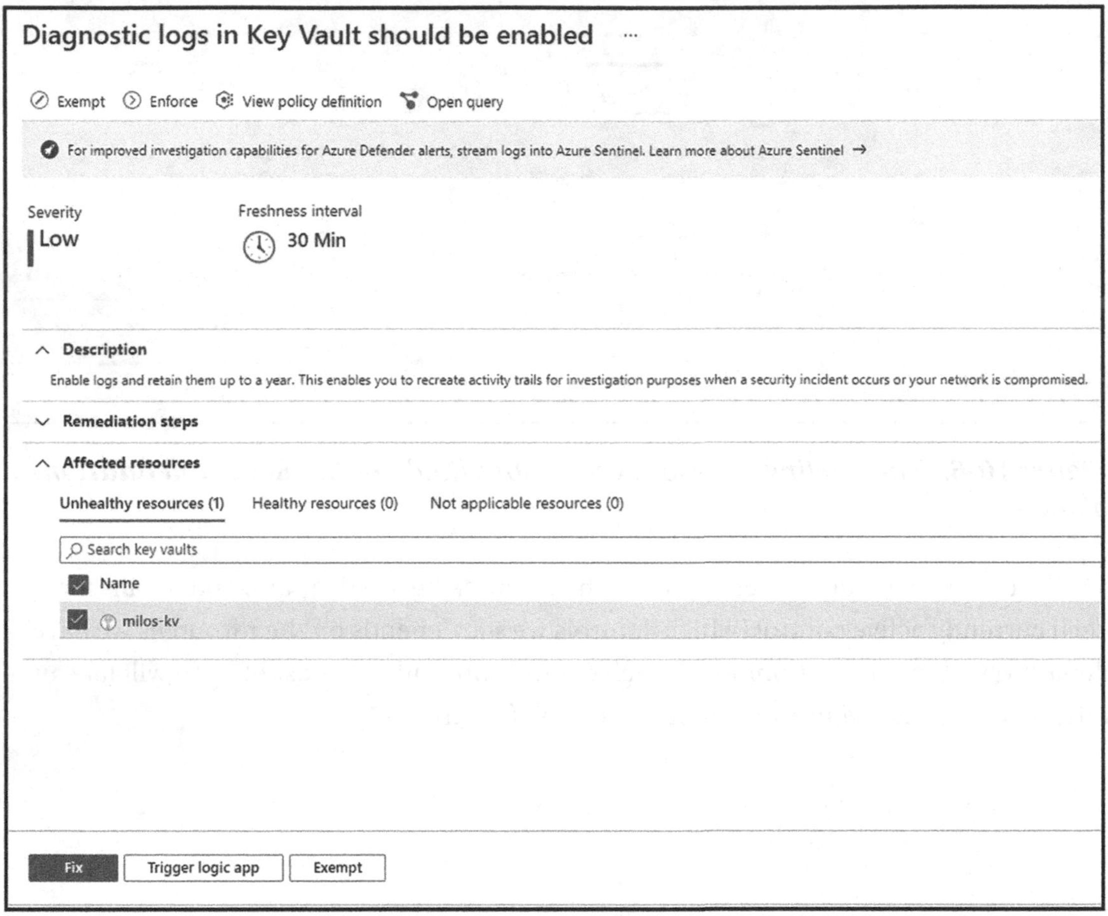

Figure 10-7. *Each control sub-bullet is clickable and goes further into detailed reporting*

In the detailed overview, we will learn more about the recommendation, initiate a quick fix (not possible for all findings), follow manual steps, or decide to make an exemption out of it. (This view is summarizing all resources of the same type with the same recommendation.)

If we look closely, we can notice that there is a **View policy definition** button. That means that all these findings are based on, already mentioned, built-in policies. There we can see the policy definition, and if needed, we can make a copy and adjust it to our needs (e.g., retention policy for KeyVault logs is 365 days). Also, we might want to keep them longer because our company has specific rules. Perfect example for building a custom policy.

For an additional overview of all recommendations for one specific resource, we should go to the **Inventory** tab (Figure 10-8).

Figure 10-8. *An additional overview of all recommendations for one specific resource*

If we go to our resource now, we will get all recommendations for that specific resource (Figure 10-9).

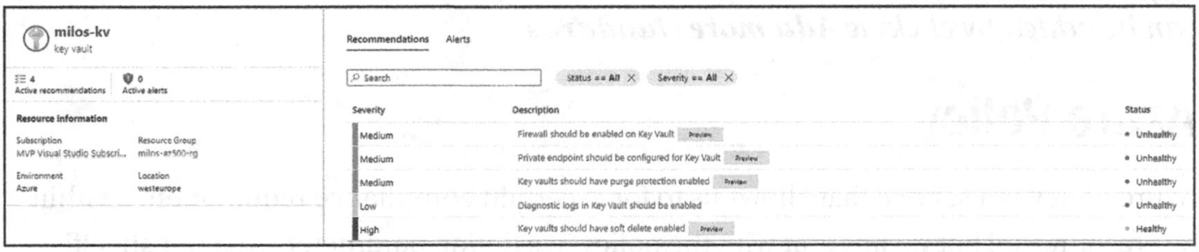

Figure 10-9. *All recommendations for a specific resource*

One more great value that Security Center brings is that it teaches us what we might need to implement in our Infrastructure as Code. That way, we will have our future deployments secured by default.

If we are building infrastructure for a healthcare or financial institution, for example, there might be additional compliance standards that we need to follow. The most used ones can be added if we go to the **Regulatory compliance** tab, click **Manage compliance policies,** and choose a subscription. From there, we will be able to see which standards are already included and will be able to add new ones by clicking **Add more standards** (Figure 10-10). That would activate new controls and generate additional reports on our deployed services and infrastructure.

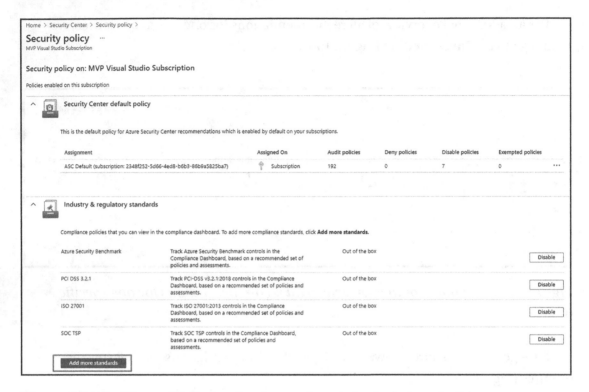

Figure 10-10. *View which standards are already included and where new ones can be added by clicking **Add more standards***

Azure Policy

Azure Policy is a service that allows us to force certain compliance requirements within our resources. That means that with the policy, we define parameters that our specific resource must have (enabled and/or populated with a specific value). That helps organizations to have a consistent resource across different environments.

A JSON file in which we describe the desired state is called policy definition. As we already mentioned, there are certain built-in definitions, but we may create custom ones too. The second part is a policy assignment – this is a scope on which we want to use the previously created definition.

We may also hear about the "Policy initiative." That represents several definitions grouped to simplify management. Policy definition or initiative can be assigned on all organizational levels:

- Management group

- Subscription

- Resource group

- Resource

Times when our resources get evaluated based on the policy:

- When a resource is created or modified

- When policy is assigned to a certain scope

- When assigned policy is updated

- Once every 24 hours (standard evaluation cycle)

To understand what a policy can do, we shall analyze one definition:

Note   This one and many other examples can be found in the Microsoft documentation – `https://docs.microsoft.com/en-us/azure/ governance/policy/samples/built-in-policies`.

```
{
  "properties": {
    "displayName": "Allowed virtual machine size SKUs",
    "policyType": "BuiltIn",
    "mode": "Indexed",
    "description": "This policy enables you to specify a set of virtual
    machine size SKUs that your organization can deploy.",
    "metadata": {
      "version": "1.0.1",
      "category": "Compute"
    },
    "parameters": {
      "listOfAllowedSKUs": {
        "type": "Array",
        "metadata": {
          "description": "The list of size SKUs that can be specified for
          virtual machines.",
          "displayName": "Allowed Size SKUs",
          "strongType": "VMSKUs"
```

```
        }
      }
    },
    "policyRule": {
      "if": {
        "allOf": [
          {
            "field": "type",
            "equals": "Microsoft.Compute/virtualMachines"
          },
          {
            "not": {
              "field": "Microsoft.Compute/virtualMachines/sku.name",
              "in": "[parameters('listOfAllowedSKUs')]"
            }
          }
        ]
      },
      "then": {
        "effect": "Deny"
      }
    }
  }
}
```

In this example, we define which VM SKUs can be deployed (depending on the scope of the policy assignment). The **parameter** section is where we set the list of desired values, and the **Rule** is where we decide what to do with provided values.

As we can see, in the Rule section, we are pointing toward virtual machine resources, and we are comparing the SKU with defined parameters. In case there is a mismatch, our **effect** takes place. In this example, deployment of the VM with non-allowed SKU would be denied.

There are other types of effects, but besides *Deny*, the most used ones are *Audit*, *AuditIfNotExists,* and *DeployIfNotExists*.

Policies are a very important service because they are not just helping us stay compliant with certain standards (public or company internal ones) but can also protect our environment by raising security awareness. They can help us with cost management by defining the type of resource or SKU for each resource type.

Chapter Recap

This chapter discussed general security principles in Azure, such as identity and access controls. Since security is a vast topic that cannot offer any kind of standardization, every project in Azure will have different security requirements. This chapter helped us understand how security works and what our starting point should be.

Since this chapter is the last one in this book, now is time for the conclusion. As we already mentioned, Azure is one of the biggest public cloud providers, and changes and improvements are constantly happening. At the time of writing this book, some services and resources work in one way, but in a few months, that may not be the case. Nevertheless, this book has provided us with all the needed information to start our journey with Microsoft Azure and start one of the most significant transformations.

Index

A

Active Directory (Azure AD)
  definition, 247
  Enable Security defaults, 248
  licensing tiers, 247, 248
  Microsoft, 248
  security settings, 248

Amazon Web Services (AWS), 2

Application Gateway
  Apress GitHub account, 235
  Azure portal
    auto-scaling, 227
    Azure Load Balancer, 229, 230
    back-end pool, 229, 230
    deployment, 234
    error pages, 231
    front end, 229
    HTTP2, 227
    HTTP settings, 232, 234
    probes, 232
    routing rule, 231
    specified listener, 232, 233
    standard parameters, 227, 228
    TLS, 234
  definition, 226
  modes, 226

App Service
  ARM template/PowerShell/
    Azure CLI, 102
  Azure portal, 101

definition, 99
  languages, 99
  plans, 99, 100

ARM template
  definition, 30
  deployment, 34, 36, 37
  example, 31, 32
  file, 33
  forms, 30, 31

Attribute-based access
    control (ABAC), 251

Azure administration
  Azure Cloud shell, 24, 25
  Azure portal, 19, 20, 22, 23
  CLI, 28, 29
  PowerShell, 25–27

Azure Cloud Shell, 24

Azure Container Registry (ACR), 118

Azure Firewall
  creating, 174, 175
  definition, 173
  features, 173, 174

Azure Front Door
  creation
    Apress GitHub account, 241
    Azure portal, 240, 241
    preview mode, 240
  definition, 238
  routing policy types, 238
  SKUs, 239, 240

© Vladimir Stefanovic and Milos Katinski 2021
V. Stefanovic and M. Katinski, *Pro Azure Administration and Automation*,
https://doi.org/10.1007/978-1-4842-7325-8

Printed in the United States
by Baker & Taylor Publisher Services

Printed in the United States
by Baker & Taylor Publisher Services